DOG-FIGHT

Also by Greenhill:

THE COMPLETE FIGHTER ACE:
ALL THE WORLD'S FIGHTER ACES, 1914–2000
Mike Spick

FLYING FURY:
FIVE YEARS IN THE ROYAL FLYING CORPS
James McCudden, VC

THE RED AIR FIGHTER
Manfred von Richthofen

SAGITTARIUS RISING
Cecil Lewis

DOG-FIGHT

AERIAL TACTICS
OF THE ACES OF WORLD WAR I

NORMAN FRANKS

GREENHILL BOOKS, LONDON
STACKPOLE BOOKS, PENNSYLVANIA

Greenhill Books

Dog-Fight: Aerial Tactics of the Aces of World War I
First published 2003 by Greenhill Books,
Lionel Leventhal Limited, Park House, 1 Russell Gardens,
London NW11 9NN
www.greenhillbooks.com
and
Stackpole Books, 5067 Ritter Road, Mechanicsburg,
PA 17055, USA

British Library Cataloguing in Publication Data
Franks, Norman L. R. (Norman Leslie Robert), 1940-
Dog-fight: aerial tactics of the First World War
1. Fighter plane combat – History
2. Fighter pilots
3. Fighter planes
4. World War, 1914-1918 – Aerial operations
I. Title
940.4′4

ISBN 1-85367-551-2

Library of Congress Cataloging-in-Publication Data available

Edited, designed and typeset by Roger Chesneau
Line drawings by Barry Weekley
Printed and bound in the UK by MPG Books Ltd,
Bodmin, Cornwall.

Contents

Introduction

This is the story of the development of aerial warfare in 1914–18, bringing into focus some of the tactics introduced, discovered and employed by the airmen of both sides of the conflict. Everything, of course, was new; there had never been an air war before, and so whatever the flyers did, it was for the first time. Probably most early tactics were developed individually, just in order to survive, and if a manoeuvre seemed to work, it may have been passed on to comrades in the Mess as a matter of interest. Certainly there was no dissemination of these tactics from an official level for some time.

Before war came, pilots did little more than fly straight and level, with gentle turns and climbs to change direction and height. A few rash aviators had tempted fate by 'looping the loop', more as a display to thrill a crowd. However, to understand fully how the various tactics developed, it is also necessary to realise what was happening in the air war. Therefore, the work undertaken by the various arms of the flying services must be mentioned—reconnaissance patrols, artillery observation, photography and contact patrols, coastal patrols and anti-submarine warfare by the Navy, and so on. It is no use trying to understand how tactics needed to be worked out unless the basic reasons behind them are at least brought into the equation.

From the early air actions which developed into combats, a few airmen on both sides began to achieve above-average success and became the first 'aces', a term generally associated with five victories in air combat. This yardstick, while accepted today, is not fully understood

7

in the original First World War perspective, so, in dealing with aces and their tactics, several things have to be taken into account. What, for example was fairly easy for some pilots in the later years of the war, was extremely difficult for the pioneers in the first years. It should also be remembered that many airmen did not engage in aerial fighting resulting in victories; the bombing and reconnaissance airmen had other priorities.

Therefore, this book covers not only these elements, but also the way in which the air war progressed, necessitating the constant need to improve, change and develop. In the beginning, aeroplanes were for the most part fragile and motors were not totally reliable; machines were often built for stability, not combat, and as such were unarmed. The need for manoeuvrability, armament and reliability came as a matter of course, during which time the airmen had to adapt to the rapidly changing events around them.

That most took the developments in their stride—and eagerly—helped to change for ever the way wars were going to be fought, and these were achievements in themselves. The airmen of the Second World War, the Korean and Vietnam Wars, the Falklands War and conflicts in the Middle East all benefited from what the early fighting aviators learnt between 1914 and 1918.

Today they have all gone, and we shall not see their like again. They were faced with a new dimension and overcame, and in some way conquered, the elements that were pitted against them. Theirs was a special war, and they were special people. War in the air has become very sophisticated, but the long journey had to start with a single step—a single flight—with men unafraid of taking to the skies, into an element that was not for the faint-hearted.

In the 1960s and 1970s I was privileged to meet or correspond with a number of First World War fighter pilots, many of them aces. The letters and tapes have remained almost unused in my files since then, and this book has provided the chance of using them, giving some authority to how they fought their air war some eighty years ago. A number of them had also written books on their participation in the conflict, and, wanting myself to be a writer, I was obviously keen to talk to some of them about their work. Several of them told me to take what I wanted from their books if it helped (at this time, Chris Shores and

I were working on a book which was later published under the title of *Above the Trenches*). These were books by Arthur Gould Lee, MC; Leonard Rochford, DSC, DFC; Sir Gerald Gibbs, MC; Willy Fry, MC; Bill Lambert, DFC; Ed Crundall, DFC, AFC; and Charles Bartlett, DSC. All have been pored over and digested.

I hope I have not done any of these men a disservice in discussing what they—and scores of others—achieved. One thing, however, becomes clear in reading books written by the airmen of the time, and in reading old combat reports, etc.: there is almost no mention of specific tactics being used. From the moment hostile aircraft are sighted, it takes but a few words to find the writer attacking. There is no build-up, no prelude, no mention of what was needed. This suggests either that a specific tactic, to be used in a certain situation, was so obvious that there was no need to mention it, or that the only real tactic was to engage the enemy in the shortest possible time.

However, there can be no doubt that some thought went into what was about to happen—a careful check of the sky above and behind, into the sun (as far as that could be viewed); the nearness of cloud, both for hiding in and obscuring more hostile machines; the position of the sun was in relation to one's own approach; the distance to the safety of the lines (or, from the German airman's perspective, can I get my man before he runs to safety?). What sort of aircraft am I attacking. Is it better than mine? Just how many are they? Can I see them all? Have I fuel and ammunition left for a prolonged fight? Is that enemy pilot better than me? Will my aeroplane burn? And (possibly in the dark recesses of the mind) am I going to die in this fight? The kaleidoscope of thoughts must have either galvanised or numbed the mind.

And for many, those fleeting thoughts of danger—what to do, and how to do it—would have been their last.

ACKNOWLEDGEMENT

I wish to thank my good friend Mike O'Connor for reading the draft of this book and making several useful comments during infrequent periods of sobriety.

N.F.

ONE

Learning by Experience

I T IS ALL too easy to look back and read what happened many years ago and forget to take into account what we know now. In other words, hindsight in all things is wonderful, but to really appreciate how things happened, how events occurred and how people reacted, it is important not to be influenced, nor have a perspective coloured, by accrued knowledge.

When the 'Great War' broke out in August 1914, the French, British and Belgian Armies went into the field against the Germans in France and Belgium, while the Italians, in May 1915, after a period of neutrality, defended their northern borders against the opposing Austro-Hungarian Empire, which were at war with Serbia. On the Eastern Front, the Germans faced the Russians.

On the Western Front, the war started, as has many others, with sweeping movements of troops and cavalry, engagements with artillery and clashes to gain high ground and take strategic villages and road junctions. The one new factor which now came into the equation of open warfare was the machine gun.

Rapid-firing guns had slowly been developed during the late 1800s. The most famous example—frequently seen in movies about the American Civil War or Red Indians—was the Gatling gun. By the latter part of that century, Germany, France and Britain, amongst others, had developed the machine gun to a very high degree, and whether called the Spandau, Maxim, Hotchkiss, Vickers, or indeed, the American Lewis gun or Colt-Browning, they were all deadly.

Infantry, and more especially cavalry, became increasingly vulnerable to the machine gun. As the 1914 winter came, with no end of the war in sight, the two opposing sides did what no major warring nations had done before in Europe: they dug in. With often elaborate flair in construction, the trench system quickly scarred the French and Belgian landscapes from the North Sea coast down to the border with Switzerland. In order to defend these 'trench lines', mile after mile of barbed wire was quickly produced, hurried to the battle front and strung out in spikey coils and strands, making it very difficult for infantry to penetrate in a straightforward assault. Behind this irritating and cruel invention sat the machine guns.

Once the trenches became established over the winter of 1914/15, they effectively precluded any war of movement, and, in reality, stalemate ensued for the next four years. During those years each side tried, again and again, to punch a way through, and if any gains were made they were often be measured in yards and with massive casualties. There were some breakthroughs, gaining a few miles—at a tremendous cost in lives—but if one side achieved these, such was the surprise at the success that there was no real back-up to support the opening, and by the time support arrived the other side had managed to react and stem the advance. Often a huge counter-attack would force the line back to the original position, and the whole process had to start again.

Meanwhile a second new factor in the first major European war of the twentieth century had emerged—the aeroplane. The aeroplane had evolved rapidly since the Wright Brothers had first put a man-carrying, powered flying machine into the air in 1903. By 1912 the whole concept had advanced to a stage where the British Army had formed the Royal Flying Corps, including a Naval Wing. This was no doubt influenced in part by the arrival of a French aviator, Louis Blériot, in a forced landing near Dover Castle on 25 July 1909, having taken off from Les Baraques, France. Suddenly, Britain no longer had the English Channel as a defensive moat.

The year 1909 also saw the birth of what became the French Air Service, while in Germany the previous year a Technical Section had been formed to further the development of aviation. All these services took interest not only in aeroplanes, but in airships too, although it would ultimately be the aeroplane that would dominate.

The First Warplanes

One could almost say that when the war began there were no real warplanes, merely civilian aeroplanes adapted for war. Once war had been declared, however, practically anything that could fly was pressed into service, some machines being donated by patriotic aviators. In 1914 the RFC had just seven squadrons, six equipped with aeroplanes and the seventh with airships. By August the airships had been detached to the Navy, and the remaining squadron—No 1—equipped with aeroplanes. Not that the squadrons had uniform equipment: each had a variety of types as they flew off to *La Belle France*.

Numbers of aircraft were small. France and Germany had the largest air forces, the former having around 138 machines spread through 21 Army escadrilles while the latter had some 230, interspersed among 33 field sections (*Feldfliegerabteilungen*) and eight sections attached to frontier fortresses.

In the main, few machines carried any armament. The performance of the early aircraft was adversely affected by the weight of a machine gun and ammunition, and the most a pilot or crew might carry was a pistol or perhaps a carbine. Some of the younger pilots were more warlike, but the older commanding officers in the RFC, strictly 'old-school', generally forbade any initiative in this direction. In some ways they were right, as there was nobody to fight. The job of the early airmen was one of reconnaissance and observation. French and German airmen had the same task, flying over the battle areas, reporting back what they had seen, and endeavouring to be generally useful.

It has to be said that most Generals were rather sceptical about what they thought these flying 'chappies' could see. Few had any concept about what view airmen had of the ground, some thinking that the mere speed of the flying machine must make most things a blur! Luckily, there were some forward-thinking commanders who came to trust the reports the aviators brought in, and used the information to advantage. Meanwhile, the others still preferred to use the traditional method of reconnaissance—the cavalry.

However, with the coming of trench warfare and barbed wire, together with the machine gun dominating the battlefield, the cavalry became reduntant by the spring of 1915. Suddenly, the Generals were turning to the aviators to tell them what was occurring 'on the other side of the hill'.

Some of the important information the generals needed related to how the enemy's lines of communication were being used. Increased traffic usually heralded an attack or a major offensive. Two advantages lay with the Germans. The first was that British communication lines ran north and south (because the British used the Channel ports), roughly parellel with the front lines, so it became easier for German two-seater crews to keep them under observation. The German lines of communication however, proved to be mainly fan-shaped, and these also had important 'nerve centres' which needed to be kept under a watchful eye. Some of these could be as much as 50 miles behind the front line, so air reconnaissance sorties were constantly conducted over such towns as Brussels, Ghent, Valenciennes, Douai and Lille.

The other German advantage was the direction of the wind. For the British and French, the predominant westerly wind helped carry aircraft into the German side of the lines, but blew against them as they flew back. German recce crews, flying high, might have to struggle to get into Allied air space, but, once finished, or threatened with air attack, they could quickly break off and head eastwards with a good wind behind them.

The sun was another problem, although it was an advantage and a disadvantage to both sides. In the morning, on good-weather days, the sun, rising in the east, was in the eyes of the Allied airmen, while the Germans had it at their backs and could use it to conceal themselves. In the afternoons, this was reversed, the Germans having it in their eyes, as the sun travelled west and down.

Both sides were faced with the same dilemmas and had quickly to entrust reconnaissance to the men who flew the not altogether reliable flying contraptions that the generals occasionally saw buzzing overhead. They quickly proved their worth, but also came to the realisation that what their own airmen could see, so could the opposition's flyers. There were not, of course, masses of aeroplanes in the sky, but there were enough. It was not an unusual occurrence for a crew to see a hostile machine, its crew doing their work in a similar fashion to themselves. And this work increased. Visual reconnaissance was still undertaken, but gradually aerial cameras began to be taken aloft, the photographic prints being examined by up-and-coming experts on photo-interpretation. The ranging of artillery fire and the fall of shot soon became an important daily topic, and if there was a battle, the contact patrol became an important factor.

These contact patrols were, as the term suggests, flown to make contact—with ground troops. The Generals needed to know how far their own troops had advanced in an attack, and where the enemy was. The first task was not very difficult, but the second, requiring airmen to fly at low level in order to see the colour and style of uniforms and helmets, was rather more exciting, as hostile troops would, naturally, fire up at the aeroplane. The airman need to double-check, as he could just as commonly be fired on by his own side.

As this developed, co-operating with the infantry became essential, and the troops on the ground had a number of ways of attracting the attention of the aviators. One was by using Popham Panels (invented by Colonel R. Brooke-Popham, a future Air Chief Marshal). These looked a little like venetian blinds that could be stretched out on the ground and, by quick adjustments, formed into a variable chequerboard pattern in black and white. A simple code told the airmen above what assistance was needed, and the aeroplane crew could send Morse messages back to headquarters on the soldiers' behalf, or take the information back. Sometimes, of course, if hostile aircraft were about, the infantry would be reluctant to show their positions and they stopped using the panels in case enemy guns pinpointed them.

Ranging artillery was fairly simple. Pilot and observer would fly over the battery with which they were co-operating at a certain time, ready to engage a previously agreed target. The pilot would then call up the battery on his Morse set and look for a reply by means of strips of white cloth laid out on the ground. Once the flyers saw a message 'Signals clear, carry on', they would position themselves nearer the target, and when the first shell burst the crew would signal the position of the explosion by means of a clock code, the 12 o'clock position indicating due north, six o'clock due south, and so on. The gunners could then adjust their fire by reference to their own map. This continued until either the target was hit or the battery became fed up and ceased firing.

In turn, the aircrew could change targets, especially if a better or more important one was sighted. If it became vitally important, the crew could signal a 'Zone Call', whereupon all gun batteries in the area would range on the new target. Everything would go wrong of course, if the ranging aircraft were either driven off by hostile aircraft or shot down by gunfire or hostile aeroplanes. What is sometimes not appreciated (or is sometimes forgotten) is that in using the Morse key, the observer in the two-seater had first to wind out a 120-foot copper aerial, with a three-pound lead weight on the bottom to assist it to trail behind. If his aeroplane were attacked in the air, the observer had either to wind this back in—if time permitted—or jettison it. If the latter, then whatever the outcome of the attack, the two-seater crew's job was effectively ended.

Ranging a 15-inch howitzer battery, which of course had only a single gun, was spectacular. From the air, the airmen could see the huge shell leave the gun muzzle as it set off in a wobbling trajectory, moments before being lost to sight. About a minute or so later they would observe a great explosion on or near the target, which would leave a tremendous hole in the ground.

The aeroplanes were not armoured, and there were no bullet-proof fuel tanks. Random gunfire could just as easily hit the occupants (in their wicker seats)—or engine or petrol tank, or could cut control wires—as miss altogether. And at, say, 50 feet on a contact patrol, an aeroplane was not a difficult target, compared to later and faster aircraft. To coin a later phrase, it was a hell of a job, but someone had to do it!

The Aeroplane and the Machine Gun

Once it became important to stop the opposition from carrying out its task—or to try and shoot it down if it had—the airmen of both sides actively sought out the other's aircraft and engaged them, using pistols and carbines. However, the more aggressive individuals saw the need to affix a machine gun to their aircraft if they were to inflict sufficient damage to bring the opponent down.

Mounting a machine gun on an aeroplane was not a new idea. The necessity to oppose a hostile aeroplane in the air was being discussed as far back as 1909 at least. It was only the method that was the limiting factor at first, but once the idea had become desire, a big problem was the propeller. Most aircraft were 'tractor' types, that is to say, the engine was at the front and the propeller 'pulled' the machine through the air. It was obvious to everyone that the best method of attack was for the pilot to aim the aircraft at the hostile machine and fire at it along the line of flight, i.e. through the propeller arc.

Several ideas were put forward and some were adopted. One of the most successful was to fit the gun obliquely so that the bullets would fire slightly off to one side, missing the blades. This meant that the pilot, instead of aiming his machine directly at the enemy, would aim it a few degrees to the left or right. A better idea was to fit the gun to the top wing of a biplane (or a parasol—a monoplane with a high wing), angled to fire downwards but *over* the propeller, and still enabling the pilot to aim his machine at the enemy.

The First Fighting Aeroplanes

It is not often realised that, in an age dominated by biplanes, many of the early aircraft were in fact monoplanes. In fact, it was monoplanes which first became the first successful fighting aeroplanes. The French produced the Morane-Saulnier series of aircraft. This company produced four monoplanes soon after its formation in late 1910, and from these came a succession of rotary-engined machines given the type lettering L, G, or H. One notable pilot who flew them was Roland Garros, who had become a company pilot in 1912. The following year the Types G and H emerged: the G was a two-seater and the H a single-seater, but otherwise they looked identical.

Looking at photographs of the H model, one can be forgiven for thinking that the aircraft is a Fokker E (for *Eindecker*, i.e. 'single-wing', or monoplane). Both Morane types flew with the French in the early days of the First World War, and at least one H model served with the RFC. However, it was the Type L which saw more service, although this was a high-wing ('parasol') rather than a 'shoulder-wing' monoplane, that is, the wings were attached to the fuselage sides adjacent to the cockpit. The Type L was a two-seater and was used by both French and British services early in the war, as did a more refined model known as the LA. Both types were able to carry a Lewis machine gun.

These were followed by the Type N, which, in early 1915, became the first single-seater to carry a fixed machine gun firing through the propeller arc. It was Roland Garros, now a military pilot, and another French pioneer, Adolphe Celestin Pégoud, who were credited with developing a method of firing their guns between the whirling blades of a propeller, firstly with a Type L and then the N. (Pégoud had already enjoyed victories, scored with his observer.) Both men, and no doubt one or two others, agreed that the best method of attack was to aim the aeroplane, and the logic was that the majority of bullets fired through the arc of the airscrew would not touch the blades. Therefore, it only needed some form of protection on each of the two blades against those few bullets that would strike them. The answer was to fit metal deflector plates to the area of each blade opposite the gun's muzzle, and those bullets that hit would be parried away.

Garros had seen early experiments of this system before the war, but they had not been a success. Once Garros was a Sous-Lieutenant, flying with Escadrille MS 26 in the spring of 1915, he was able to develop the theory further. He had his first success on 1 April, shooting down a German two-seater whilst flying a Type L near Westkapelle. (His Type L was subsequently lost during a storm, so he transferred the device to a Type N.) On 8 April Garros scored a probable victory, then destroyed another enemy aeroplane on the 15th and finally, on the 18th, shot down his third. However, the Frenchman was brought down by ground fire this same day, near Inglemunster in Belgium, again in a Type L, and taken prisoner.

With his Morane virtually undamaged, the secret of his device was discovered by the Germans, and shown to the Dutch aeroplane designer Anthony Fokker, who was producing aircraft for the Germans. Tasked with producing something similar, Fokker was quick to determine that a strict copy would not do, and he and his design team concentrated on making a true interrupter gear. This idea was not new, but it had not yet been perfected by other designers. In a very short time, however, Fokker and his men produced a gear which satisfactorily stopped the gun firing once a propeller blade was directly in front of the muzzle, and in order to test their theory they had the system fitted to one of Fokker's own single-seat designs, the Eindecker, or Fokker E.

Despite its important place in military aviation history, the Eindecker was an unspectacular aircraft built purely for unarmed reconnaissance. It was almost indistinguishable from the early Morane Type G, except for the shape of the fin, and one might be tempted to say that Fokker copied the French design. However, what changed the Eindecker and gave it a place in history was the synchronised machine gun.

Sent to the front for evaluation, the Eindecker soon proved itself as a fighting machine, especially in the hands of a few aggressive pilots like as Oswald Boelcke, Max Immelmann, Otto Parschau and Kurt Wintgens. It became a veritable scourge amongst French and British airmen for a year, from mid-1915 to mid-1916. However, although this period was termed 'The Fokker Scourge' in reality only a comparative handful of German fighter pilots—the first German fighter pilots— created this scourge. While a number of other pilots flew Eindeckers, once the type was seen or engaged in air combat it was quite natural for Allied airmen to assume that their opponent was Boelcke or Immelmann, who was about to shoot them down.

Yet these first German fighter pilots had to learn everything from scratch. There were no manuals on air tactics, no experienced airmen to ask, no lectures to attend: they had to find out for themselves how to do the job. They had to learn by trial and error.

TWO

Air Fighting Begins

MENTION was made in the previous chapter about the weight of a machine gun affecting an aeroplane's performance and some commanding officers actively curbing certain of their pilots from becoming too enthusiastic about engaging enemy aircraft. The job in hand, as they saw it, was one of reconnaissance, not of indulging in personal conflicts with opposing airmen.

However, some pilots and commanding cfficers chose to pursue ideas of combating hostile aircraft, and one pilot, Louis Strange, flying with No 5 Squadron RFC, fitted a Lewis gun to his Avro 504 biplane. Strange argued that so long as he was not required to climb above 7,000 feet, performance would not be unduly affected.

The gun was mounted on top of the fuselage decking, with a piece of rope lashed about its centre of balance. This was passed up over a metal tube and then fixed to the cross-member of the front seat petrol tank bearer. A pulley on the rope enabled his observer to sling the gun up into mid-air and fire it all round as well as back over the pilot's head, with the aid of a wooden stock tucked into the shoulder. He, of course, sat in the front cockpit, which was not ideally suited as a gun position, but the Avro, like the B.E.2 series, had been designed primarily for reconnaissance at a time when it was thought best that the observer be seated in the front cockpit for a good forward view. Obviously the observer, surrounded by struts and wires, and with a whirling propeller in front of him, did not have an easy task when firing his Lewis gun, nor did he command a tremendous field of fire.

Oddly enough, a few aeroplane designers had given thought to the problem of taking guns into the air *prior* to the First World War, and had overcome the problem of the engine being in front by simply placing the engine behind. The Vickers company had produced a design to meet an Admiralty request for such an aircraft, and it was first seen at the Olympia Aero Show in February 1913. These aircraft, built with the engine behind the pilot rather than in front, became known as 'pushers'— for obvious reasons. To get round the fuselage problem, the actual area in which a pilot and observer sat became a bathtub-like nacelle. The rear of the aeroplane was merely two large booms with struts either side of the propeller, stretching back to where rudder and elevators needed to be.

The result was an aeroplane with an almost unlimited forward field of fire of 180 degrees, although the major problem was the remaining 180 degrees at the back—and, of course, the majority of attacks upon the machine by hostile aircraft would come from the rear. Provided the crew kept a keen vigil behind them, a surprise attack could be avoided, but it was still a case of solving one problem only to create another. Nevertheless, the developed Vickers F.B.5 (called, much later, the 'Gunbus') became the first true gun-carrying aircraft to see service with the RFC, arriving in December 1914, and it was eventually used by six squadrons in France. Maurice LeBlanc-Smith flew the Vickers F.B.5 with No 18 Squadron. He was born in 1896 in Leatherhead, Surrey, survived the early air fights with this pusher and later became an ace on Sopwith Camels with No 73 Squadron, winning the DFC. In 1974 he told me:

> Having learnt to fly on a Maurice Farman, the Vickers doubtless seemed a more robust aircraft, but my chief recollection, apart from the smell of castor oil that blew into our faces and probably helped to keep us fit, was the unreliability of the 100hp Gnome engine. One great fault was the breakdown of the expanding piston ring, shaped like an L, the short bit fitting into a groove within the piston. It frequently would not stand up to the heat and would buckle or break, with consequent loss of power, the visible sign always being the 'blueing' of the cylinder wall outside. Plug trouble was equally prevalent.
>
> As to the aircraft's general performance, I have no particular recollections. I was inexperienced and not above average as a pilot, though I seldom broke anything. I see from my log book that I once reached 11,700 feet, but it was mostly 6,000 to 9,000 feet or lower. We met hardly any enemy aircraft—three

A Vickers F.B.5 (later known as the Gunbus) of No 11 Squadron, 1915. The 'AJI' indicates the observer—Lieutenant A. J. Insall. Note that the engine/propeller is turning.

encounters—so its ability as a fighting machine was scarcely tested, but we did a lot of photography and artillery co-operation, for which it performed adequately. In all, I did about 150 hours on them.

The Germans also had a 'pusher' type in 1915, from the AGO factory, but it was not produced in any significant numbers and was used only for reconnaissance. It, too, had a machine gun in the front cockpit, but this was used for defence, not offence, although it did help if its crew made an attack.

Meanwhile, the air war was hotting up. It was difficult to curb the enthusiasm of airmen from both sides of the lines for engaging their opposite numbers. It was a splendid game, fought out amidst the clouds in the crisp air above France. Not that being armed with a machine gun, however mounted, brought instant success. Reading combat reports of the period, one learns that observers could empty drum after drum of Lewis-gun ammunition and had finally to break off and go home with no illusions whatsoever of having hit the enemy. Some got in a lucky shot with a rifle; others totally missed with hundreds of rounds from a machine gun. Tactics were hardly thought about—it was all too new.

Things changed, however, in the summer of 1915, once the Fokker Eindeckers arrived at the Front. They did not arrive in large numbers: they had to be built, tested and then fitted with the synchronisation gear before they could be used. Any form of mass production was still way in the future. At first, those that did arrive were sparsely distributed amongst the various two-seat reconnaissance units on the Western Front—the *Feldfliegerabteilungen*. Their task was to help protect the unit's two-seater crews whilst the latter carried out their assigned tasks of reconnaissance, artillery co-operation or photography, and ward off the nasty British or French airmen who might try to interfere with their work.

Pilots who were assigned to fly them were, for the most part, merely volunteers, men who felt that their task gave them adventure and a bit of freedom, away from the rigidity of their normal two-seat duties. Because of the relative few numbers of Fokkers in service, and because the synchronisation gear was still very much a secret, there were no Fokker Staffeln, only one Fokker, perhaps two, attached to each two-seat Abteilung. Moreover, the pilots that flew them were forbidden to take their machines across the lines for fear of being brought down on the Allied side and the interrupter secret being revealed. In essence, this was the start of the German fighter arm's mainly defensive war.

This in itself was significant—although far from apparent in 1915. With the gradual build-up of the British and French air forces, plus the small Belgian force, it was easier, and then virtually necessary, for the Germans to fight a defensive-type of fighter air war. General Hugh Trenchard, who commanded the RFC in France from August 1915, waged an offensive war, almost daily sending his airmen across into German-held territory to reconnoitre, direct artillery fire upon, photograph and bomb the enemy.

Significant Factors in the Air War

As this scene was being set, it soon became apparent that the airmen of both sides would have to cope with, adapt to, and quickly learn about the conditions under which they operated.

Maurice LeBlanc-Smith flew Vickers F.B.5s with No.18 Squadron in 1915–16.

The weather was always going to be a problem. In the early days of flight, aviators generally chose to fly first thing in the morning, or last thing in the evening, as at these periods the weather was often calm and relatively wind-less. In a war situation, men had to fly at all times and in all weathers. Rain, certainly heavy rain, and fog, would always curtail flying. Cloudy weather, like broad sunlight, were two-edged swords. One could hide in clouds and use them to approach a ground target or a hostile aero-plane, so long as one remem-bered, with the latter, that an enemy pilot might also be creep-ing up on one. Similarly, bright sunlight might make visibility better, but the sun's glare held dangers, for in its rays could be hiding an enemy pilot waiting for his chance to pounce.

Cold weather, particularly during the winter months, made flying especially uncomfortable. There were no enclosed cockpits, no heating, nor, at this stage, heated flying clothing. A pilot might have a small windshield to help protect him from the blast of propeller and slipstream, but he still had to look about him in order not to be taken by surprise. An observer, too, had to keep careful watch in every direction for enemy aircraft, while still carrying out his assigned task—which meant leaning over to look at the ground. Thick layers of flying clothing helped, and whale oil smeared on the exposed areas of facial skin was some protection, but it was still difficult. How many airmen died because the cold made them just a little less watchful for a moment? Anyone today given the chance to fly in the front open cockpit of a Tiger Moth (as I have), will quickly learn how cold and inhibiting the blast of the air can be.

The RFC, while taking the war to the enemy, exposed its airmen to hostile anti-aircraft fire and enemy aircraft. Hits upon themselves or their machines could spell disaster. At best they might become prisoners of war, and at worst their end would be either a hideously fiery death or a bone-crushing impact following a fall from height. There were no parachutes—at least, at first.

The British and French had also to contend with a prevailing westerly wind or airstream, as already mentioned. This meant that as they flew across the trenches, any sort of breeze or wind helped them along, but as they flew back again it hindered them. In an air combat, a pilot might easily lose all sense of location as he tried to ensure that another human being would not kill him, and the wind would take him deeper into hostile territory without him fully realising it.

German fighter pilots, flying a defensive war, had the advantage of being able to wait for the 'customers to come into the shop'. Later, once dedicated fighter Staffeln were in being, the pilots could wait until Allied aeroplanes actually crossed the lines or were seen working above the trenches, before they had to take off. This gave them an advantage in fuel consumption—they knew almost exactly where to find their opponents—and because any air actions were almost always over German-held territory, if they had to come down themselves to make a forced landing, they would not end up as prisoners.

The Fokkers Strike

July and August 1915 saw the first Fokker victories. Two pilots in Fliegerabteilung Nr 62, Oswald Boelcke and Max Immelmann, based just outside Douai, had volunteered to fly its Eindeckers, On 1 August, Immelmann shot down a British B.E.2c aeroplane near Douai, recognised as the first pure fighter victory by what would soon become known as a fighter pilot. However, history may be confused here, and perhaps in reality it was the first victory by a pilot of FA62, for another German Fokker pilot, Kurt Wintgens, with Fliegerabteilung Nr 6, was credited with downing a Morane Parasol on 15 July, having already claimed two others earlier in the month which had

Max Immelmann seated in his Fokker Eindecker. The wing in the picture (right) is that of the F.B.5 of No 11 Squadron he forced down on 26 October 1915.

not been confirmed. Whoever was the first is not particularly significant: what *is* important is that the Allied airmen were about to face a period where they, as minnows, were about to encounter sharks.*

By the very nature of early flight, aeroplanes were designed and built to take off, fly in straight lines, make gentle curves, and then to land. While this in itself did not become too difficult, it was still something tremendously new, and so docile aeroplanes—machines that did not surprise pilots and send them spinning into the ground—were much preferred. Therefore, almost all the early warplanes were built to be friendly to the pilots that flew them, and this also assisted in their crews being able to concentrate on flying their reconnaissance missions from a submissive and stable aerial platform.

The British, with their B.E.2s, plus a variety or Moranes, Avro 504s and B.E.8s, and the French, with their Caudrons, Farmans and Voisins—both also having a number of lesser machines for a while—did not have what one might call 'battleplanes'. None was designed for stressful manoeuvring in what was quickly becoming a combat situation. Not that the Fokker was designed for anything over-stressful either: in fact, it was a fairly innocuous aeroplane. Its only superior

* This Fokker period is covered in my book *Sharks Among Minnows*, Grub Street, 2001.

features were that it now carried a forward-firing machine gun with synchronisation gear that enabled the gun to be fired directly through the propeller arc, and it was being flown by several pilots who were keen enough to use the airframe to its (as yet unknown) limits.

Oswald Boelcke, a 24-year old Saxon and former army cadet, learnt to fly in 1914. He achieved his first victory in an Eindecker on 19 August and downed two more in September. Immelmann, who was nearing his 25th birthday and came from Dresden, got his second on 26 August and his third in September. He, too, had been an army cadet, and had learnt to fly in late 1914 after transferring to aviation. By early August, Wintgens had three 'kills' too. Yet another former army cadet, Wintgens was 21 and had moved to aviation in 1914. By the end of the year, several Fokker pilots had scored victories, and a number of Allied aircrewmen had become well aware that the dangers of aerial warfare had changed dramatically during that late summer and autumn.

On the Allied side too, single-seat fighters—known more familiarly as scouts—had started to inflict hurt on the German two-seaters. Both the French and British used Moranes with deflectors on their propellers to attack them. Another machine in the RFC's stable was the Bristol Scout, which, like the Moranes, was known by a letter as its type. Thus

A better view of the famous Eindecker, a type which began air fighting for the German Air Service. This machine is from Fokkerstaffel Metz and is being piloted by Jakob Wolff.

Major Lanoe Hawker, VC, DSO, won his Victoria Cross for early air fighting, but was shot down by Manfred von Richthofen on 9 November 1916.

the Bristol B and C Scouts were in action, although they were biplanes, not monoplanes.

At this stage, those airmen keen to arm their aircraft were experimenting with all kinds of gun mounts, the RFC in particular using the Lewis gun, which had an ammunition drum, rather than a Vickers-type which was belt fed. It was far easier to change a drum than have to worry about housing a long belt of bullets. Lanoe Hawker, flying with No 6 Squadron RFC used Bristol C Scouts with his machine gun attached on a bracket to the port side of the fuselage by the cockpit, fixed to fire at an angle to miss the propeller, and aimed slightly downwards. Hawker had been a Royal Engineer officer who had transferred to the RFC before the war. He had already been awarded the DSO for a lone bombing raid on a German airship shed in April 1915, using bombs and hand grenades. On 21 June he forced a German two-seater down; then, on 25 July, in a Bristol (No 1611), he forced another to land in German lines, and another to land inside British lines. For these feats he was awarded the Victoria Cross.

Another Bristol C Scout, this time with No 12 Squadron, had a Lewis gun mounted on the top wing, above the cockpit, set to fire over the propeller, while a No 5 Squadron Bristol had a Lee-Enfield rifle, minus its stock, fixed the opposite side to Hawker's gun but again aimed out and downwards to miss the blades. This particular machine also had a Mauser pistol in an external holster fixed by the cockpit rim.

The Vickers gun was eventually fitted to Bristol Scouts in 1916, located in front of the pilot on the top forward fuselage decking. It was set to fire between the blades of the propeller with the use of one of the early British synchronisation gears known as the Vickers-Challenger system. It worked, and one of its early successes was achieved by Lieutenant Albert Ball of No 11 Squadron on 16 May 1916, driving down a German two-seater. This was Ball's first credited victory, although the Bristol was struck off in a crash the following day. Whatever the airmen were putting on their aircraft by way of offensive or defensive armament, the war in the air was certainly becoming interesting—and more deadly. And Albert Ball's name was soon to become famous.

Eventually the British invented their own interrupter gears, the first practical system being that developed by a Romanian, George Constantinesco and a British Major by the name of G. C. Colley. This emerged as the 'CC gear' (Constantinesco-Colley gear)and proved more successful than some others being designed and became the standard issue. Meanwhile in France the Alkan gear was being developed. This was essentially a copy of the Fokker gear, designed by one Sergeant Mechanic Alkan in collaboration with a Navy engineer by the name of Hamy.

THREE

Air Fights and Victories

THE QUESTION of what contitutes a victory may seem a simple one, and easy to answer, but in 1915–16 it was not. This was mainly because nobody had imagined that such a thing would be important. However, once individual pilots began to bring down numbers of hostile aircraft, it began to seem, no doubt to the media of the day, that this achievement was similar to scoring goals in football or a large number of runs in cricket—the higher the score, the 'better' the man. Nevertheless, any aviation historian can name dozens of airmen who achieved great success in the First World War through being good leaders or useful tacticians. They may not have shot down more than, perhaps, one or two enemy aircraft, but this did not make them any less valuable to their air forces.

A 'league table' of victories therefore, however awe-inspiring, tells very little of the story. If one takes the cold facts that the famed 'Red Baron'—Manfred von Richthofen—scored 80 victories before his death in 1918, and that Max Immelmann scored fifteen (or seventeen, depending on how one makes the count), then, on the face of it, von Richthofen must have been a far better airman than Immelmann. However, this assumption would not take into account the conditions under which each fought, the time period, the aeroplanes used, nor several more factors which would come into the equation.

For example, a victory in 1916 was very different from a victory in 1918 —and, for that matter, different from a Second World War claim or victory. I, for one, was quickly caught out in my early days as a historian in trying to relate one war to another in terms of pilot victories. My first interest was the Second World War, and, as I began to study the First, I assumed similar yardsticks for both conflicts. This confused me for a long time.

Between 1914 and late 1916, a victory did not necessarily mean a hostile aircraft destroyed: merely sending an opponent down was thought to be an achievement of a sort, for if a fighting aircraft of one side forced a two-seater reconnaissance aircraft to abort its mission, this was a 'victory'.*

In the early days, too, while there were comparatively few aircraft in the air and before the air war became more deadly, a pilot of either side, if he felt that he were in serious trouble with a hostile aeroplane and was over his own side of the lines or could quickly get to it, might easily call it a day and land. This course of action may have ended his chance of taking photographs or directing artillery, but at least his aircraft and his observer were safe—if a little sweaty! On the other hand, a crew may have been wounded in a combat, and the pilot (or the observer) may have managed a good landing on his own side of the lines. Perhaps, indeed, the crew had been killed in combat. Did these circumstances represent a more worthy 'victory'? Moreover, whether or not a fighter pilot was credited with a 'kill' depended upon who saw it and how it was reported.

In the early days of the First World War, therefore, an attacking pilot— certainly in the RFC—might be credited with a 'victory' even if no material damage had been inflicted: the scale of damage could vary between 0 and 100 per cent, and the victorious pilot might well have had no idea where the percentage lay. Nor did he particularly care.

There were a number of well-known pilots on both sides who were killed in combat but where credit for their demise was not given to an opposing pilot simply because nobody knew what had happened. This was more often true of German losses than of Allied, because, fighting their defensive war, German victories more frequently fell on their side

---

*From now on I shall refer to 'working' two-seaters as 'Corps aircraft', to describe the work their crews carried out—reconnaissance, photography, contact, bombing, artillery observation etc.—as these squadrons operated for a specific army corps, and the comparison between each side is similar.

of the lines where wreckage, bodies or captured airmen were found more readily. If a German pilot reported that a B.E.2 that he had attacked had crashed near Bourlon Wood, and later a wrecked B.E.2 was found near that famous landmark, with either dead or captured airmen, and no other German pilot had made a claim, the 'kill' was confirmed.

For the British and French, an attack upon a German aircraft which was then seen to spin away, its pilot looking as though he were dead at the controls, but which then disappeared into low cloud, was more difficult to confirm as a victory: the aeroplane may well have continued down through the cloud to smash itself to pieces in the French countryside, its end unseen. As far as the British pilot was concerned, he could only claim what became known as an 'out of control' victory. It does not take a genius to realise that the same spinning German pilot, once clear of the action, and below the cloud, might easily correct the spin and head for home, with nothing more serious than soiled trousers, a grateful and a wiser man. Yet if another British pilot in the fight had witnessed a comrade firing at a German machine which had then spun down into cloud, seemingly out of control and about to splatter into the ground, he could confirm this once back home and his fellow pilot would be given credit for a 'victory', which would be added to his score. Meantime, the 'victory' was back on his aerodrome, telling his pals how lucky he had just been.

The French, on the other hand, were more strict in their confirmation policy, and unless an actual crash had been seen, or the aircraft had burst into flames, or the pilot had been observed to fall or jump out, then any aircraft looking remotely to have been 'out of control' would be noted and credited as a 'probable', much like the 'probables' in the Second World War: although noted, it would not be included in the French pilot's total score. Often—although one suspects not always—the number of witnesses to a machine's destruction required by the Frenchman was at least two. On a two-man patrol over the German lines, this was immediately difficult, for the third witness would have to be either a third airmen who just happened to be in the vicinity and see the battle, or an observer on the ground, that is, in the trenches or just behind them. There is a reference to a French pilot downing his first German aeroplane while in company with the famous ace Georges

Guynemer, but even corroboration from this hero of France was not sufficient for a full credit.

Often a squadron's intelligence officer, who was responsible for confirming fallen aircraft claims, would telephone through to the nearest front-line army position, or gun battery, in order to ascertain if anyone could confirm an aircraft crash near a certain location at a given time. It must have driven many front line officers crazy to think that, within the turmoil of war, flyers back in their comfortable billets, miles behind the lines, were interested only in knowing if their prowess had been seen, so that they might add another medal to their chests. Generally, however, if they could confirm something, they did— although we know from research that what an army witness, who might hardly know which end of an aircraft held the propeller, actually saw and what he thought he saw (or possbily what he could be persuaded he saw) could be two vastly different things. This, of course, happened on both sides of the lines.

As a good example, Manfred von Richthofen, on 27 December 1916, claimed an F.E.2b two-seater shot down into British lines. Front-line observers confirmed its fall and therefore he had his 15th victory. For historians, the problem is that no F.E.2b machine fell in the area, nor indeed anywhere at the time stated. Reading between the lines, one can see that because there was another fight near the location between some German aircraft and some F.E.2s— although none was lost, or even damaged—the front-line officer reacted to a call from von Richthofen's adjutant asking if he'd seen a *Gitterrumpf** go down, had confirmed it. In fact, he had probably seen the F.E.s in a combat, and had at some stage seen a 'pusher' aircraft going down: the Germans called any 'pushers'—that is, an aircraft with no fuselage, only rear booms—*Gitterrumpf*. However, nobody had thought to ask if the pusher had been a single-seater or a two-seater *Gitterrumpf*—and would the man have known the difference? The actual aircraft von Richthofen had fought was a single-seat pusher, a D.H.2 (which we will read about later), flown by none other than future VC winner James McCudden, then still a lowly NCO pilot. McCudden had had his gun jam and, seeing no future in waltzing around with an armed German fighter, had

---

* Literally, 'lattice fuselage'.

put his machine into a spinning nose dive and fallen an estimated 9,200 feet!

Obviously, von Richthofen had declined to follow his victim down, especially as he was now inside British airspace, likely to be fired on from the ground as well as being in danger from aircraft from above. He headed for home, reporting that his opponent had last been seen at 1,000 metres, still spinning, and had obviously crashed. McCudden, feeling out of immediate danger, levelled out at low level and flew home—where it had already been reported by his comrades that he had been shot down!

We can see from this action the classic 'claim', which in fact was no claim at all and certainly no victory. Every one of the 300 rounds that von Richthofen had fired at McCudden had missed him and his fighter, but, wanting the 'kill', the Baron had was convinced that the spinning British machine, going down for such a long distance, must have crashed.

This sort of scenario confused many pilots and observers, and has introduced doubt into many fighter pilot's scores. No nation was immune, not even Germany. Hundreds of Allied machines fell within German territory, but in a particular action we often find, for example, three German pilots claiming the only two Allied aircraft lost. The Germans also frequently confused the issue by resisting any confirmation of aircraft that went down on the Allied side of the lines, although many victories were credited where this *did* happen—even where there is no corresponding loss of an Allied aeroplane.

It was a question of the *interpretation* of witnesses as to what they saw. However, if the artillery (of either side) could see a downed aeroplane which looked more or less intact, their shellfire could reduce it to matchwood, making a dubious victory a certain one. Later, the Germans also employed the term 'z.L.g.', *zur Landung gezwungen—* forced to land on the (Allied) side. These types of 'victories' do not appear in a pilot's tally, yet earlier, before the term became well used, they did. In similar fashion, the British used the terms 'driven down' or 'driven down and forced to land'. Prior, certainly, to 1917, some of the early aces had scores which included 'driven downs' as well as 'out of control' victories. Albert Ball, of whom we shall read more later, had an overall score of 44 'victories', which is is sometimes interpreted as his having destroyed 44 enemy aircraft—which is incorrect. In the First World War, certainly on the British side, one should not confuse victories with aircraft destroyed. Ball's total of 44, for example, comprised 27 and one shared aircraft destroyed, one balloon destroyed, six aircraft 'out of control' and nine deemed as 'forced to land'. In the Second World War this score would probably be interpreted as 27½ destroyed, six 'probables' and nine damaged, with a balloon also shot down. The shared victory might confuse the historian too, since, in many cases, certainly on the British and French sides, an aircraft shot down by two, three or four pilots would be noted as a 'kill' (or at least a credit) each. Therefore a pilot could share in five individual victories and, without a single victory scored on his own, still be deemed an ace.

A successful French fighter pilot's score should generally reflect all confirmed 'kills'. The ace René Pierre Marie Dorme—known affectionately as 'Pére' (he was 22 in 1916)—was credited with 23 confirmed victories, that is, enemy aeroplanes deemed as destroyed. In addition, but not included in his tally, he was supposed to have had some 70 'probables', of which some 17 can be found in records, plus two more forced to land. In all, he had some 120 combats between June 1916 and his death in May 1917.

From 1917, the British did not register 'forced to land' or 'driven down' in an overall total of victories, merely 'destroyed' (including shares) and 'out of control', plus balloons. Balloons were always counted. They were dangerous targets to attack because they were always well defended, not only by anti-aircraft guns but also, more often than not, by aircraft patrolling nearby. The Germans did not always venture behind the Allied lines, but in order to attack balloons they had to, for they were always located a few miles back. If two or more Allied pilots attacked and a balloon was destroyed, then again it was shared and each pilot would received a victory credit.

British balloon observers were RFC (after 1 April 1918, RAF) men, often assisted by artillery officers. To be effective they needed to be at around 5,000 feet, and were generally about three or four miles behind the front lines. With field glasses and telescopes they had a fairly good view over the other side of the trenches, and like airmen, they could direct artillery fire by the use of the telephone. Naturally, the weather affected their efforts: high winds or inclement conditions made their task impossible, while low cloud made them more vulnerable to sudden aircraft attack. Unlike their compatriots in aeroplanes, balloon men did have parachutes and could save themselves in the event of their balloon being set on fire.

The Americans of the US Air Service, more or less attached to the French in 1918, used the French victory method, so only confirmed victories were counted, with shares in a 'kill' counted as one victory per participant. For example, John Sidney Owens, with the 139th Aero Squadron in 1918, gained five victories—two shared with six others, one shared with five others and two shared with two others. He made no individual 'kills', but the system nevertheless allowed his admittance into the ranks of the aces.

Better Fighting Machines

The success of the Fokker Eindecker pilots between August 1915 and August 1916 started a race to produce better aircraft for both sides. Once the Allied side discovered, through capturing an Eindecker in the spring of 1916, that the secret of its success was the interrupter gear, it only helped to spur on their own race, not only to have a working gear themselves, but to design and build machines created specifically for air fighting.

The Vickers F.B.5 soon began to disappear, but, keeping the same basic layout, a single-seat pusher, the Airco De Havilland 2, arrived in France during November 1915, and like the German Fokker, was assigned in ones and twos to existing squadrons, until No 24 Squadron arrived fully equipped in February 1916, followed by Nos 29 and 32 Squadrons. This nimble fighter, along with a new French biplane, the Nieuport Scout, is credited with ending the period of Fokker monoplane dominance, and no doubt this is true—up to a point. However, it may also be one of those popular myths that become historical 'fact', for there does not appear to be any evidence for droves of Fokkers shot down by victorious D.H.2 pilots. It is more probable that by the time the D.H.2, and the French Nieuport Scout got into their strides, the Eindeckers were being replaced by new German biplane fighters, which began to appear in August.

The French Nieuport, the other new fighter at the front, came, like the Moranes, in a number of variants, both two- and single-seaters.

The Nieuport Scout was a successful fighter machine in the hands of a good pilot. This No 1 Squadron aircraft shows the Lewis gun in the 'pulled down' position. The photograph was taken when the aircraft was in German hands.

They were tractor biplanes, or more correctly 'sesquiplanes', the lower wing having a much smaller chord than the upper . In consequence, the interplane struts were 'vee'-shaped.

The more familiar types were the Nieuport 11 single-seater and the Nieuport 12 two-seater. In addition there was the Type 16, one of which went to No 11 Squadron RFC in the spring of 1916 and was flown by Albert Ball, setting him on his road to fame. The most numerous variant was the Type 17C1 single-seater. In the RFC and RNAS, Nieuports generally carried a Lewis gun on the top wing, although the French, once they had acquired an interrupter gear, favoured a machine gun in front of the pilot. Firing the wing-mounted gun was accomplished by Bowden cable. The cocking lever and trigger was attached to the cable, which hung down inside the windscreen, alongside a wire which freed the front of the gun, thus allowing it to be pulled down for reloading with a new drum.

Another British pusher-type was the Royal Aircraft Factory's F.E.8, similar to the D.H.2. This arrived in France during August 1916, although it only equipped two squadrons before the Nieuport and later the D.H.5 replaced it. However, by far the most amazing pusher type was the F.E.2, a large two-seater which went to France in late

A D.H.2 'pusher', showing the pilot's good field of vision. Note the rack for storing spare magazines for the machine gun, located by the cockpit. The D.H.2 began to wrest air superiority from the Fokkers in 1916.

1915 (as the F.E.2a), quickly replaced by the superior F.E.2b (and then by the F.E.2d) in early 1916. Its wing span of 47 feet 9 inches (14.7m), was 11 feet (3.38m) greater than that of the Vickers F.B.5, and it sat 1½ feet (0.46 m) higher. It was, with a 3,037-pound all-up weight, 1,000 pounds heavier, and its three-hour endurance, while more than an hour less than that of the Vickers, still gave it a long patrol time.

The F.E.2 also had additional defence against attack from the rear, as the observer now had a second Lewis gun mounted on a pole between him and the pilot's cockpit, which enabled him to fire back over the top wing and propeller arc. In the main this had probably no more than a 'scatter gun' effect, which an experienced German fighter pilot could no doubt avoid by dropping below the F.E., thereby keeping out of the cone of fire. Of course, the observer had to stand up to fire the weapon, stepping up on to his seat for better effect, or even on to the rim of the cockpit. Despite this, there are no known incidents of observers being thrown out during an air fight, although it no doubt concentrated the mind and helped one keep a firm grip on the gun, with the other hand on the pole. Sometimes, too, the pilot had a fixed, forward-firing machine gun, on what was called a No 4 Mark IV

(Clark) mounting, on the right-hand edge of the front cockpit (looking forward).

Back in 1972 I was in touch with W. C. (Bill) Cambray, MC, who had been an observer with No 20 Squadron in F.E.s. He sent me an article that he had written about this aircraft and his time on the Squadron:

> The FE2d, despite its ungainly appearance, was wonderfully strong, and I did not see one break up in the air even during strenuous manoeuvring.
>
> An observer's 'wing' was not just given automatically. It had to be earned in action, and many observers were killed before they were able to fill the conditions. These included the drawing from memory of a map of the area—in our case Ypres to Armentières, and as far over as Tourcoing, Roubaix and Lille—and putting in all the enemy aerodromes, gun emplacements where known, roads, rivers, etc. Photographs had to be taken with the necessary overlap, so that when they were developed they showed a continuous picture. At this point a request was made to Brigade HQ, and if all went well an extra five shillings a day flying pay was granted.
>
> The aspirant, too, had to have one fight with the enemy and return. As No 20 was mainly a fighter squadron, an observer quite often 'went west' during that first encounter. If he was lucky enough to return, he was good for one more; and if he returned after *three* fights, he was so experienced that, with luck, he would last six months and return to England for Home Establishment.

The F.E.2b and 2d equipped several squadrons in 1916, including Nos 11, 18, 20, 22 and 25, which used them very much in the fighter and fighter-escort role as well as for reconnaissance and photography. Indeed, in terms of aircraft claimed as having been shot down, No 20 Squadron held the record. F.E.2s were still in action during 1917: if they were allowed to form one of their defencive circles, as they edged along towards the safety of the Allied lines, they were hard to engage. Baron von Richthofen was wounded during an attack on an F.E.2 in July 1917.

The reader will have noted in the foregoing paragraph the phrase 'if they were allowed to '—or one could say 'if they could do'. One often reads about aircraft manoeuvring into a favourite, or a favourable tactic, but this always assumes that the *circumstances* are favourable, and more often than not pilots and crews were unable to do so. Patrols or escorts of, perhaps, five F.E.2s might easily be reduced to four if one fell out with engine trouble, and if another was then hit in an initial attack by German fighters the remaining three could hardly put up an effective defence by flying in a circle. It also assumed each pilot was able to fly such a manoeuvre, whereas in practice at least one of the pilots would be new to the front with only a few hours of flying time. Heads up, chaps—smell the daisies!

Lord Balfour once invited a friend and me to tea at the House of Lords. During the First World War he had won the Military Cross, and Bar, flying Moranes with No 60 Squadron, then Sopwith 1½-Strutters (so-called because they had an unusual interplane strut arrangement)

The F.E.8 'pusher' fighter. Although the pilot was protected to some degree by the rear engine, this was vulnerable to stern attacks, as was the fuel tank.

and Camels with No 43 Squadron. In his book *An Airman Marches*, Captain H. H. Balfour refers to flying defensive circles with the Strutters, noting that:

> After some weeks we learnt the best tactics: as soon as ever we saw a gathering crowd of Huns above us, we would go round and round in a circle, the whole formation of us, each one chasing the tail of the machine in front, until we had formed a perfect revolving wheel. The wheel would then edge slowly towards the lines, and woe betide any German who tried to come down on top of that circle. He would get the concentrated fire of six observers' guns, and, brave fighters as they were, no German could face that with impunity. But, equally, woe betide any one of our people who got out of the circle. I saw this happen twice. On one occasion the wings were shot off a machine in my Flight, and one of my best young pilots . . . and his observer were pitched out into space as the machine disintegrated. The other occasion I think the pilot must have suffered from engine trouble and have been forced to leave the circle. His petrol tank must have been punctured and the aeroplane soaked with petrol, for an incendiary bullet struck it. One moment it was gliding away from the wheel and the next it was a mass of flame from wing tip to wing tip.

The Americans later named a defensive circle a 'Lufbery', after Raoul Lufbery, the American ace who flew initially with the French in the American-manned N 124 Lafayette Escadrille. This tactic, too, was of aircraft flying in a moving circle, each pilot defending the tail of the machine ahead of him. Again, as with the Immelmann turn (see below), the origins of neither the name nor the manoeuvre are clear. In 1916, when Lufbery was with the Lafayette, he often flew alone or with just one or two pilots, so it is difficult to see how a circle could be developed. When he was with the Americans in early 1918 he had hardly got into combat before his death, so could not have invented, nor encouraged, such a manoeuvre then.

The Fokker Aces

Before we leave the Fokker period, and the so-called 'Fokker Scourge', we must review the Fokker menace and the men who created it. There is no doubt that the mere sight of a Fokker monoplane coming into view was enough to tighten the buttocks of the most ardent Allied aviator.

Despite the fact that there were comparatively few about, those that were flown certainly made their presence felt—although many Fokker pilots flew and fought with keen anticipation of a victory but achieved none. When one actually analyses the period, the 'Scourge' was created by just a handful of German pilots, who, as a result, became the first fighter aces, and the first recipients of the prestigious Ordre Pour le Mérite—the 'Blue Max'. This was the highest honour Prussia could bestow upon its fighting men.

These first aces were Boelcke, Immelmann, Wintgens, Parschau, Höhndorf, Frankl, Berthold, Leffers, Buddecke, von Althaus and von Mulzer. Boelcke scored eighteen Fokker 'kills', Immelmann fifteen (or seventeen, depending on the source), Wintgens at least a dozen of his eventual nineteen, Höhndorf eleven, Max Mulzer ten, von Althaus eight, Frankl eight or nine of his overall twenty, Parschau eight, Berthold six (of a total of 44), Leffers at least five of his nine and Buddecke five or six over France and Gallipoli. As these pilots became famous in Germany, so their names and actions also became known to French and British aviators, and before long every Fokker met in the air was seen as being flown by one of these aces. Often this was indeed the case, but, just as later every red Albatros or Fokker Triplane was von Richthofen's as far as the Allied flyers were concerned, the truth was that such an adversary could have been *any* Fokker pilot.

So famous became the name of Immelmann at this time that a manoeuvre was named after him. Immelmann himself made no apparent reference to any manoeuvre he developed, so one must assume that the RFC airmen, seeing something rather new—probably little more than a steep bank or a climb and stall—felt that it was this manoeuvre that was defeating them in the air. Others who said they saw it described it as a climb, a roll off the top of a half loop and than a dive, bringing the aircraft behind the opponent once more. However, if the opponent had made a sharp turn in either direction, or a steep climbing turn, the Fokker would be out of position.

By far the most logical manoeuvre was a climb, wing-over and dive; this has also been described as a *chandelle* by the French. The Fokker monoplane did not have ailerons. To put the machine into a rolling attitude it used wing-warping, that is to say, control wires flexing the mainplanes. Ailerons were much more effective and quicker in operation than wing warping. Thus the Eindecker pilot did not have a quick-roll ability, making this manoeuvre something of a struggle. Immelmann

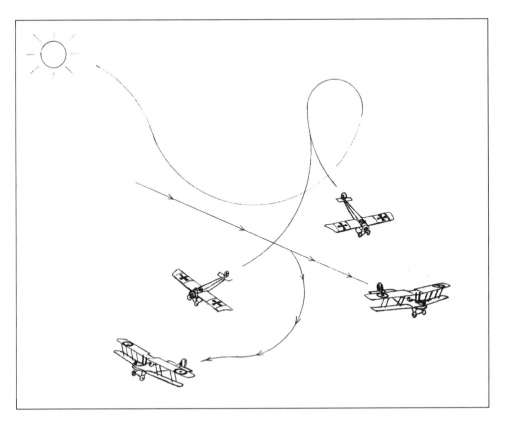

The Immelmann Turn. While this turn is supposed to have been invented by Max Immelmann in a Fokker Eindecker, it does not seem likely and he certainly never made mention of it. Most probably it was a manoeuvre that was no more than a steep climb and stall turn as seen by some Allied pilots, and, as *all* Fokkers must have been flown by Immelmann at that period, his name was put to it. The true Immelmann Turn, developed later, came from a failed attack from height and from behind, forcing the attacking pilot to climb and then turn back towards the opponent. As most Allied—or, for that matter, German—pilots in the early days did not appreciate that it was far better to turn into an attack rather than merely turn away, it was easier for an attacker to get back behind an opponent who was trying to head away as fast as he could, rather than stay in a turning circle. Later, with opponents making tighter turns following a surprise attack, a rapid climb without increasing engine power initiated a stall, at which stage the pilot would kick the rudder, producing a quick falling turn. With the power back on, the resulting dive would quickly bring him back down on the target aircraft, which by this time had probably started to head away.

and his brethren would soon have found that the quickest way to turn in order to reverse direction would be almost a stall-turn, pulling up and kicking the rudder as the stall approached, thereby coming back down in the opposite, or roughly opposite, direction. The French *chandelle* was a more fluid wing-over and turn.

A good deal has been written about the Immelmann turn, much of it contradictory; many flyers who described it had never flown a wing-warping machine and so had little idea of how that sort of aeroplane performed in the air. A so-called 'Immelmann turn' might therefore in fact be no more than a manoeuvre in which a pilot attacked from height, gained speed and, if his initial burst of gunfire did not appear to 'do the trick', dived under the target, pulling up steeply beyond it, going into a stall-turn or *chandelle*, and coming back to face his opponent.

All this, of course, assumes the target to be—ideally—a B.E.2-type machine, from which there could be no direct forward fire from the gunner (positioned in the front cockpit, behind a propeller). If the Fokker pilot attempted this manoeuvre on a 'pusher' machine, he would leave himself open to a forward attack, having lost the advantage of speed in the climb and wing-over process. It also presupposes that the B.E. pilot was still lumbering along in a more or less straight line, whereas the natural thing to do would be to break one way or another and dive like mad for the lines. While this might give the Fokker pilot a chance then to continue pursuit on a now retreating enemy, it did at least over come the risk of a collision: if he came down from the turn, the B.E. pilot having closed the gap, he was now almost head-on to his antagonist. In fact, it would be far better, from the German's point of view, if the target aircraft had turned. Therefore, since the Fokker was unable to execute a rapid aileron turn, the manoeuvre reported was probably no more than a quick *chandelle* turn-and-chase towards a fleeing aircraft.

As we shall read, any tactic developed was—and could only be—used if circumstances were favourable for that tactic. Often they were not. Moreover, whatever the manoeuvre, everything depended on position, or on what modern fighter pilots call 'tactical awareness'—otherwise a pilot had to attack from the most favourable angle possible, and hope for the best.

Observers of attacks on RFC aircraft by hostile scouts noted a dive from height, which took it below the target aircraft, whereupon the enemy pilot zoomed up to rake the target from below. After firing into the target aircraft, the attacker would continue upwards in a steep, climbing turn. Often an attacker, if unsuccessful in downing his opponent, would simply continue away, while others would proceed to make another approach and attack. It could be argued that either pilot might fall into the category of 'press-on', aggressive types, who continued until their opponent went down or they ran out of ammunition. Or was it more sensible to cast around for another target—one that had not been alerted by a near miss?

FOUR

Loners and Organisers

UNTIL MID-1916, at least, the sky was not full of battling aeroplanes. There was plenty of action, but for all sorts of reasons flying was a fairly solitary affair. Two-seater reconnaissance machines flew out alone; artillery observation duties were flown alone; and attacks by fighter aircraft, of both sides, were flown mostly alone.

What changed this was the losses. It soon became apparent that aircraft flying on their own were far more likely to be shot down than if there were two or three machines flying together for mutual support. This in turn, as far as the Fokker fraternity was concerned, and especially as a few more Eindeckers became available at the front, led to German fighter pilots engaging the opposition in twos and threes, while the defenders flew in small groups for mutual protection.

For the German pilots, there was no real need to fly patrols along the front. There were always targets about, and patrolling was not only tiring but a waste of fuel. It was far better to wait until Allied aeroplanes were reported, or even visible from front-line airfields: fighter pilots could then take off, intercept and engage. Most front-line airfields had high-powered binoculars on a tripod, with an observer constantly watching the skies above the trenches. During 1916–17, German fighters were seldom seen above 15,000 feet, because their targets were generally low-flying Corps aircraft. Allied fighter patrols, too, needed to be fairly low to protect the two-seaters, but if crossing over the lines they rarely went below 14–15,000 feet, so as to avoid anti-aircraft fire.

Once over German-held territory, they could, provided the leader felt the upper air was free of enemy aircraft, drop lower to try and engage German fighters making themselves a nuisance with the Corps or bombing aircraft.

Early in 1916, Trenchard had been forced to order aircraft to escort reconnaissance machines, but this was never easy work to undertake. Unreliable engines, poor weather, combat—anything could upset the routine for the escorting aircraft. However, this directive showed how things were developing in the air. It also showed how the Fokker menace was affecting the overall effectiveness of the RFC, forcing it to reduce the numbers of aeroplanes available for Corps work by requiring other aircraft to fly escort.

This escort problem did not go away, and although some effort was made, the main problem was one of communication in the air—or , rather, the lack of it. Even by 1917 it was all pretty 'hit-and-miss'. A new CO of No 45 Squadron, who happened to know several COs of single-seater units in the area, promised:

> I would get you escorts if I could, but I can't, so we must do the best we can. . . I know the COs of the scout squadrons and, although I can't get you an escort, I'll ask them to tell their boys to keep a look-out for you whenever they've got a patrol detailed with orders to go across the lines at the time you go out.

Fine words—but could it work? In any event, the scout pilots had a lot of other things on their minds besides hoping that they might run into the Strutter crews, somewhere, sometime. Moreover, the German fighter pilots would be watching and waiting.

Artillery observation missions were still, nevertheless, lonely affairs in the main, but reconnaissance, photo 'shows' and bombing began to be carried out in small formations as 1916 progressed. Trenchard had also ordered squadrons to practise close-formation flying—something that had hitherto not been tried to any great degree. Often a photographic reconnaissance mission would be flown by five machines, perhaps two with cameras and the other three flying as escort. Five observers firing at an attacking Fokker was a better bet than one. Bombing, too, would be carried out by small formations of five or six, although if he happened to be flying a docile old B.E.2 type, in order to carry bombs the pilot had frequently to dispense with the observer. Thus a possible five B.E.s out bombing might have three aircraft without observers, and just two with one each. Whichever scheme was tried, engine trouble quickly made a nonsense of it, especially if the escort machine or machines had to abort the sortie. A B.E.2 pilot with a revolver was no match for a German monoplane—and nor even were two pistol-packing pilots.

The RFC and RAF had two main cameras for use in the air, one that captured, in minute detail, a small area of about 1,000 square feet, and another, with less detail, that would reveal main points of interest over a larger area—say, two to three miles—whilst the pilot was flying at around 16,000 feet. The vertical pictures were usually taken at this higher level, while oblique shots were taken at much lower altitudes. The camera operator had to take into account the strength of the wind, while the pilot had to keep the aircraft as level as possible, without varying the height. Often a series of overlapping pictures would later be laid out to form a mosaic of an area that was of interest to the generals at headquarters.

The pilot on 'photo-ops' was a busy chap. Once over the 'target' area, and if there were no sign of hostile aircraft, the pilot would keep his docile B.E. flying straight and level with his left hand while operating the camera with his right. The actual camera, being fixed to the outside of the cockpit, was, in the early days, not unlike a studio apparatus, complete with leather concertina bellows. It carried a box of 18, sometimes 24, glass photographic plates, and the pilot pulled a toggle as he leant out into the 70mph slipstream in order to look down through a rudimentary 'ring and ball' sight.

Of course, most fighter pilots on both sides preferred to hunt alone. There was something of the adventurer about it—the 'white hunter'—and, once gained some experience had been gained, it was deemed challenging good fun. Trying to locate a hostile machine amidst the clouds, or by hiding in the sun's rays was akin hunting wild boar in a German forest, a stag in the Scottish highlands, or a tiger in the jungle. With so few aeroplanes about, it was expedient to hunt singly, and as pilots had no way of calling another comrade in the air—there was no airborne radio—it seemed logical to go it alone.

Some men excelled at it. Albert Ball's name quickly comes to mind. This 19-year-old from Nottingham had claimed seven victories before his twentieth birthday, and he had already been in France as a pilot for six months before he reached that age. Not only was he a 'loner' in the air, he generally kept to himself on the ground, and, despite the adventure of it all, he hated war and killing. However, this did not stop him from doing what he saw as his duty for his King and Country.

Once Ball began flying a single-seat Nieuport Scout with No 11 Squadron (delivered in order to escort the unit's F.E.s), his first victories were over German two-seaters, a Fokker Eindecker and an observation kite balloon. Of his first seven claims, three were credited as destroyed, two 'out of control' and two more forced to land. In August 1916 he doubled his score, all against two-seater types. He began to excel at stalking his opponents, creeping up on them from positions which made it difficult for a two-man crew to spot him coming—down through cloud, out of the sun or from below, keeping in the crew's blind spot.

The upward-firing gun. Initially a light machine gun was installed on the top wing of RFC fighter aircraft so that the bullets would pass harmlessly over the propeller blades. Even after synchronisation gear was brought into use, this wing gun was still used, especially by pilots adept at stalking hostile aircraft. Aces such as Albert Ball and, later, James McCudden were remarkably good at stalking tactics, which enabled them to get up underneath an opponent, pull down the wing gun and fire up into the German machine. The first the recipients would know of the attack was bullets coming up through the bottom of the fuselage of the aeroplane, often causing death or injury, holing petrol tanks and crippling engines. The gun, being fed by a drum of ammunition, could also be reloaded in its pulled-down position, the pilot having two or more spare drums located in his cockpit.

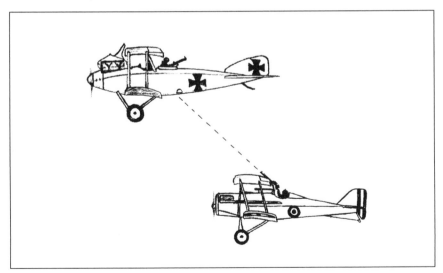

The Nieuport had its single Lewis gun mounted on the upper wing, ideally placed to enable the pilot to pull it downwards using a Foster mounting, so that it could (a) be fired upwards and (b) have an empty ammunition drum replaced when required. Once the pilot had manoeuvred himself into a position immediately below and behind a German two-seater, the first the enemy crew knew of his presence was bullets slashing into wood, fabric, metal and flesh from beneath. By September 1916 Ball's 'score' of victories had topped 30, of all categories—destroyed, out of control and forced to land. But 'victories' they were. Any two-seater driven down, damaged or not, was preventing its crew from working. Stopping bombs falling on soldiers, stopping cameras taking photographs of Allied positions, stopping artillery shells being directed on to men and equipment—all made life for the British Army easier.

If one should think his job was easy, then why were there not many more Albert Balls, downing victory after victory? Certainly he had an exceptional, aggresive talent, not found with every fighter pilot. There were a few others, but none as successful as he at this stage. Alan Wilkinson, who flew a D.H.2 with No 24 Squadron, did achieve a measure of success. He downed ten German aircraft between May and August 1916 and won the DSO. When he first went out to France he thought it would be beneficial to carry two Lewis guns in the front cockpit of his pusher, but was quickly told to carry one like everyone else. Weight over firepower.

Before moving on from the subject of the wing-mounted Lewis gun, I must not leave the reader with an impression that pulling down, reloading the gun and then pushing it back into position was an easy task. No machine guns are so light that they do not require considerable effort to carry or even lift them. Added to this is the weight of the ammunition drum. The first drums held 47 rounds, in itself somewhat weighty, but the RFC later modified its drums to hold 97 rounds. The usual load was three drums in all. To manipulate the gun to a position in front of his face, change a drum, place the empty one in its stowage in the cockpit and then push the gun back into position, was no easy task for a pilot—even on the ground.* Whilst flying, or in the middle of a

---

*Nieuports, D.H.2s and F.E.8s had a selection of 'pockets' in which to stow apparatus.

dog-fight—well, think about it! The pilot would also, of course, need to keep one eye on the skies about him.

Immelmann Falls

After achieving fifteen victories, Immelmann fell in combat during the evening of 18 June 1916 while in a fight with F.E.2 pushers of No 25 Squadron. On the same day, he had shot down two more F.E.s, but his death prevented their being credited properly, and at least one was then claimed by another Fokker pilot. Controversy has raged ever since about how he met his end. Perhaps it had all happened too quickly? The Germans reported that his interrupter gear had failed and that he had shot off a blade of his propeller, causing sufficient vibration to shake his monoplane to pieces.

The RFC claimed that one of their F.E. crews had attacked and shot him down. Their fire may, of course, have hit his propeller, although apparently he had damaged the propeller of another Eindecker shortly before the 18th. Just why he did not immediately switch off his engine and glide down if he had shot off his own propeller is still a valid question. If the F.E. crew did get him, it was certainly a case of the observer in the pusher F.E. having a clear field of fire as the Fokker flew across in front of him.

As it turned out, almost every Fokker ace was to die before the year 1916 ended, and only von Althaus survived to middle age. They had all risen to a challenge and were a product of their moment in the first air war.

Two-Seat Fighters

In the early days, before the single-seater's agility made it the preferred fighting machine, some aviators were of the opinion that two-seater fighters gave the best chance of success. This was due solely to the fact that it could carry a gunner in the rear cockpit to defend against attacks from the rear, leaving the pilot free to engage aircraft to the front. Later, this concept found great success in the Bristol F.2b fighter.

In 1916 the Sopwith 1½-Strutter arrived in France and Nos 43, 45 and 70 Squadrons employed them for fighter recce missions, while the RNAS also had some in France and in the Aegean. The French, who built them under licence, used them for similar operations. At first they were employed more or less defensively—just as the Bristol F.2bs would be in April and May 1917—rather than offensively. One individual in No 45 Squadron who did particularly well with the Strutter was Geoffrey Hornblower Cock, MC. In just 97 flights over the lines he and his observers scored nineteen victories, of which fifteen he regarded as certainties.

His success was due to the fact that he decided early on to handle his Strutter like a fighting scout, attacking enemy aircraft with his front gun with his gunner/observer equally free to engage the opposition from behind. On 9 May 1917, Cock was flying at the rear of a formation and spotted German aircraft behind. Firing a red Very warning flare, he immediately turned to engage, sending one Albatros down and with another starting a spinning nose dive. He swerved to one side, and his observer then fired at another of the enemy aircraft, which began to break up in the air. Later, at the foot of his combat report, someone wrote: 'This is gallant, but is all against orders and common sense.' Nevertheless, his tactics worked, although in the end he was shot down and taken prisoner on 22 July by Willi Reinhard of Jasta 11—the German's first victory of his total of twenty. Geoffrey Cock told me in 1967:

> The 1½ Strutter was a good aircraft, but the front gun was quite useless. I, however, was lucky in getting the Ross interrupter gear on trial, and this speeded up the rate of fire of the front gun to almost normal rate, and I got most of my victories with it.
>
> Of course, both front and rear guns were operating in a fight, but if the Hun was shot down while the rear gun was firing at him, the gunner got the credit, and very rightly too.

The Ross gear was used only on Strutters, but it was popular with No 45 Squadron because if a pilot found himself in a tight spot he was able to fire the front gun without engaging the gear, even though this meant putting bullets into his propeller! It was obviously a case of expediency over common sense. It was apparently invented by a Captain Ross and an armourer in No 70 Squadron, which also flew Strutters. Therefore, with Cock saying he could fire at a rapid rate, he was also saying that he deliberately fired through the propeller arc, without synchronisation. Norman Macmillan, MC, a Flight

No 45 Squadron's Strutter Formations. The two-seat Sopwith 1½-Strutter crews of No 45 Squadron had enough problems without the ever-present attentions of 'Archie' (German anti-aircraft fire). At the start they flew in pairs, stepped up (right), but German gunners could predict height and speed, and shells could explode at any height amidst the formation and still cause damage. In order not to split themselves up, the aircraft would have to turn in formation, remaining vulnerable to AA fire. To avoid the exploding shells, therefore, they flew with each aircraft at a different heighs while in 'vee' formation, each crew occupying their own piece of sky (below). Once the first AA shells came up near them, the leader could easily make a rapid vertical bank-turn, with the other pilots doing the same in precise order whilst turning outwards from each other. The formation therefore came together in their same order but flying in the opposite direction. This could be effected quickly, and could not be anticipated by the AA gunners. Several other two-seat units adopted this tactic.

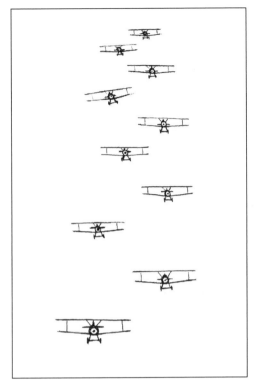

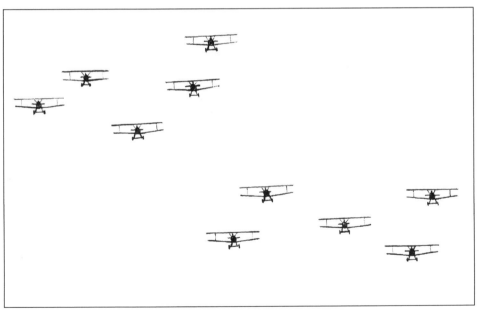

Commander with No 45 and later a well-known flyer and writer, recorded that although several pilots returned home with as many as twenty bullet holes in their propeller blades, no one was known to have been lost because of a shot-off blade.

In No 45 Squadron, a system was developed in order to try to avoid exploding AA shells. The crews discovered that they could often outwit the enemy gunners by having each aircraft fly at slightly different heights in their 'vee' formation, so that each pilot had his own particular area of sky. Before this they flew in pairs, stepped up from the rear, but in this case the whole formation could only make wide sweeping turns. With the new formation, the leader could easily make fast vertically banked turns, the other aircraft doing the same in precise order, turning outwards from each other. Thus the formation came together in the same order but facing the opposite direction. So swift was the manoeuvre that the ground gunners could not anticipate it.

As 1916 moved into autumn, several D.H.2 and F.E.8 pilots began to accumulate victories, each slowly mastering the task of learning how to fight and survive in the air. Nos 24 and 32 Squadrons began to inflict casualties upon the Germans, while the F.E.2b units, too, were winning through. Times were about to change, however, not only becaue of an increase in overall aircraft numbers, but also because airmen were beginning to think more about how to improve tactics. History says that aircraft like the D.H.2 helped to defeat the Fokker monoplane: as mentioned earlier, this was no doubt due to the fact that, having wing ailerons, they were able to turn much more quickly than the wing-warping machines, and in a turning fight the Eindeckers would lose.

There Has to be a Better Way

By the spring of 1916, most of the Allied squadrons were at least receiving standardised equipment. Gone were the days of a unit having a mixture of machines. This was particularly so with the scout (or fighter) squadrons. The RFC now had dedicated squadrons of Nieuports, D.H.2 and F.E.8 fighters, Sopwith 1½ Strutters and the multi-purpose F.E.2b and 2d machines that could, and did, fly all sorts of missions with almost equal efficiency.

Gone now were the Vickers F.B.5 pushers, and so too the B.E.12s; the B.E.12 was, after all, no more than a B.E.2 with the observer's front cockpit covered over and one or two Lewis guns fitted to the top wing to fire over the propeller. Unfortunately, they were little better than B.E.2s, and although Nos 19 and 21 Squadrons used them for a time as fighters and escort machines, they were too docile for air combat and were quickly outclassed by the opposition.

The French still operated their two-seater types, but they, too, now flew single-seaters—Nieuports and the new Spad VII. By the autumn of 1917 these two fighter types equipped not only all French escadrilles, but also some in the RFC. Spads replaced the B.E.12s of No 19 Squadron, and replaced No 23 Squadron's F.E.2bs in early 1917. Of course, the French were using Nieuports long before the RFC, whose first examples were the Type 16. The RNAS used Type 11 single-seaters at first.

On the German side, the Fokker monoplanes, still operating but slowly being overwhelmed by the RFC fighter types, were still attached in small numbers to the two-seater Fliegerabteilungen. For the Battle of Verdun in February 1916, they were being grouped together in Kampfeinsitzerkommando units (KEKs) at various locations. Generally they were known by their base airfields, for example KEK Vaux, KEK Bertincourt, KEK Habsheim, KEK Sivry and KEK Jametz. There were still only a handful of pilots and aeroplanes in each KEK, which were nothing like the size of Allied squadrons, but they could continue to help protect the two-seaters which operated from the same airfield or area, as well as providing fighting machines to engage Allied two-seaters over the front. RFC squadrons generally operated with three Flights, each with a Flight Commander and five other pilots (totalling eighteen flying men). The CO of the unit did not necessarily lead or even fly with his men. Some did; some remained purely a figurehead. At times, COs were actually forbidden to cross the lines, it being deemed too risky since their loss would be a blow to overall leadership and experience.

Grouped together, the KEK pilots were better able to combat the increasing size of Allied formations. These units were generally commanded by senior officers of Oberleutnant rank or above, who may or may not be one of the up-and-coming aces. Oberleutnant Rudolf

The B.E.12 was the fighter version in the B.E.2 series—and was next to useless in that role. This photograph photo shows a Home Defence B.E.12 with twin Lewis guns on the top wing. The pilot is Freddie Sowrey, DSO, MC, who, apart, from downing Zeppelin L 32 over Billericay, Essex, later scored heavily as a Spad pilot in France.

Berthold had commanded KEK Vaux until injured in a crash, but with the Germans—and the British—rank almost always overrode experience. As the war progressed, some top German aces were operating as NCO pilots while their unit was being led by a pilot with no victories at all and little combat experience.

However, experience was a factor in determining a successful fighter pilot. With the British, a trainee pilot was generally assigned as a two-seat or single-seat pilot once he had passed through the training system. Once in France, he would go to a pilot pool to await a slot in a front-line squadron, that is, he would wait to fill a dead man's shoes, or replace a pilot who was going home on rest. Aptitude seemed to be only a minor consideration, for within the training schools the instructors knew they had to produce Corps, bomber and scout pilots in established proportions. Each task had its dangers, but that of the single-seat pilot was perhaps the most dangerous, although, provided he were not surprised and shot down, he might at least be best placed to run for the comparative safety of the lines. Once in France and assigned to a squadron, he had either to learn quickly or die. Not that the Corps pilots had it that much better, but at least they had the chance of flying with an experienced observer who could help watch the sky. However, this was not always policy: after all, no veteran—pilot or observer—wanted to entrust his life to a novice.

Newcomers took time to 'see' things in the air. There are many stories of pilots returning from their first sorties having seen nothing, while their comrades had come across hostile and friendly aircraft and engaged in air battles while the embryo pilot had sailed along oblivious to everything. Nor was it a case of retaining an edge just because of past experience. A considerable number of experienced aircrew were lost soon after returning from extended leave or from a period spent as an instructor. That honed edge had dulled, and the air war had progressed: aircraft and situations changed.

The German system was different. Once the war progressed into 1916, it was rare for a pilot to be considered for single-seaters unless he had been flying two-seaters for some time. Many observers, too, had long experience in the back of a two-seater before they were considered for pilot training—those who wanted it: they might turn out to be useless as fighter pilots, but at least they could survive in the air far better than shiny new Second Lieutenants in the RFC straight from training school.

This is not to say that RFC observers did not become pilots. The point is that German airmen had generally to go to single-seaters via two-seaters, whereas the British pilot could go directly to a two-seater or single-seater unit from flight training. The French had a similar system to the Germans, many pilots progressing via two-seaters before going to fighter escadrilles.

One experienced fighter pilot who did not fly with or command a KEK was Oswald Boelcke. His friend Max Immelmann had fallen in June 1916, and, following the start of the Battle of the Somme on 1 July, he had been rested after gaining his nineteenth victory. Whether or not he needed a rest, the main reason for taking him away from the front was to protect Germany's first aviation Pour le Mérite winner, awarded on the same day as that of Immelmann, who was now dead. The loss of Immelmann had already been a severe blow to the Air Service, and Boelcke's demise was unacceptable.

Boelcke was whisked away to the Balkans, but, while engaged on mainly an inspection tour, his organisational brain, already full of ideas as to how the German fighter force might be changed, came up with his Dicta Boelcke, and a report to his masters at Headquarters on how the fighter force should be arranged in future. Taking the KEK idea a step further, he felt that larger—but still dedicated—fighter units should be formed, independent of the Fliegerabteilungen, but still under the control of, and assisting, the various German Army establishments.

Ideally, each unit, which became known as a Jagdstaffel (hunting squadrons), should have a commander and at least a dozen pilots of various ranks. No longer would they be responsible for two-seater escort duties, but employed solely for hunting out Allied aircraft raiding German territory, or attacking those they found engaged in intercepting German two-seaters.

His Dicta Boelcke was published and distributed to KEKs and the new Jagdstaffeln—or Jastas, as they became known—once they were indeed established. It read:

1. Always try to secure an advantageous position before attacking. Climb before and during the approach in order to surprise the

Oswald Boelcke wearing his Ordre Pour le Mérite, the ribbons of the Hohenzollern House Order with Swords, and the Iron Cross 2nd Class. The Iron Cross 1st Class and his pilot's badge are lower down.

enemy from above, and dive on him swiftly from the rear when the moment to attack is at hand.

2. Try to place yourself between the sun and the enemy. This puts the glare of the sun in the enemy's eyes and makes it difficult to see you and impossible for him to shoot with any accuracy.

3. Do not fire the machine guns until the enemy is within range and you have him squarely within your sights.

4. Attack when the enemy least expects it, or when he is preoccupied with other duties such as observation, photography, or bombing.

5. Never turn your back and try to run away from an enemy fighter. If you are surprised by an attack on your tail, turn and face the enemy with your guns.

6. Keep your eye on the enemy and do not let him deceive you with tricks. If your opponent appears damaged, follow him down until he crashes to be sure he is not faking.

7. Foolish acts of bravery only bring death. The Jasta must fight as a unit with close teamwork between all pilots. The signal of its leaders must be obeyed.

Some of these recommendations will be self-evident to today's readers, but in 1916 these words of wisdom from Germany's top ace were read and digested avidly. However, some comment might be worth making.

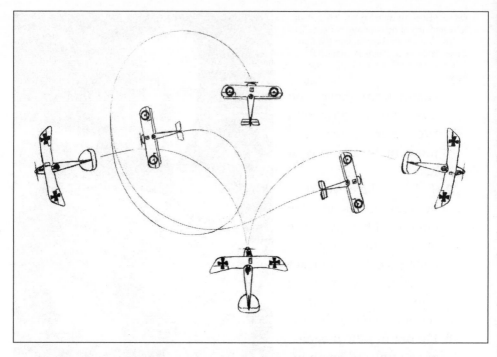

Attacked from behind. It did not take long for pilots of both single-seater and two-seater aircraft to discover that the natural inclination to dive when attacked courted almost certain disaster. A tight turn was far better, as it put the attacker into a position of having to turn more tightly—if he were able to—in order to fire a deflection burst ahead of his target. With more experience, the pilot being attacked, or one who saw an attack coming, began to realise that a turn into the approach, and a slight dive, gave an even more difficult approach shot to the attacker. The latter's angle of turn made a deflection shot almost impossible, and he was thrown on to the back foot; if he turned too steeply, he lost sight of the target below his own aircraft, and the target could then half-roll and dive from trouble. By the time the attacker realised his opponent had done so, the latter was generally out of range and out of danger.

Considering the first 'rule', there has to be some advantage of attacking from below, the way Albert Ball liked to. Attacking a two-seater from above and behind gave the enemy observer a good chance of getting in a telling burst at the attacking fighter, and, of course, surprise was lost immediately the enemy crew saw you diving upon them. Diving gave the attacker speed, but it was often useful to try and keep the hostile machine's tail between you and the observer's gun. There is no argument with No 2, which continues to apply to this day. As for No 3, firing at close range was always better than firing at long range, no matter how good a shot a pilot was (although most were not). The more experienced pilots also knew that if an opponent opened fire too soon, it was generally a sign that he was new and inexperienced. Knowing this gave the experienced pilot an added advantage in that he was probably superior to his opponent during a one-on-one combat. However, occasionally a long-range shot by an experienced pilot was fired for a purpose, especially if the machine he was attacking was, in turn, attacking a comrade's aircraft: his fire became a distraction. Nevertheless, one needed to be on one's guard. An experienced pilot in a tail chase, and realising that he is not going to close the range, might begin firing at long range in the hope that his opponent, in order to avoid being hit, takes evasive action, thus losing speed and position and allowing the pursuer to close the gap.

In No 4, the danger always was that a crew was so busy carrying out their job that they were taken by surprise. Watching out for hostile aircraft became secondary for a few moments, and it was these moments that could spell life or death. Watching for the fall of artillery fire or handling a camera with its photographic glass plates needed special attention. The two-seater pilot was responsible for watching the sky during these seconds, but he too could be distracted, and often the top (or bottom) wing of a biplane put the enemy in a blind spot.

No 6 needs some clarification. Anyone who has studied combat flying will immediately say that this is wrong—that one should not follow an opponent down. However two things should be remembered. When Boelcke wrote this, combat was still mostly a one-on-one affair, with no other aircraft about let alone in sight. Moreover, once the Jasta formations came into being, they had a definite way of fighting, wherein the attacking pilot was generally covered by his men. We shall discuss this further later on.

As to the last item, covering signals, it is important to understand that we are talking here of a period before air-to-air wireless came into being. Communication between pilots in the air was by means of signal flare, wing-waggling or hand movements. This, of course, always assumed one was watching for them, and not looking in a totally different direction (for a good reason). Despite the comparatively slow speeds of First World War aircraft, things still moved quickly, and if a pilot was not careful his whole flight of comrades might suddenly turn and disappear while he was looking in another direction.

Both sides employed a signal flare system in the air. In the RFC, firing a red flare meant 'danger' or 'attack', or, after a fight, 're-form'. A white flare meant 'let's go home'. A green light would be fired by any member of a formation if he needed to abort the sortie and return home with an engine or other problem.

There was no point in any pilot straggling along trying to keep up, for the machine would stick out like a sore thumb and he would be quickly picked off by an opponent. If a pilot did abort, for whatever reason, it was highly unlikely that he would be escorted back by another aircraft. Patrols were, in general, too small to allow this luxury, as this would then open up the remaining members to attack by superior numbers. The ideal answer would have been for the whole patrol to abort and escort the 'lame duck' safely home, or at least to the lines, but that would leave the Corps two-seaters open to attack from a gap in the overall cover.

If there were enemy aircraft about, a green light would attract them, so the more experienced flyer, if in trouble, would simply slip away and hope the Germans did not notice him. On rare occasions, if his guns jammed in a fight, an experienced pilot, rather than break off and head west, might climb way above the mêlée and wait for it to end, all the while keeping a good look out overhead. He might also be able to rectify the jam and return to the fray.

Later in the war, some two-seater crews painted individual red, white and green circles on the trailing edge of the wing's centre section, so that if the observer saw a flare that his pilot had not noticed, a tap on the head and a finger jabbing at the appropriate paint mark would make the pilot aware of what was happening. It might also be necessary to fire more than one flare to ensure that everyone had 'got the message'.

The Jastas

By the time the German air commanders had decided to endorse Boelcke's ideas of forming fighter Staffeln, the introduction of new fighters was under way to replace the Eindecker, which was being outclassed by the better British and French counterparts. Oddly enough, despite the success of the monoplane, all the new machines were biplanes.

Boelcke seated in his Fokker E.IV
Eindecker, fitted with two machine guns.

Fokker produced the Fokker D.I, followed by the D.II and III; Halberstadt brought out their D.II and D.III and LFG their Roland D.II; and then the Albatros company added their D.I and D.II types. All had synchronised machine guns firing through the propeller arc, and by the late autumn of 1916 the Albatros machines were replacing virtually everything.

These types, together with the last remaining Eindeckers, equipped the first fifteen Jasta units in August and September that year. Boelcke himself was given command of Jasta 2, and had the good fortune—and standing—to be allowed to select most of his pilots. Having been rested and on a tour of inspection, he had had the time to meet and interview several men who would later become aces with his unit. Among these was a certain Leutnant Manfred von Richthofen, who would become the German ace of aces, and Erwin Böhme, who would feature in Boelcke's demise.

Some of these first Jastas were formed with pilots from Flieger-abteilungen, some from KEK units, others from nothing, save perhaps a senior airman as leader and perhaps one or two experienced pilots from a KEK or Kampfstaffel.*

At first, few of the new aircraft were available to some of the Jastas, while others, formed from KEKs, at least had what equipment they had been using previously. Boelcke had two Fokker D.IIIs and later an Albatros D.I. He began scoring 'kills' in September, and as new aircraft started to arrive, so his novice pilots began to emulate him and started to score victories. His skill and words of wisdom encouraged his young

---

* Literally, 'combat squadron'.

63

The streamlined Albatros Scout, although heavy, proved a good fighting machine, from the D.I through to the D.Va. This one is an OAW-built D.III with the rounded tailfin more in keeping with the D.V. The initials on the fuselage, 'KP', are for its pilot, Kurt Petzinna, of the Bavarian Jasta 32.

flock and instilled in them the desire to do better and to bring intelligence and thought into air fighting, not to just go bull-headed at the enemy.

With his score of victories at 40, Boelcke was killed during an air fight with DH.2s of No 24 Squadron RFC on 28 October 1916. He and Erwin Böhme collided, and although a distraught Böhme landed safely, the great air hero of the Fatherland fell to his untimely death. The Father of the German fighter arm, and inspiration to many, remained undefeated in combat, and although the war was to last for another two years, only nine German pilots would better his score and two others equal it.

FIVE

The Air War Gets Serious

BY THE LATE autumn of 1916, the first handful of German Jastas were getting into their stride. Jastas 1 and 2, in particular, flying their new biplane fighters, had started to cut a swath through the RFC on the British front flying their new biplane fighters. Jasta 1 claimed 30 victories by the end of that year, while Jasta 2—now named 'Jasta Boelcke' in memory of its famous late commander— scored an incredible 86 victories. Jastas 4 and 5 were both into double figures by the end of December, despite the arrival of winter.

Although the German fighters, in the main, remained behind their lines, there were short periods, certainly in the early days, when pilots would encroach on Allied airspace. This is evidenced in a letter Erwin Böhme wrote in December 1916. In the same letter, he told of the two subsequent commanders of Jasta 2:

> We have already had two Staffel leaders since Boelcke. The current is a Bavarian Oberleutnant named Walz, whom we chose as commander ourselves. His predessor Kirmaier (also a Bavarian), who assumed command of the Staffel after Boelcke's death, we unfortunately had to leave behind enemy lines on November 22nd. Our English clientele is now somewhat intimidated. We have to fly ever deeper over their lines to locate them. At that time there were five of us on patrol when we were simultaneously attacked by two large squadrons. Each of us was involved with multiple opponents. I saw Kirmaier still. He was in pursuit of a smoking Vickers two-seater while he himself had a number of opponents on his tail—such a thing corresponded with his Bavarian tastes.
>
> I myself was attacked at that moment by a Morane monoplane. The foolish fellow quite tactlessly attacked me from the front. Now he lies in the vicinity

of Longueval, where the Delville forest formerly stood. That was my seventh 'confirmed' victory. That is because [of] the three Russians which I shot down, since they lacked 'ground observers' [witnesses], in other words confirmation by a disinterested party, I was only credited with one. They are very exacting in crediting a victory, but that is good, since it precludes the temptation of boastfully padding one's totals.

This period, during which the Germans had to go looking for the enemy, was at the start of the 'Jasta era', their new Albatros and Halberstadt scouts being superior to Allied aircraft. It lasted until about May/June 1917. In the fight on 22 November 1916, Böhme's victim was a two-seater crew from No 3 Squadron on a photo 'op'. Jasta 2 engaged D.H.2s of No 24 Squadron, Stefan Kirmaier being shot down by Captain J. O. Andrews, MC, and Second Lieutenant K. Crawford. It was Andrews' seventh victory and Crawford's second. The Albatros fell near Flers, south of Bapaume, just inside the British lines.

In the New Year of 1917, the Albatros D.III started to arrive, and it quickly replaced all earlier German fighters—Albatros D.Is and D.IIs— as well as the Halberstadts. The main visual differences with the D.III were its new upper wing and, almost copying the Nieuport's example, much narrower-chord lower wing ,which, as with the Nieuport, necessitated 'vee'-struts between the two. The RFC soon began to call the new machines 'vee-strutters'. With an improved Mercedes 160hp engine, two synchronised machine guns and a two-hour endurance, the

By 1917 the Germans were almost wholly equipped with Albatros Scouts. This photograph depicts Hermann Göring's Jasta 27. The nearest machine is his D.Va, while the next is a D.III.

D.III became the standard German fighter on the Western Front for most of 1917, supplemented also by the D.V and D.Va, which had a new, rounded fuselage and better tailfin.

As the winter of 1916/17 gave way to spring, both warring sides in France were planning offensives as soon as the weather improved. Better weather in March saw the German Jasta pilots honing their skills in the air. They were eager for more targets to shoot at—targets that were sure to come in any future battles. And come they did. In fact the Allied side struck first, on Easter Monday, 9 April 1917, opening the Battle of Arras. The objective, apart from attempting to break through the German trench systems, was to take the high ground of Vimy Ridge which overlooked much of the French countryside, with Lens in the immediate forefront. Lens, of course, being an industrial town, was important to the Germans for coal.

Anyone who has travelled in northern France will know how flat the landscape is, so it is no surprise to understand that any high ground was essential to take and hold because of the advantage it gave the occupying side. Many battles of the First World War were over fought the occupation of high ground. The Canadians took the Ridge despite heavy casualties and some advances were made into German-held territory to the south, the ground troops being strongly supported by the airmen of the Royal Flying Corps. However, the air battle soon presented the opportunity the German fighter pilots had been straining at the leash for since the New Year began.

'Bloody April'

A few miles further east from Arras and Vimy was the town of Douai. It was from an airfield near here—Brayelles—that Max Immelmann and Oswald Boelcke had flown their Fokker monoplanes in the summer of 1915. It now housed an even more deadly airman— Manfred von Richthofen.

Von Richthofen, whose mentor, Boelcke, had taught him so many things about air fighting while he was a tyro with Jasta 2, had by the spring of 1917 achieved a personal score of 39 victories. He had been given command of Jasta 11 on 15 January, having thus far achieved sixteen 'kills' with Jasta 2. Jasta 11 had scored not a single victory since its formation in October the previous year. The Staffel had been based at Brayelles since its formation, under the command of Oberleutnant Rudolf Lang, who had previously been with Kampfstaffel 31. On leaving Jasta 11 he had moved to command Jasta 28, but was then given command of a fighter school in April. By the time he left, Jasta 28 had only scored two 'kills', neither by Lang. His unit was taken over by a Jasta 11 protégé of von Richthofen's, Karl Emil Schäfer. By constrast— and to possibly put things into perspective—Schäfer had, between 4 March and 25 April 1917, shot down 22 British aircraft under the Baron's tutelage!

Jasta Tactics

Jasta tactics had, by this time, started to emerge. A Jasta was smaller than a RFC squadron, which generally comprised 18 pilots (plus a CO) in three Flights—A, B and C. So, whereas the RFC would usually patrol in Flights, each generally of five aircraft, under the leadership of a flight commander or his deputy, a Jasta would fly in more or less full strength of anything between five to nine or ten machines. It was led by the Staffelführer, unless he were on leave, taken ill or on some official business, in which circumstances the next most senior pilot would take charge.

As on most occasions, the Jasta chose its moment of combat—unless it were surprised by British or French aircraft—it was always the leader who made the initial assault and had first crack at the opposition, protected by the rest of his men. In this way he could concentrate on the target without worrying about an attack from behind. Once combat had been joined and the aircraft of both sides begun to dog-fight, then it was every man for himself, although invariably someone would be looking out for the leader. This is why, in general, Jastas had one or two 'star turns' in terms of victories and others managed only the occasional 'kill'.

While this may not have spread the victories nor the honours that went with them, it did produce good results in terms of downing the opposition, because the 'stars' were able to knock down aircraft in good numbers as their experience in doing so grew. German pilots, flying over their own territory, were also able to break off the action far more readily and return to their aerodromes, whereas Allied airmen had to fight their way out of trouble and then head back west to re-cross the lines. Unless there was a burning reason to engage, the Germans were more inclined not to attack if terms and situations were unfavourable, which led Allied pilots to comment that the Germans had 'the wind up' (a catchphrase of the time), whereas, in fact, this was a reasonable tactic and good common sense.

The Germans could always wait until the opposition had finally to turn for home, perhaps with that prevailing west-to-east breeze or wind hindering the flight home. The famous action in which von Richthofen downed Major Lanoe Hawker, VC, DSO, on 9 November 1916 (whilst the German was still with Jasta 2) was a classic example of this, for although both men were able to evade each other's fire, Hawker had finally to make a dash for the lines or face capture with an empty fuel tank. Once the D.H.2 began heading for the lines, Richthofen was able to get in a telling burst of gunfire, killing Hawker in the air with one round out of 900 shots he had fired during the combat! Far from being evenly matched, Hawker was certainly at a disadvantage in more ways than one. He carried four 97-round ammunition drums, which had to be changed, whereas the German had two synchronised, belt-fed guns and was flying a much superior aircraft. Moreover, although Hawker was an experienced pilot, he was under-matched in terms of fighter-to-fighter combat. Richthofen was still very much learning his trade by this time, but his shooting was good, and improving.

It seems apparent that the Staffel tactics were developed from the former KEK days in 1916, where the Experten like Boelcke and Immelmann, then operating with a small number of other pilots in order to combat the growing size of Allied formations, attacked first on account of their proven skill, rank and position, whilst being protected by the other Fokker pilots. Only occasionally did the others score 'kills', either because the leader had missed in his first pass and broken away, or in a general air fight, the chance to attack another Allied machine had presented itself.

In his later career, von Richthofen wrote down some of his experiences and tactics, which we shall read about later, but of this 'Boelcke period' he related that Boelcke usually divided his pilots into two Flights, each of five or six machines—six or seven being, he felt, the most that one leader could effectively manage in the air.

Jasta Tactics. A German Jasta was not equivalent in size to a British or French squadron: in many respects it was akin to a large Flight. Despite some Allied airmen continually reporting 30 or 40 hostile scouts engaging them, this was probably nothing more than several Jastas banding together once they had seen the opportunity for a favourable attack. Most Jasta leaders did not engage unless circumstances were favourable: there would always be other chances, and often the mere sight of a group of German fighters would be sufficient for an Allied recce machine, or artillery spotter, to break off and head west, curtailing the job in hand. If circumstances seemed favourable for an attack, the Jasta leader—not necessarily the Staffelführer—would lead the approach and generally make the initial firing pass. He could do this in the knowledge that his men were coming along behind and keeping a watchful eye on the sky. He was therefore totally free to concentrate on his approach and attack, which, more often than not, succeeded in bringing down the hostile machine—or at least damaging it. Attacking more than one opponent, once the initial attack had been instigated—and whatever the result—a general mêlée usually ensued, in which the other attacking pilots could engage individual aircraft: the classic dog-fight. Almost without exception this would take place on the German side of the lines, the Jasta pilots knowing that if things started to go badly they could quickly dive or fly away westwards, and that the Allied pilots would not relish pursuit so far over enemy-held territory.

However, Jasta 11 appears to have broken the developing mould of the leader being the main attacker, because, during April 1917, several of its pilots scored large numbers of 'kills'. Obviously, von Richthofen had been encouraging his fledgelings to make their own attacks once the first pass had been made. (Boelcke had encouraged this too.) It was always a good tactic to split up an enemy squadron and then to pick off individual opponents. With two-seaters, it also lessened the danger of cross-fire from several gunners. Of the fourteen highest scorers amongst the German fighter pilots during 'Bloody April', a month which saw the RFC lose something in the region of 250 aircraft (and the French around 50) in air combat and from ground fire, five came from Jasta 11—Kurt Wolff with 23, von Richthofen with 22, Schäfer with 21, von Richthofen's younger brother Lothar with 15 and, finally, Sebastian Festner with 10.

Heavy Losses

Jasta 11 scored 89 victories during April. Its next nearest rival, Jasta 5, achieved 32, while Jastas 12 and 2 accounted for 23 and 21, respectively. Jasta 11 had scored more than three times the number the next three Staffeln had scored together; and, of course, the vast majority of these victories received confirmation as they mostly came down inside German lines.

The RFC were meanwhile still struggling with their B.E.2 variants, at least 75 of which were shot down during April. Despite the type's reputation, 58 F.E.2b pushers were also lost. Even Nieuport Scout pilots were not immune: 43 were shot down during the month. These losses were due to some extent to the inexperience of fighter (scout) pilots, whereas, as mentioned earlier, German fighter pilots invariably came via two-seaters where they had at least gained some experience of combat flying and had learned how to 'see' in the air.

There were a few new British types coming to the front, and more were promised, but not all were a match for the new Albatros scouts. Gradually replacing the B.E.s were R.E.8 two-seater Corps aircraft, but they were only a slight improvement on the B.E.s. They had started to arrive in late 1916, and if nothing else at least they did have the observer in the rear cockpit and were thus better able to defend themselves from rear attacks. The pilot also had a forward-firing, synchronised Vickers machine gun.

The Sopwith 1½-Strutter, which had started to trickle into France in mid-1916, was another two-seater used both for long- and short-range reconnaissance sorties and fighting patrols. Both occupants had a machine gun, the observer being seated in the rear cockpit. Fourteen of these aircraft were lost in April.

A new two-seater was the Bristol F.2a, also referred to as the Bristol Fighter. No 48 Squadron brought this machine to France during April 1917, but its potential had not yet been recognised, and its pilots and observers, once under threat from German fighters, started to close up their formation in order to put up a defensive stance. Jasta 11 themselves shot down several of the new type (in all, nine were lost during April), von Richthofen later commenting that they posed no real danger. As things developed, however, the Bristol became a superb two-seat fighter when handled aggressively, the fire from a forward-firing Vickers and one, sometimes two Lewis guns in the back proving to be a deadly combination. The Bristol Fighter was an immensely strong machine and it performed much better with its water-cooled Rolls-Royce 'Falcon' inline engine rather than with a rotary one.

Another Sopwith machine, the single-seat Pup, had also started to arrive in France in late 1916. Armed with a single Vickers gun firing through the propeller arc, it was a 'nice' machine to fly, and for a period did much to combat the Albatros scouts, provided it was flown by an experienced fighter pilot. However, it was a little too docile and lacked performance in some respects, so it failed to provide a challenge to the Albatros machines. Seven were lost in April, along with eight of the French Spads being used by the RFC.

The French lost eighteen Spad VIIs during the same period, and twelve Nieuport Scouts, the rest being a combination of single and two-seater types, including fifteen Caudron and Farman machines.

As for the British two-seater Corps aircraft, their tactics had developed slowly during 1916, becoming a little more concentrated during the Battle of the Somme which began on 1 July and lasted until the winter. During the Arras battle, they were again in the air, constantly ranging artillery, making photographic reconnaissances, conducting general

The arrival of the Bristol Fighter in France was not auspicious. This F.2a of No 48 Squadron was brought down by Richthofen's Jasta 11 in April 1917, but in later months pilots developed the machine's potential and it became a tough opponent for the Germans.

reconnaissance sorties and carrying out bombing missions on the German rear, checking supply routes and bombing transport and supply dumps, and also flying contact patrols.

With no air-to-air communications, and because Corps aircraft worked over the battle front more or less flying singly, these machines were extremely vulnerable to fighter attack from the German Jasta pilots. With only half an eye on the sky and the remaining one and a half on the ground, it was not an enviable position. Direct escort in any real sense was out of the question, for, whilst ranging artillery, the Corps machine needed to circle constantly over and around the targeted area, often under direct shellfire from the ground. This made close escort impossible; and, of course, had it been carried out, the escort would have become just as vulnerable to attack flying in more or less leisurely circles above the two-seater, particularly at medium to low altitudes.

Nor was it always possible for such an escort to locate a two-seater in the often cloudy sky, with smoke from gunfire rising to operating altitude and occasionally rain, not to mention ground haze, mist and fog. The general tactic was for Allied fighter aircraft to patrol constantly above the battle area in the hope of engaging any German fighters (or two-seaters doing work similar to that of British Corps aircraft), before they could attack or drive off the Corps machines. This was fine if it all worked, but the German fighter pilots were by now masters of the surprise attack and could bide their time, waiting for an opportunity to pounce during a break in the RFC patrols, or when a patrol was being engaged by other German aircraft.

During 1917, RFC pilots were often warned to be on the look-out for traps. Whilst on patrol they might see a German two-seater flying along, or perhaps a couple of Albatros scouts, and, in attacking them, find themselves under attack by more hostile aircraft from above. It is easy to explain this as a trap, but it is rare to find any reference to German, or for that matter British, airmen doing such a thing. In attacking and then being attacked, it was, usually, simply a case of a patrol spotting would-be aggressors and coming to their comrades' aid. These 'traps' would have worked better if the 'bait' could have been contacted by wireless and warned of the impending danger, but, unless this were carefully planned, it was more likely that the 'bait' would be shot down before the 'trap' could be sprung. However, aircrew saw or imagined all sorts of opposition tactics if they came off second best, feeling that the 'dastardly Hun' had caught them out.

However, traps cannot be discounted altogether: much later, the RAF did endeavour to use such tactics on occasion. On 2 July 1918, Richard Wenzl of Jasta 6 made an agreement with Jasta 11 that he and his section would fly low and 'act stupid' while Jasta 11 covered them at high altitude. Jasta 6 managed to lure down several American fighters, but unfortunately Jasta 11 arrived a little too late, and although Jasta 6 claimed four of the enemy, they were unable to get confirmation of their victories.

The RFC fighter pilots often derided their German counterparts for not engaging in combat. This, of course, occurred at a time the Germans might feel they were at a disadvantage. However, far from being cowardly, they were in reality being immensely sensible. There was no point in a Staffelführer diving headlong into a fight in which he might lose two or three of his pilots if he could fly away, come back and find another attacking position much more in his and his men's favour. If all the stories one reads are true, then often the British pilots were the ones who attacked with 'flare, dash and disregard for personal safety'. This was fine if they shot down a German and came home victorious, but not so good if they were shot down—and less so if they failed to score beforehand.

It has to be said that there appears to be something of a 'blind spot' regarding what Germans were doing and what British fighter pilots did, or thought they should be doing. An example of this is in claiming an opponent shot down. Let us consider the 'out of control' victory, which, if confirmed by another pilot, or someone possibly a couple of miles away in the trenches, was credited as a true 'victory' and added to a pilot's overall score. Picture this scenario. Lieutenant Bloggs is in his Pup and gets into a scrap with his comrades. Suddenly an Albatros crosses in front of him and Bloggs opens fire. The German Flieger, hearing bullets hitting his machine, realises he is in trouble, half rolls and puts his machine into a spin, hoping that he will both get away from the danger and put off his attacker by making him think he is going down to crash. Bloggs in the meantime stops firing, curves into a climbing turn, checks the air about him to make certain another Albatros is not lining him up and, seeing that his tail is clear for the moment, looks down and is lucky enough to pick out a spinning Albatros some distance below, gyrating madly towards the ground haze. Feeling wholly satisfied with his actions, he breaks off and, upon landing, informs the Recording Officer that he has shot down a German fighter, which was last seen spinning down to within a few hundred feet from the ground and would have smashed to pieces as it hit. Lieutenant Didsee lands and tells the R.O. that he saw Bloggs fire at an Albatros and it went spinning into the ground. 'Did you see it crash,' asked the R.O? 'Well, no, but it must have done so!' 'Good show, Bloggs,' says the R.O., 'I'll write up the combat report and let you sign it.' Another 'kill' for pilot and squadron.

Meanwhile, Oberleutnant Wiseman lands his Albatros back at base and, upon being questioned by his pals about the fight, says he had a lucky escape, as he was caught napping and had several bullets go through his elevators, and two through the fuselage just behind the cockpit—'Look,' he says, 'you can see them,' pointing to the six holes through the tail and top decking of his Albatros. 'You were lucky,' says one of his friends. 'I saw you start to spin down and thought you'd been hit yourself.' 'No,' says Wiseman, 'I just threw the machine into a spin, and just above the ground levelled out and came home.'

This could happen—and did! But the very next day, shall we say, Bloggs is caught by an attacking Albatros, also hears bullets punching holes in the fabric of his machine, and kicks his Pup into a spin and heads down. Going through low cloud, he rights his machine and flies home safely. Does it never occur to him that the previous day 'his' German did exactly the same thing?

All this is somehow condoned by Headquarters, who acknowledges Bloggs' victory, which may or may not help with an award of some description. If he does this sort of thing half a dozen times, he might be termed an ace, and win a medal, but has he ever downed one German aircraft?

The Germans, of course, actively encouraged the 'ace system' and their decorations were scaled to victory totals. The British never acknowledged aces, and the Squadron Intelligence Officers completed combat reports and then sent off information on downed German aircraft to HQs in order to establish how many hostile aircraft might have been lost. It was only later that aviation enthusiasts sought to make issues of aces and their claims.

SIX

Early Air Fighting

THERE IS LITTLE doubt that Albert Ball was the first successful British scout pilot, and as such captured the imagination not only of other airmen in the Royal Flying Corps, but also of the civilian population at home. Although the RFC did not openly encourage hero-worship of its fighting airmen, enough of what he was doing and achieving was released to whet the appetite of journalists, and they did the rest.

Ball was also such a small, shy and seemingly unassuming young man, and in his way quite good-looking, that he quickly conquered the hearts of those he met and others who read about him in the newspapers. He often flew alone, but that was the way of air fighting in the early days. Only later in his career did he form part of offensive patrols, although even then he would often slip away, or be so engaged in combat that he simply did not stay with his brother pilots. That he could fly well was unquestioned; that he could use this skill together with a superb 'shooting eye' made the combination almost unbeatable; and these qualities, added to the thought he put into his self-taught tactics, made him a veritable tiger in the air.

He also benefited from his early career as a Corps pilot on two-seaters, almost before real air-fighting pilots became a reality. Flying B.E.2cs with No 13 Squadron at the beginning of 1916, he undertook a variety of missions—not only recce sorties but also photography, escorts and artillery observation. In May he went to No 11 Squadron, first flying a Bristol Scout and then a Nieuport Scout. He now began

Captain Albert Ball, DSO, MC, seated in his S.E.5 on his way back to France in April 1917. He usually flew without a flying helmet. Note the guide rail for pulling down the Lewis gun to both fire upwards and reload.

to engage hostile machines, and gained his first seven victories between 16 May and 2 July.

In July he was moved to No 8 Squadron, back with BEs, because he had had the temerity to ask for a rest. Again on two-seaters, he added bombing raids to his repertoire, but obviously his prowess as an air fighter could not be ignored and he was back with his Nieuport in No 11 Squadron by mid-August. On the 22nd he gained three successes—three Roland two-seaters, all classified as 'destroyed'. One crew, Offizierstellvertreter Wilhelm Cymera and his observer Leutnant Hans Becker, came from Kampfstaffel Nr 1. Becker was killed but Cymera survived—wounded—and later became a fighter ace with Jasta 1; he died on 9 May 1917. Ball moved to No 60 Squadron on the 23rd, taking his personal Nieuport, A201, with him, as the Nieuports from No 11 Squadron went with their pilots to form a Flight in the newly formed No 60 Squadron.

Roland C.II two-seaters seemed to be his main adversaries during this summer period, another two going down after his attentions on the 28th. Remarkably, he wrote out no fewer than six combat reports this day, the first timed at approximately 0930 during an OP (Offensive Patrol). He wrote:

> Two Rolands seen S.E. of Bapaume. Nieuport chased and got underneath nearest machine, which had a three-ply fuselage. Nieuport fired one drum at

about 20 yards, turned to change drums and fired half a drum, after which
the Roland dived and landed in corner of corn field.

Machine did not fire when diving, although Nieuport followed it down to
3,000 feet. The second machine ran, and fired off back mountings.

Unknown to him, the Roland was a machine from Fliegerabteilung
(A) 207. The observer, Leutnant Böhme, had been wounded and the
pilot, Leutnant Joachim von Arnim, killed, but Böhme managed to
land near Transloy. As it happened, von Arnim had just been assigned
to Boelcke's Jasta 2, and this was to have been his last flight with this
two-seater unit.

By 10 a.m. Ball, still near Bapaume, chased another Roland, but lack
of fuel made it impossible to go further, and although he exchanged fire
with the two-seater crew, they made off.

On the evening patrol, between 18.30 and 19.30, he had more scraps
while escorting some F.E. and B.E. machines on a bombing raid. He
forced two to land after firing up underneath them—both, he thought,
made good landings—and then he found four German aircraft, two
Rolands and two LVG two-seaters:

Four H.A. seen in formation S.E. of Adinfer Wood. I dived and formation
was lost at once. I got under nearest machine and fired one drum. H.A. went
down. I followed, firing another drum at about 20 yards' range. H.A. crashed
on its nose East of Ayette. I was out of ammunition so had to return, the
remainder of H.A. followed [me] to lines, but did not come near enough to
fire.*

By the end of August, Ball himself reckoned he had seventeen
victories, and, in a summary of his combats since May, Brigadier-
General J. F. A. Higgins, commanding 3rd Brigade, RFC, noted that
Ball had had more than 25 combats. In these he had forced twenty
German aircraft to land, of which eight had been destroyed, one seen
to descend in flames and eight more seen wrecked on the ground. He
had also forced two balloons down, one being destroyed. As can be
seen, not all 'forced to land' victories had been acknowledged as
victories, and one suspects, too, that not all the eight 'wrecked on
ground' were much more than forced landings. Ball himself noted his
score as seven destroyed, three out of control and six forced to land,
plus the balloon.

---

* 'H.A.' was the term used to abbreviate Hostile Aircraft; the later abbreviation, evident
in other extracts quoted in this book, was 'E.A.', for Enemy Aircraft.)

A German kite balloon. Balloons were not new in the First World War, but all sides used them extensively for aerial observation and for directing artillery fire. They were dangerous targets, although they were also tempting. While many pilots on both sides attacked them with regularity, it is noted that some *never* attempted an attack.

Balloons, as mentioned earlier, were not easy targets, and as the war progressed attacking them became even more dangerous. Two weapons had been developed to try and ignite these gas-filled airbags, Le Prieur rockets and special incendiary bullets made by, and known as, Buckingham. The rockets were one of those grandiose ideas that did not quite work as designed. They looked like large rockets that one might see on Guy Fawkes' Night, and aircraft, especially Nieuports, had four fixed to each interplane 'vee'-strut. The pilot, attacking a balloon, would fire them electrically and hope a hit would result in the kite balloon catching fire. However, the rockets were not very accurate, and they suffered from a relatively short range.

Buckingham bullets were, in theory, only permitted (by international law) to be used during attacks on balloons, not against aircraft. If a pilot or observer were hit, the bullets would burn through clothes, flesh and bone, producing hideous injuries. One can imagine the niceties surrounding the concept of forbidding their use against targets other than balloons, although men trapped in an aircraft set on fire by conventional means would not have had a less unpleasant end. At one stage, a card signed by the General Officer Commanding in the field had to be pinned to the instrument panel of aircraft assigned to attack balloons, in case the pilot were brought down and captured and his aircraft found to carry Buckingham rounds. The Germans used Ph-ammunition (phosphorus). A small lead plug at the base of the bullet, forced forward on impact, ruptured the shell case and showered the target with burning phosphorus.

In his book *Fighter Pilot*, William MacLanachan (No 40 Squadron) wrote about a patrol in which his Flight Commander, Capt W. A. Bond, DSO, MC, had been killed with a direct hit by an AA shell, and also about seeing a German aeroplane go down in flames:

Bond's death filled us with consternation. It was an unwritten code that we did not discuss the deaths of our friends, but the fact that the indomitable Bond had been killed by a direct hit from *Archie* meant more to us even than the loss of a friend.

Later in the morning, really ignorant of what I intended to do, I asked my mechanics, Davidge and Biggs, to fill my tank, and while waiting for them to bring the petrol wagon my thoughts about the war and the Germans fell to the lowest dregs of bitterness. I had seen the wounded in hospital, the dead near Avion, and seen new pilot after new pilot arriving at the Squadron, had seen the bright promising youngster going down to a horrible death of flames, and had been within forty feet of my flight commander as his machine was shattered in a savage, black, shell-burst.

I remembered my own squeamishness on seeing the Albatros going down in flames, Anyway, I had got *him* properly.

It was then a fiendish idea came into my mind. The German pilots, as far as I saw, used only incendiary ammunition. When they hit us we were 'finished', but two or three mornings previously I had emptied a drum of our own clean ammunition into a two-seater without apparent effect. I decided to remedy this by a concoction of my own, by filling my drums with three types of ammunition, 'armour piercer', 'tracer' and Buckingham [incendiary]. Such a mixture would certainly prevent the next enemy's escaping.

The first indication of the level to which my 'morality' had fallen was provided by Davidge. He was a very clever mechanic, much older than myself; his greyish hair always gave me the idea that our positions should have been reversed as far as rank was concerned. He did not refuse to full my drums as I wanted, he drove it home to me much more effectively.

'I'll do it if you order me to, Sir, but if you are caught with such ammunition on you it will mean death for you on the other side and court martial for me here.'

Determined to have the mixture and prepared to accept full responsibility, I carried three drums over to the armoury hut and locked myself inside. It took me ten minutes to fill the first drum, for I had to lay the cartridges out in order, and test each for a sunken or defective cap. This was a frequent cause of stoppages, and as it very often jammed the gun beyond remedy in the air, we had to take every precaution. I was surprised by a knock at the door.

I asked who it might be, and Mannock's voice replied: 'Let me in, I want to speak to you.' On my opening the door for him, he came inside, shut the door slowly after him and stood leaning against the post. Conscious that I was doing something 'dirty' I could feel the tension in the air as I waited for him to speak first.

'What are you doing here?' he asked, knowing very well, because he added, 'Your mechanics have just told me.'

'Mixing some filth and corruption for the Huns,' I said angrily. 'I'm going to make sure of the next one I hit.'

Filling the remainder of the drum, mechanically, 'one tracer. one armour, one Buckingham', I glanced at him several times without meeting his eyes. Something had upset him, his face was haggard and he was nervously pulling the strap of his Sam Browne [belt].

When I was about to commence filling the third drum he put his hand on my arm. He was trembling.

'Look here, Mac. If you have any affection for me, forget about last night and this morning and let me empty out that stuff.'

I stopped and sat down on the bench, facing him.

'They've never fired anything as me but incendiary; and two mornings ago I missed a two-seater. If I had had my drums loaded with this I'd have got him—properly.'

He stood silently looking at me—almost tearfully—and, in support of my own wavering brutality, I continued:

'I'm out to do as much damage as I can, and the surest way, no matter what it means, is the best for me. Besides—it isn't like you care about how they die as long as we kill them.'

Again his challenging eyes met mine.

'Do you mean to say, Mac, that you would coolly fire that much into a fellow creature or, worse still, into his petrol tank, knowing what it must mean?'

I realised then that the hardening effect of the war had been greater on me than on Mick; or that he was attempting to play on my emotions.

'Well, if I can't do anything with you I may as well go and leave you to it, but I'll give you one last chance. If you won't chuck it for humanity, will you for me?' He had come down to our old footing.

'If *you* will tell me exactly why you are so upset about it,' I replied.

His eyes filled with tears. 'Because that's the way they're going to get me in the end —flames and finish. I'm never going to have it said that my own right hand ever used the same dirty weapons.'

Poor old Mick. He was obviously in a highly strung emotional state that I laughed.

'All right, you darned old sentimentalist, if that's how you fell about it, I'll empty my drums.'

MacLanachan and Mannock walked from the armoury, and Mannock confided in his friend the reason he carried a revolver with him in the air: 'The other fellows all laugh at me carrying a revolver, think I'm doing a bit of play acting in going to shoot a machine down with it, but they're wrong. The reason I bought it was to finish myself off as soon as I see the first sign of flames.'

Fire in the air was a very real and constant worry for airmen in the First World War, and Mannock was not play-acting. Many airmen preferred to jump from their burning aircraft rather than face a slow death in the flames. Mannock's own prediction proved correct in July 1918, when he fell in flames. Whether or not he had time to carry out his own threat of shooting himself we shall never know.

Of course, it was not always possible to adhere to the letter of the law, or have a friend talk you out of carrying incendiary ammunition on anything other than balloon attacks; some airmen would not have bothered in any case. Many thought that death to the enemy was still death, and the more that died the more quickly the war would be over. William C. Campbell, DSO, MC and Bar (23 victories), flying with No 1 Squadron, had no compunction about using incendiary ammunition, and one pilot, flying with rockets, actually shot down an aircraft by firing them at it. Ball, in his early days, is known to have fired both rockets and Buckingham ammunition at enemy aircraft, despite his feelings of abhorrence about inflicting death on his foes. But, in the heat of the moment . . .

On 22 September 1916 he used incendiary ammunition. One assumes that he carried a drum of Buckingham in case he observed a balloon, rather than being on a specific balloon strafing sortie, for he was on a normal 'OP'—or perhaps at this stage the use of Buckingham against aeroplanes had not yet been specifically prohibited. He spotted a single-seat Roland over the Bapaume–Cambrai road:

H.A. appeared through clouds. Nieuport dived and got underneath machine, firing a drum at about 10 yards' range. H.A. turned and went down through clouds in a half dive, half side-slip. Nieuport could not follow H.A., but as the Buckingham bullets were used, and they were seen to enter the machine under pilot's seat and engine, it is thought it was most likely destroyed.

Just over a week later, however, he was on a balloon hunt, and the additional remarks on his combat report by his CO are of interest:

Nieuport went over to fire at balloon S.E. of Haplincourt. On getting down to 2,000 ft, three 'A' types [Albatros Cs] came towards Nieuport. Nieuport at once turned and got under the nearest, firing 97 rounds of Buckingham ammunition at about 15 yards' range. H.A. went down in a spin and crashed in an open field near Haplincourt.

Nieuport came back at 2,000 ft climbing on way to lines. [Other] H.A. only followed a short distance.

Captain Ball fired at the balloons in order to attract the patrol which protects them. He will not attack them [balloons or aircraft, using Buckingham: this is unclear] without instructions in future.

It does seem as if his CO, Major R. R. Smith-Barry, was trying to protect his flight commander's indiscretion, not even making it clear whether Ball would not attack balloons without orders, or aircraft, if he had Buckingham ammunition. How he would seek instructions in future —whilst in the air?—is equally not made clear for us at this distance.

Two days later however, Ball got a two-seater in flames, again with Buckingham ammunition:

Nieuport saw one Type 'A' at about 5,000 ft and at once dived at it and fired a few rounds, after which it ran with nose down.

Nieuport turned, and saw another Albatros just above. Pulling gun down Nieuport fired about 5 Buckingham bullets. E.A. came down in flames. An F.E. was very close to this machine, so may have hit it too, but Lieut. Bell-Irving and Lieut. Walters [No 60 Squadron] saw the fight and say the Nieuport got it.

The report was signed by Ball, and countersigned without comment by Smith-Barry. The victory was shared with an F.E.2b of No 11 Squadron.

Ball, by this time, not only had the DSO and MC, but was about to get a Bar to the DSO, followed by a second Bar shortly afterwards. Ending his first fighter tour of duty, he came home to England in

October, his victory tally standing at 31. He would return to the front in April 1917.

★ ★ ★

The Alan Duncan Bell-Irving mentioned in Ball's combat report was a Canadian from Vancouver, born in August 1894. By the autumn of 1916 he would be an ace with seven victories before being wounded by a Jasta 2 pilot. He would survive the war and was one of six brothers in service, three being in the RFC, one in the RNVR and two with the Army. There was also a cousin in the RFC.

On 21 October he became the second victory for Leutnant Alfred Mohr, the leader of Jasta 3, who was born in January 1889 and came from Oberremmel. Details of Mohr's early flying career are unclear, but he had taken command of the Jasta on 15 September, gaining six victories before his death on 1 April 1917.

Bell-Irving had been out escorting bombers in his Nieuport Scout, and on the return trip spotted what he identified as a Roland D scout. Bell-Irving turned to engage, but, owing to the cold, he found that his Lewis gun had frozen up, and, as he described the Roland as more powerful and better armed than his Nieuport, the Canadian dashed for the lines. He later wrote home:

> He put a bullet in my petrol tank—petrol poured out onto my lap. I had to stop trying to fix the gun jam and plug up the hole with one hand. Then he hit my right strut ,displacing it badly. I went down all agley [sic] but with my engine off and rudder and cloche [stick?] hard over and by sticking myself out over the side as if I had been sailing, I got things fairly level again. I had no directional control left but luckily under heavy Ack-Ack fire crossed the line about 50 feet up. I was doing a gentle curve and if I'd been any higher would have headed back to Germany.
>
> As it was I plunked down between the front and support lines. I jumped out before the machine went into a communications trench and turned over. I rolled over myself a few times before I got to my feet and ran like a rabbit for the trench. There I made a severe dent in the 8th Kings Royal Rifles' supply of brandy. Salvage parties are trying to get the instruments and engine. It was A203, the first and only Nieuport I've had and one of the best. However, I got a new one today.

As it turned out, when Mohr was killed in 1917, he too fell inside British lines, following a combat with a B.E.2c of No 12 Squadron. His crashed Albatros Scout was given the British code 'G18', as most captured or wrecked German machines in British lines were given an intelligence code number for reference. Bell-Irving had scored six of his victories in A203, his first claim being made while flying a Morane. He received the MC and is acknowledged as the first Canadian-born ace of the war.

Oswald Boelcke

Often called the Father of the German Fighters, Boelcke came from Giebichstein, near Halle in Saxony, where he was born on 19 May 1891. He was one of six children of a schoolmaster, and he joined the military in 1911 as a cadet . Becoming interested in aviation, learnt to fly in 1914, and therefore was an aviator as the First World War began.

Flying two-seater reconnaissance aircraft, sometimes with his brother Wilhelm as observer, he flew many sorties. With another observer, he gained his first combat victory on 4 July 1915 in a two-seater LVG, with Fliegerabteilung Nr 62. With the introduction of Fokker monoplanes, two were assigned to FA 62, where he and Immelmann flew them.

During the autumn of 1915 and into 1916, he and Immelmann vied for victories in their nimble, gun-carrying Eindeckers. With a total of nineteen 'kills' by 27 June 1916, and following the death of Immelmann, he was taken away from the war front. Following his ideas for fighting units—rather than a piecemeal distribution of fighters among the two-seater Staffeln (a move already under way with the advent of KEKs), the Jagdstaffeln were formed, and fifteen were soon in operation.

Like Ball, Boelcke often flew alone, although, at the start of operations with his Jasta 2, he was the only pilot with an aircraft and soon began to score more victories; as more machines arrived, so his fledgelings started to score. With 40 victories, Boelcke was killed in a collision on 28 October 1916.

The First Two Air-Fighting VCs

To give an indication of the importance attached to air fighting—or perhaps it was merely a case of new and outstanding achievements—two of the first VCs to be awarded in the First World War were in recognition of air combat. The two Victoria Crosses awarded went to

Major L. G. Hawker, DSO, and G. S. M. Insall. Hawker, who received the third air VC, has already been mentioned, and Gilbert Insall gained his VC for an action he fought on 7 November 1915.

Insall was born in Paris on 14 May 1894, and educated there, intending to follow his father into the dental profession. He enlisted in the Army when war came, but he and his brother Algernon joined the RFC and in the summer of 1915 went to No 11 Squadron, which was equipped with the Vickers F.B.5. Flying all manner of sorties, he and his observers still had time for combat. Although no 'kills' emerged, several enemy aircraft were driven off or driven down.

On 7 November, with Corporal T. H. Donald in the front cockpit, Insall attacked a German two-seater, which was forced down after a long chase and landed in a field. As he circled, the downed crew seemed to be preparing to fire up at him with their rear gun, so Insall dived, allowing Donald to fire at the pair. Nearby German ground fire started to come up at the Vickers, so Insall dived again, dropping an incendiary bomb on the stricken machine and later noting it to be obscured by smoke. Heading back to the lines, Donald strafed the trenches, but then the Vickers' petrol tank was hit and he was forced to land just inside British lines. Despite artillery fire from the Germans, the aircraft survived, and that night, having erected a screen, he and Donald were able to repair the machine by torchlight. At dawn, the pair took off and flew home. Insall received the VC, Donald the DCM.

Just over a month later, both men were wounded, brought down in a fight with another two-seater, and captured. Insall, recovering from his wounds, later escaped from captivity and managed to find his way to Holland. He was rewarded with the Military Cross.

A Third Fighter Pilot VC

Lionel W. B. Rees was not only the third fighter pilot to win the Victoria Cross but the most senior, being, at the time, a Major. Born on 31 July 1884, he was brought up in Wales before becoming an army cadet in 1903. By 1913 he was serving in the West African Frontier Force but was seconded to the RFC just before war was declared.

With No 11 Squadron in 1915, he and his observers engaged in several aerial actions, starting with one involoing a Fokker monoplane 'driven down' on 28 July, then, on 31 August, an LVG two-seater 'destroyed'. Two more two-seaters were 'driven down' in mid-September, followed by an Albatros two-seater of Fliegerabteilung 23 forced down inside Allied lines, the crew being killed. With another LVG 'driven down' on 31 October, Rees's victory tally for official purposes came to six—two destroyed and four driven down—for which he was awarded the Military Cross.

In 1916 he took command of No 32 Squadron, flying D.H.2 pusher fighters, and although officially he was not allowed to fly over the lines he was often to be found in the air. On 1 July—the day the Battle of the Somme commenced—he flew out and attacked four German two-seaters, which were then joined by two or three more. In the fight which ensued, Rees shot down one 'out of control' and forced another to land, also hitting the observer of third, but he himself was wounded in one leg and had to break off the attack. Seeing the other Roland two-seaters heading away, he made a final attack to help them on their way, effectively clearing the sky over the battle zone of enemy aircraft. For this action he received the Victoria Cross.

While there was no massive indoctrination in the techniques of air fighting given to new scout pilots in the First World War, other than the handing down of knowledge by instructors at fighting schools, a few reports had been compiled. However, it was up to the individual trainee to read them, and to try to understand them: there were no lectures on the intricacies of air fighting.

One of these reports was written by Rees. This runs to some pages, but, reading it, one suspects that he had been asked to give an overall view of what the new scout pilot might meet over France, for much of it appears very fundamental. There follow selected extracts from the report, and these demonstrate not only his thinking on tactics, but also, apparently, the thinking of the time—July 1916. It is established early on, for example, that the target should be the pilot of the enemy machine, not the machine itself.

Fighting in the Air

These notes are based on experiences of last year, so that it is impossible to lay down any hard and fast rules, as the conditions alter so fast. The deductions are based on the experiences of many RFC officers to whom I am greatly indebted.

On Sighting the Enemy

A scout should be able to get within 100 yards (or less) of the enemy without being seen, if it keeps between the enemy and the haze over the horizon, climbing to attack as the Fokkers do.

When you have seen the enemy, do not bank the machine more than is absolutely necessary. At long ranges the sun shining on the planes [wings] makes the machine very visible, and at short ranges banking makes one's marks [roundels] more visible.

Keep end on to the enemy as long as possible, because that position is the most invisible, and the end on target is the smallest. If the character of the machine is doubtful, the marking on the tail [a large black cross] usually shows up before anything else. Scouts approaching from 2,000 feet above are very often not observed.

When within 800 yards of the enemy do not fly straight unless you have reason to think that you are unobserved, because it is not known what range and speed-finders the enemy uses. If there is reason to think that the enemy has seen one, open fire before the enemy, as one always runs the risk of being hit by stray bullets at 400 yards range. Always so long as you do not open fire at a longer range than that at which you know you can obtain hits.

Close to within 100 yards if you can. Having decided to open fire, go all out. This gives the best chance of hitting, and intimidates the enemy.

The above statements are in places contradictory; it depends on one's temperament what one should do.

Having taken every possible precaution, trust to one's luck as far as possible. It is well known that Napoleon considered unlucky men of no use as fighters.

Usual Enemy Tactics

The single-seater Fokker tries to approach from behind. If seen or fired on he dives, to come up again a short time after. They attack in this fashion time after time.

The slightly larger Fokkers [*sic*] dive at their target from any angle. Having fired they go straight down. Sometimes now they dive under one, and then climb quickly, so that when next seen they are above and behind one's machine. To prevent this, hustle the enemy to prevent him coming up again.

Reconnaissance machines dive for the nearest [friendly] AA Battery and fire over their tails. The heavy fighters aim at bringing all their guns to bear. Machines seldom fly straight and make a proper attack.

The Engagement

Open fire before the enemy.
Open fire at the shortest possible range.
Open fire under the most favourable conditions.
Try to disable the enemy at once.

Close as soon as you can, so as to prevent the enemy setting his sights and taking aim. It is useless expecting to hit successfully at ranges over 400 yards.

Reserve your fire till within 100 yards of the enemy, but if discovered open fire before the enemy.

At ranges of 50 yards and under, if attacking from the flank, aim at the enemy's leading edge as you see it (one or other wing). This statement is only a guide.

If one must collide go straight up, as the enemy nearly always goes straight down. Then if one hits the enemy one hits him with one's undercarriage.

Do not collide unless by accident. If the enemy pilot is disabled the enemy machine may travel quite normally for a long time, so that one runs the risk of wrecking one's machine uselessly.

If it is necessary to change drums, dive under the tractor, as that upsets his aim.

As a rule it does not pay to follow a machine below 3,000 feet. At that height the machine guns from the ground become dangerous, and if the enemy machine is not disabled before that it will probably not be disabled at all.

It is dangerous to cross the trenches below 2,000 feet.

Kurt Wintgens

Another of the successful Fokker monoplane aces was Kurt Wintgens, born 1 August 1894 in Neustadt. He was also a pre-war Army cadet, transferring to aviation after the war had begun, firstly as an observer in France and in Poland, but in early 1915 he trained as a pilot and because of his flying ability became a Fokker pilot attached to the Bavarian Fliegerabteilung Nr 6.

Wintgens' first victory on 1 July appears not to have received official confirmation, nor did another three days later, but on 15 July he had his first confirmed 'kill'. Number three came in early August, but then illness kept him away from flying until early 1916, However, by June he had eight victories.

He joined KEK Vaux and brought his score to thirteen by the time the Jastas were being formed, KEK Vaux becoming the nucleus of Jasta 1. He gained a couple more Fokker 'kills' before the new biplanes started to arrive, and on 24 September he had nineteen victories. Next day he was in combat with French aircraft and went down in flames after an attack by a French Spad thought to be flown by Lieutenant Alfred Heurtaux of the well-known Escadrille N 3. Photographs of

Wintgens often show him wearing spectacles. Many First World War flyers flew with eyeglasses, showing that using them did not automatically preclude a man from piloting an aeroplane.

Alfred Heurtaux

The fall of Wintgens, again flying a Fokker Eindecker, was Alfred Heurtaux's eighth victory, and he was at the time flying a Spad VII: Escadrille N3 was about to become Spa 3, changing its equipment from Nieuports to Spads. Heurtaux came from Nantes, born on 20 May 1893, and had been through the military school at St Cyr pre-war. He was a cavalry hussar officer early in the war—he was cited for bravery—then transferred to aviation. His first unit was MS 38, flying

Four French aces, who between them scored 102 victories: Mathieu Tenant de la Tour (8), Alfred Heurtaux (21), Albert Deullin (20) and Georges Guynemer (53), all flying with Spa 3.

Moranes, but in early June 1915 moved to N 3 to fly Nieuports and then Spads.

During the summer of 1916 he became an ace pilot, and by the end of the year he had achieved sixteen combat successes, with three more as 'probables'. In May 1917, with his score standing at 21, he was severely wounded, sustaining an injury which almost put him out of the war. His victor was Ernst Udet of Jasta 15, a pilot who would survive the war with 62 victories, making him the second highest scoring ace after Manfred von Richthofen. Heurtaux was his sixth victory, and the Frenchman was fortunate to come down inside his own lines. He later returned to his command but was again wounded on 3 September, and this finally ended his front- line service.

Ernst Udet

Born in Frankfurt on 26 April 1896, Udet only joined the military after having been rejected several times. Beginning as a motor-cyclist, he suffered an injury which led him to transfer to aviation. After yet another rejection, he learnt to fly at his own expense.

After a period on two-seaters he went to one of the new KEK units at Habsheim, and during a raid on Mülhausen on 18 March 1916 by 22 French aircraft, he shot down a Farman while flying a Fokker monoplane. Then, attacking a Caudron G4, his gun jammed after knocking out one of its engines, and the quarry escaped.

After KEK Habsheim had become Jasta 15 in the late summer, he downed his second victory on 12 October and made it three on Christmas Eve. Two French Nieuport Scouts in the spring of 1917 made it five, then came the fight with Heurtaux's Spad. At around this time (as Udet later wrote in his book, *Mein Fliegerleben*), he met a similar light brown Spad, both pilots being out alone over the front. They began to circle one another, each watching the other for a move, or a sign of weakness; the first one to get behind the other might well be the victor. They passed by each other so closely that Udet was able to make out the pilot's helmeted head and, on the fuselage near the wings, two words in black lettering. Finally, he was close enough to read the words—'Vieux Charles' (Old Charles). The man who flew a Spad so marked was known to the Germans: it was Georges Guynemer, the French ace, who at this time had around 40 victories!

Udet knew that he was up against it. He understood that Guynemer, like all dangerous predators, usually flew alone, would sweep down on an opponent and rarely missed with his first attacking pass. Udet went into a half loop in order to try and come down on the Spad from above, but Guynemer was not to be outfoxed and also looped. Then he executed another steep turn, but the enemy was still with him and in fact was able to fire. Bullets thudded into Udet's Albatros, holing the starboard wings and hitting the 'vee'-strut. Udet went into a series of turns, stalls and side-slips, but the Frenchman anticipated every manoeuvre and Udet began to realise not only that the Frenchman was better than he, but that his Spad was superior. Then, suddenly, the Spad came into his sights and Udet jabbed at the gun button—but his guns had jammed.

Unable to clear his guns, Udet thought he might dive, but knew that with a pilot like Guynemer behind him he would be shot down in seconds. The turning and twisting continued, while Udet still tried desparately to clear his stoppage. Then the Spad stopped turning and flew alongside; Guynemer had seen that the German pilot was having trouble with his guns. Udet watched as the Frenchman waved across at him, then broke away and dived to the west. At this stage of the war there was still some chivalry between airmen, although, contrary to the views of many writers of pulp fiction, chivalrous acts in the First World War were few and far between.

Udet had been lucky. Guynemer was deadly in the air: once he had sized up a situation, no matter the position or angle, his Spad would head directly for anything with the black cross painted upon it, his guns blazing.

Georges Guynemer

By mid-1916 the slim, somewhat frail-looking Georges Marie Ludovic Jules Guynemer was the hero and the darling of France. France, like Germany, lauded its air heroes. In Germany, in particular, one could buy postcards of all the famous airmen, not only of fighter pilots but also of successful two-seater men as well. The more their deeds were publicised, the more the adulation and the more the hero worship rose. France, too, eventually had postcards on sale depicting her heroes of the air.

Guynemer was born in Paris on 24 December 1894 and volunteered to fly in November 1914. By June 1915 he was with Escadrille MS 3, which, upon change of equipment, became N 3 and then Spa 3. He was to remain with this unit until his death in combat on 11 September 1917.

His first victory was achieved whilst in a two-seat Morane, on 19 July 1915, but by the winter he was flying Nieuports and by Christmas had achieved three more 'kills'. In the New Year his score began to rise slowly, so that by the end of 1916 he had secured 25 'kills', many over two-seaters operating above the French lines. In 1917 his prowess continued to improve, and by September he had 53 confirmed victories, with numerous 'probables'.

In air fighting there were many different types of men. Some went straight into the attack almost without thinking. Others, perhaps, thought too much. Guynemer was well known for his calm, calculating approach to a combat, but, once he had decided to engage, his actions were swift, almost instinctive, albeit reasoned. Some days he scored more than one 'kill', and on 25 May 1917 he gained four.

Nor was he the flamboyant hero. If he had to be in Paris, he hated being seen in public because, it seemed' everyone knew his face. He much preferred to drive into the centre of the town at night, where he might escape the attentions of both men and women alike. Once, at the height of his fame and with a chest full of medals, he was asked what further honour could he possibly win. He replied, 'The wooden cross!' Some say this was because he felt certain that his ill-health would deny him a long life

Even this, in the end, was denied him. Finally shot down in combat on 11 September 1917, his Spad fell into the battle area, and, although a doctor was able to inspect his corpse, the battle became so fierce that his body and aeroplane were obliterated by shellfire and lost. Only his identity card survived, and this was returned to France in 1938.

Guynemer had a couple of special Spads for his own use, including one equipped with a 37mm cannon—the aeroplane was designated Spad XII—which he used on occasion in the summer of 1917. The cannon was difficult to operate and was smoky, and only experts could fire them successfully, so not many were used at the front. Guynemer still carried the normal machine gun in addition to the cannon. A single hit by a shell from this latter gun was usually enough to bring a German aeroplane down.

However, the lone scout pilot's days were now numbered. The sky was becoming too full of aircraft, and the danger lay in being surprised, especially by more than one attacking enemy aircraft. Many of the big aces could fight their way out of trouble, but, sooner or later, a chance hit, or a much better air fighter, would end the 'lone wolf' tactic and terminate a gallant flying career. Guynemer had become separated from his companion on 11 September, and had fallen.

Guynemer would have been like so many other successful air fighters. Their great attributes were self-confidence, determination, flying and shooting ability, and not a small amount of luck. Some pilots, even in the Second World War, came to realise that , although their shooting skill was below par, their piloting ability was good, and they could use this to get in close.

One imagines, too, that such men, once they had become successful, had that overwhelming urge to continue. There was no way in which they could stop, and if they were ever to suggest something of the sort, they believed they might be thought cowards. Success breeds success, and creates excellence. Some pilots liked the adulation—the glory, if you like. They pressed their luck, and for many, they chased it just that little bit too far.

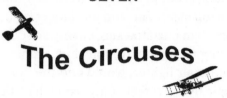

SEVEN

The Circuses

THE GERMANS started a new trend on 26 June 1917 with the formation of Jagdesgeschwader Nr I. The Geschwader consisted of four Jagdstaffeln, Nos 4, 6, 10 and 11. While this official grouping of Jastas was new, there had already been temporary unofficial groupings. or example, towards the end of April 1917, Jastas 3, 4, 11 and 33, under the leadership of Manfred von Richthofen, had been formed, if not in any permanent way. With JG Nr I the group was to remain together for the rest of the war, and was again commanded by the 'Red Baron'.

It is easy to assume that all this meant was that, in the air, the four Jastas would fly and fight together and, subject to serviceability, might have a formation of fighters numbering anything up to 50. However, this was not the case. While, on occasion, elements of one, two or perhaps three of the Jastas might take off together, it was rare for the group to mass such a number of fighters. Indeed, without radio communication it would have been impossible for any one leader to control such a large formation, and with the others keeping one eye open for any signals or signs from the leader to turn, orbit, attack, etc., the force would be open to the dangers of a surprise attack.

In the main, this grouping of Jastas was one of administration and tactical control by von Richthofen, and of convenience. While the Baron had control over these four units, and could—indeed did—have a good deal of control over who would lead them and even who would join or leave them, the real idea behind the formation was that in this way a group of fighter Staffeln could be moved, en masse, to any given area along the battle front where they could be used to advantage. This would be either to defend a sector against an Allied offensive, or to help support a German offensive. Nor were the Jastas all based on the same flying field. As JG I was formed, and became established at the start of July, they all moved to the Courtrai (Kortrijk) area in Belgium. Jasta 4, commanded by Kurt von Döring (who at this time had three victories of an eventual eleven), moved from Ceune to Markebeeke; Jasta 6, commanded by Eduard von Dostler (with twelve victories of an eventual 26), were based at Bisseghem, just to the north, across the River Lys; Jasta 10, commanded by Albert Dossenbach (fourteen victories of an eventual fifteen), moved from Heule to Marcke, just across the road from Markebeeke; and Jasta 11, now taken over by Karl Allmenröder (30 victories) was also at Markebeeke, moving in from Harlebecke.

Von Richthofen had handed over command of his own Jasta 11 to Allmenröder on 26 June, as soon as the orders to form JG I were received. In the event, Allmenröder was shot down and killed the following day, so another of Richthofen's fledgelings, Kurt Wolff, took

This Nieuport 23 Scout (A6733) was flown by Lt H. B. Redler. Note the streamer fixed to the wing's vee-strut. Streamers on both struts denoted a Flight leader. (Bruce/Leslie Collection)

over. He had scored his 31st victory the day Allmenröder died. Von Richthofen himself, at this date, had 56 victories, actually making it 57 on 2 July.

Marckebeeke, just to the south-west of Courtrai, had the customary château nearby—in fact, just by Jasta 11's flying field, the Castle of Béthune, in which von Richthofen and his officers housed themselves. Von Richthofen, now with ample men and aircraft, immediately instigated larger patrol numbers. If a Jasta were short in any way, one of the others would also put up aircraft so that the Allied aircraft could be engaged in strength.

Virtually all the Jastas were now equipped with the Albatros D.III, and the improved Albatros D.V was also starting to arrive. While a good deal better than the old biplanes of late 1916, the Albatros was soon to be matched with the arrival of the new—and long awaited—Allied scouts (fighters). The S.E.5s of No 56 Squadron were already well established, and the Sopwith Pups, Triplanes and later Camels would add to the Allied arsenal. The French had improved Nieuports (Types 23 and 27) and Spads (XIII). The main hope for the German fighter pilots was that much of the Allied corps, recce and bombing work was still being undertaken using comparatively small numbers of aircraft, and sheer weight of Jasta numbers would let them retain both the initiative and a fair degree of superiority.

Cecil Lewis, famous for his book *Sagittarius Rising*, had won the MC with No 3 Squadron, and became a minor ace with No 56 Squadron in 1917. While he was with No 56, a captured Albatros Scout was sent round to some squadrons so that the pilots not only could see it at close quarters but also might even take it into the air. Lewis did just that, and found that it was sluggish, yet strong and reliable. Compared to the S.E.5, the cockpit was cavernous, and the aircraft altogether seemed large. However, he did not feel able to throw it about the sky in gay abandon, and he found it hard work compared with the lightness of the SE5. He knew it would make him sweat if he had to fly it in a dog-fight.

The Loss of Albert Ball

A month before JG I was formed, Albert Ball failed to return from a patrol. He had gone back to France as a Flight Commander with No

56 Squadron, on the understanding he would stay for only a month. Apart from his patrol duties, he was, because of his past record and status, allowed to have his own personal Nieuport Scout—a Type 17— in which he could indulge his passion for lone stalking patrols. His final victories were scored between 23 April and 6 May 1917—thirteen in all, with two more forced to land.* This brought his personal score to 44. The breakdown of his score could be written as 27 and one shared destroyed, one balloon destroyed, six aircraft 'out of control' and nine 'forced to land'.

On Ball's last flight, during the evening of 7 May, No 56 Squadron got into a fight with Jasta 11, led by the Baron's brother Lothar, during which some Sopwith Triplanes of No 8 Naval Squadron were in the patrol area, as well as Spads from No 19 Squadron RFC. In a darkening and cloudy sky, several skirmishes were fought amongst the cumulus, and eventually Ball came out of some cloud, very low, most probably disorientated, and inverted. Before he could recover, his SE slammed into the ground behind the German lines.

Of course, Ball's name was well known to the Germans, just as that of von Richthofen and others were known to the British, but they did not immediately announmce his death. The feeling was they wanted to establish first who had brought him down. In the event, the nearest claim was that of Lothar von Richthofen himself, of a British scout, though it was described as a Triplane. This was obviously a problem, with Ball flying a biplane, but finally he was credited with Ball's demise. With brother Manfred having downed Hawker VC the previous November, it was good propaganda to credit his brother with Albert Ball, holder of three DSOs and an MC. After his death, Ball was given a posthumous Victoria Cross for his valiant war service, while the French made him a Chevalier de la Légion d'Honneur. He was still only twenty years of age when he died—and Lothar von Richthofen had his 20th victory!

Ball's VC citation has only helped to confuse latter-day historians with the complexities of victories and victory totals. In it is recorded: 'In all, Captain Ball has destroyed forty-three German aeroplanes and one balloon, and has always displayed most exceptional courage, deter-

---

* 'Forced to land' claims were no longer allowed in 1917, unless the vanquished aircraft was so damaged as to be a write off (which was difficult to prove).

The two Richthofen brothers, both wearing the 'Blue Max'. Manfred, left, gained 80 combat victories, Lothar 40.

mination and skill.' As noted earlier, victories were not always of the 'destroyed' variety—i.e. burned, smashed or disintegrated in the air—but by describing his victories as all 'destroyed', the authorities confused the issue. On the so-called 'ace lists', if one applied Second World War victory criteria to First World War totals, Ball would be credited with perhaps 29; Group Captain J. E. Johnson, the famous Second World War fighter pilot, if employing the same First War principles, would have as many as 59 'victories' (34 and seven shared destroyed, three and two shared 'probables', and ten and three shared 'damaged').

Ball, in his last combats, whether in the Nieuport or S.E.5, was still able to use the 'attack from below' tactic, because the S.E.5 and S.E.5a both had not only one fixed, belt-fed Vickers machine gun firing through the propeller arc but also a drum-fed Lewis on the top wing. It was set to fire once again, over the propeller, and could still be pulled down in order to permit the pilot to fire upwards. Many years ago I met a First World War S.E.5 pilot who told me that he hardly ever used the Lewis gun to fire upwards, and when he did never hit anything. He was keener to fire both the Vickers and Lewis on the occasions he found something in front of him. Nevertheless, many S.E.5 pilots used the Lewis in both positions and were able to bring down aircraft when firing it upwards.

Ball's first S.E.5 victory came during the late morning of 23 April 1917. On a lone patrol he spotted five green-coloured Albatros Scouts over Cambrai and gave chase, catching them up over Selvigny:

SE5 dived at the nearest and fired about 150 rounds of 1 in 3 out of Vickers at close range. H.A. went down and was in flames before reaching the ground. Remainder of H.A. put a few rounds in SE5, after which they all cleared.

Ball much preferred his Nieuport because of its greater manoeuvrability, and he also led patrols in it. His last successful combat, in the evening of 6 May, was in the Nieuport, leading four S.E.5s of his Flight on an OP to Sancourt. He met red-coloured Albatros Scouts—a new type, presumably D.Vs—which, he noted, were slow during turns. His combat report read:

Nieuport Scout No. B.1522 on patrol with four SE.5s Nos. A.4860, 8904, 4853 and 4858. Nieuport Scout was unable to keep up with the SE.5s and lost them at Arras.

Nieuport went on towards Douai, and viewed four red Albatros scouts, new type, going towards Cambrai at 10,000 feet, Nieuport being at 11,000 feet. Nieuport got above H.A. and dived on the nearest one, getting in the centre of the formation of H.As, which broke up. Nieuport got underneath the nearest H.A. and at close range fired two and a half drums of one in one tracer which were seen to enter H.A. H.A. went down and was seen crashed on the ground near the crossroads and railway South of Sancourt.

The remainder of the H.A. kept well away and did not attack Nieuport until on its way home. Nieuport easily outclimbed H.A., and also could easily out-manoeuvre them, H.A. being very slow on turns. Nieuport could not fight again owing to having no ammunition. H.A. only got three hits on Nieuport. Nieuport returned home at 8.40 pm.

One has to wonder about this, Ball's final combat report. He was Flight Commander and he was leader, so was it not necessary for his companions to reduce speed and remain with him? Or was it a case of 'I'm going off on a lone sortie: don't bother to follow me?' Ball, being Ball, then attacked four German fighters, coloured red, which he could assume were members of the Richthofen Circus, without any apparent hesitation, and claimed one down after a fight. The scrap obviously lasted some little time, as he used three drums—that is, he emptied two and had time to pull down the Lewis gun on its Foster mounting, to take off the empty one and put on a replacement twice, which took a few moments at least.

Then, although he could not keep up (he says) with his four comrades, Ball was easily able to out-climb the new-type Albatros Scouts, presumably Albatros D.Vs, and could also out-turn them. In describing the new types prior to his narrative, he estimated that their speed was 100mph, and in fact it was around 103mph (165kph). His Nieuport's top speed was about the same, 100mph (160kph), so there was very little margin. The S.E.5's speed was around 120mph (192kph). In point of fact, Ball appears to have been attacking a formation of Jasta 20 which was not part of the Circus, for Vizefeldwebel Jäger was reported to have crashed south of Sancourt this day and been badly wounded.

James McCudden

Three months after Ball's death, another great pilot joined No 56 Squadron and flew S.E.5s as a Flight Commander. James T. B. McCudden had been in the RFC since before the war as a mechanic, and in the early days of the war was an observer in France . Becoming an NCO pilot, he flew D.H.2 pushers with No 29 Squadron in 1916–17. By the early summer of 1917 he was a minor ace with the Military Medal and the French Croix de Guerre, and after a brief spell with No 66 Squadron he became a patrol leader supreme with No 56.

However, McCudden was one of those pilots who could also operate alone in the air and became an expert stalker of high-flying German two-seater reconnaissance machines. His first few victories with his new squadron were all Albatros D.V scouts, and then came a long string of two-seaters, interspersed from time to time with Albatros scouts during patrols at the head of his Flight. Moreover, at least nineteen of these two-seaters—which of necessity were over Allied lines doing their recce and photographic work—came down inside British lines. Thus these victories were confirmed beyond doubt, the wreckage providing incontrovertible evidence. No other pilot in the First World War brought down so many enemy machines inside his own lines.

In the latter stages of his most successful period, December 1917 to February 1918, McCudden often scored multiple victories on one day. Several times he scored doubles, but on 28 December and 13 January he scored triples, while on 23 December and 16 February he downed four on both days.

He, too, was the master of both guns on the S.E.5, the fixed Vickers gun and the movable Lewis on the top wing. He had taken the time to study the best way of sneaking up on two-seaters, stalking them for as long as it took to approach without the crew seeing him, and often the first sign of his presence was bullets smashing through the machine as he came up underneath his targets.

Not all his fights were successful, but each time he learnt a little more about his art of bringing down hostile aircraft. In his famous book *Flying Fury,** he wrote of an action on 1 October 1917:

> I went up by myself soon after lunch to look for enemy machines over our lines, and whilst over Béthune at 12,000 feet I saw a German machine, 5,000 feet higher going north-west, so I followed, climbing steadily. The Hun flew over Estaires and then turned west, and by the time he was over Hazebrouck at 19,000 feet I was up at 16,000 feet and could now see that the German was a Rumpler, such as the enemy use specially for long photographic reconnaissances over our lines. The Hun flew towards St Omer, and a

Nieuport now joined in the pursuit. Just short of St Omer the Rumpler turned and flew south-east over Aire at 21,000 feet, whilst I had just got to the [my] limit of 19,000 feet. The Nieuport got a little higher, but not so high as the Hun.

After pursuing the Rumpler for the best part of an hour we lost him, for he recrossed the lines at at altitude of 22,000 feet over La Bassée. I now turned away west at 19,000 feet and then saw another Rumpler farther west and a little lower, so after him I went. At this time I had not fully developed my stalking art, and so attacked my photographic friend prematurely. He turned east as I secured my firing position. After firing some good few shots from both guns, the Hun gunner gracefully subsided on the floor of his cockpit, but I had now got a bad No. 3 stoppage in my Vickers gun which I could not rectify in the air.

Anyhow, the Lewis was going well, so I put on a new drum and closed again to effective range. I fired the whole drum at him, and thought I had him in flames, for a large cloud of black smoke answered by burst. Meanwhile, the Hun pilot still went on, and at last I left him, miles over the German lines going down in a very flat glide with his propeller stopped.

That Hun gunner must have been full of lead, but I know why I missed the machine. I had just resighted my guns before I went up and made a little error which became apparent; it was all to my future guidance and instruction. I returned from that high flight not disheartened, but with a very bad headache owing to high flying for so long at such a height without oxygen.

With the exception of a few trials, and some German experiments, single seater pilots did not use oxygen during the First World War, although some two-seaters did, as did airship crews. In any case, not many pilots had easy access to oxygen, and few liked to use it. It represented excess weight, and the oxygen tank tended to explode violently if hit by a bullet. Airmen faced enough problems as it was without worrying about this too.

★ ★ ★

In contrast, the words written down by Major L. W. B. Rees, VC, as noted earlier, gave the embryo pilot a much better understanding of what he should do and look for. Although McCudden later expanded on this initial work in his *Bring Down Your Hun*, what follows is a good example of how an experienced air fighter imparted knowledge to others in early 1918:

---

* Earlier published under the title *Five Years in the Royal Flying Corps*.

Fighting the SE, January 1918

Having been requested to write some notes under the above heading, I must ask pilots to consider them as the method of an individual (myself) and not as an effort to lay down anything like hard and fast rules when fighting [in] the SE.

Scouts: Enemy scouts are not often seen above 15,000 feet during the winter months, the reason being, I suggest, that the Albatros Scout, which constitutes the bulk of enemy scouts, is a very cold machine in comparison with the SE5, so that enemy pilots do not go up high during cold weather unless for some good reason; therefore, I usually take my patrol over the lines at anything over 14,000 feet. Nine times out of ten I am above enemy scouts during the whole of my patrol.

In attacking enemy scouts, surprise is usually aimed at, but the sun and wind direction are a great help when intelligently used. If you think the E.A. have not seen you, try to attack from the east, and when going down give the rear machines of your own formation plenty of time to close up, so that each member can attack one E.A. simultaneously.

Whilst attacking E.A. scouts, one should keep plenty of engine, so as to keep zooming above the formation of E.A. the whole time. I find that if SE's attack E.A. from above, they can remain above the whole time, but now I find that as soon as we attack scouts, one of them, more likely than not their leader, flies off out of the fight and climbs his utmost until he is above the top SE, and them comes back, and it is the thought that there is one Hun above you that divides your attention and nullifies your advantage in height, so as soon as I see the one Hun going off I climb as well, and this usually frustrates his intentions.

I consider it a patrol leader's work to pay more attention to the main points affecting a fight than to do all the fighting himself. The main points are—(1) Arrival of more E.A. who have tactical advantage, ie. height; (2) Patrol drifting too far east; (3) Patrol getting below the bulk of enemy formation. As soon as any of these circumstances occur, it is time to take advantage of the SE's superior speed over E.A. scouts and break off the fight, rally behind leader and climb west of E.A. until you are above them before attacking them again.

When any of the above circumstances occur, I fire a red light, which is a signal to my patrol to break off the fight and follow me, and we find that this is very effective.

Two-seaters: I have had many more combats with 2-seater E.A. than scouts, so hope I am able to give few tips.

I think a lot of pilots over-estimate the death-dealing qualities of the 2-seater's rear gun; at the same time, however, one should not become careless, because enemy observers are usually highly trained and can shoot very accurately, especially at quite long range. Therefore, when attacking a 2-seater, it should be a pilot's main object, after surprise, to get to close range

(100 yards) without letting E.A. gunner shoot at you. This is quite possible, because in December, I shot down six 2-seaters in succession without E.A. gunner getting a single shot at me, although in each case the E.A. had seen me approaching and had good time to make up his mind what to do. The six E.A. were not shot down in one fight but were successive combats on different days.

Two-seaters keep a very good look-out above but pay very little attention under their level. Therefore try to surprise them from underneath and climb up under their fuselages and tail plane. The position from which a pilot can do most damage to a 2-seater at the least risk to himself and machine, is 100 yards behind it and 50 feet below. If, however, you are in this position, and E.A. turns, you will at once come under his fire, and your object is to keep out of his field of fire as much as possible, so, therefore, keep in a direct line behind his fuselage, so that if he turns to the right, you turn to the left and vice-versa. To do this manoeuvre successfully, one must have superior speed to do the outside circle, which is the inevitable position if one is to use E.A.'s tail and fuselage as cover to the best advantage whilst E.A. is turning. As soon as E.A., gunner sees he cannot fire at your from this position he will try the other direction.

Now whilst changing from one bank to the other, E.A. will be in a good position to fire at if you are quick enough. Try a short burst to confuse the pilot. His tendency when alarmed is usually to dive, which is just is what you want him to do. No gunner can stand upright in a machine that is doing over 130 mph and do accurate shooting, because the wind pressure against him at this speed is enormous. In several cases I have seen a 2-seater dive so steeply and fast that the gunner has been blown flat on the fuselage. When this happens you need not worry about E.A.'s rear gun. I find that when diving on the tail of a 2-seater one usually does not need to allow a deflection, but just shoot straight into him. The chance of a decision when fighting a 2-seater are greater west of the line than east, because when a 2-seater is attacked west of the line, nine times out of ten he will push his nose down and do 'S' turns, shooting at you as opportunity offers, but after you have had some practice you will be able to sit under his tail as safe as anywhere provided that you do not become careless. On the contrary, a 2-seater attacked east of the lines only needs to keep going round in one direction for any length of time and he can then do all the shooting whilst you can do practically none. Whilst turning like this, help for the E.A. is practically certain to arrive in the form of E.A. scouts. In fighting 2-seaters west of the lines, pilots should think before attacking what the E.A.'s work is, so as to let E.A. get as far west as he wishes to, so that you will then have made ample time to shoot him down before he gets east of the line. Most 2-seaters will stand a lot of shooting about before giving any evidence of damage.

The above method of attacking a 2-seater is what I advise, but a good deal of practice is necessary before you are able to keep up with a 2-seater at close range without being shot at.

I find that is very difficult to shoot the pilot from directly behind because you probably hit the gunner first, who collapses in a heap in his cockpit, and you go on shooting and are simply filling the gunner with lead, and also a huge petrol tank which is usually situated between the pilot and gunner, and the pilot gets off without a scratch, so once you have shot the gunner you can afford to close right up and shoot the pilot at your leisure.

I have had a a lot of combats with 2-seaters and have been hit by their fire very seldom, and then only a few bullet holes.

The advantage and possibilities of this form of attack should be obvious to anyone who gives the subject thought. Even at 50 feet below an E.A. at 100 yards, one has to zoom ever so slightly to get one's sights in E.A., and it is to be remembered that the SE's guns fire at an upward angle to the line of flight.

In conclusion, I wish to point out that, although I have achieved good results with this method of attack, I think the Huns will take measures to repel it in one way or another, and I also contend that a 2-seater in which the pilot and observer co-operate well, is more than a match for a Scout, no matter how well handled.

As a final tip, one should be very alert when firing at an E.A. at close range, so that, when E.A. falls to pieces, as they very often do, after being fired at a lot, that one does not fly through the wreckage. I narrowly missed flying through a pair of E.A's wings recently.

McCudden gained 57 victories and received the Victoria Cross. Following a period of rest from the front, he was given command of No 60 Squadron in July 1918, but crashed and was killed on his way to take up his new post. He would undoubtedly have had an outstanding career in the RAF had he survived the war.

Sopwith Triplanes

The Royal Naval Air Service flew a variety of aircraft, both landplanes and seaplanes. They scoured the North Sea for submarines, occasionally engaged in combat with German seaplanes and also bombed German ships and kept watch on German ports and shipping. The RNAS had several bombing squadrons situated in France along the Channel coast, especially around Dunkirk, for use against the active German ports of Ostend and Zeebrugge.

A number of RNAS fighter squadrons were attached to the RFC and were moved south to assist during the Battles of the Somme and of Arras. Initially they flew Sopwith Pups, Nieuport Scouts and Strutters, but as these slowly became obsolete a new type was needed. The replacement was the Sopwith Triplane.

The RNAS in fact had the prototype Triplane on trial in France as early as June 1916, used by Naval 'A' Fighting Squadron at Furnes. It was not found wanting, so further production machines were ordered and these equipped No 1 Naval Squadron at the end of the year and No 8 Naval Squadron in February 1917, followed by 'Naval 10' soon afterwards .

The naval pilots, flying missions similar to those of their counterparts in the RFC, found the Triplane both a delight to fly and a splendid fighting machine. Its unusual configuration gave it a remarkable rate of roll and a fast climb. Some Triplanes were also used by the French Navy in France, but, surprisingly, the RFC never used it. With a top speed of around 117mph (187kph), its only real drawback was that it still had only a single Vickers machine gun firing through the propeller, mounted atop the fuselage in front of the pilot. The arrival of the Sopwith Camel in the summer of 1917 soon saw an end to the Triplane, RFC and RNAS squadrons quickly replacing Pups and Triplanes with the new type.

In the interim, the Triplane gave a good account of itself during the early summer of 1917. Naval 10 were exceptionally prolific in claiming victories, in particular the Black Flight led by Captain Raymond Collishaw, who would end the war with 60 claims. From British Columbia, Canada, Collishaw was born on 22 November 1893, and upon leaving school became a seaman. In early 1916 he joined the RNAS, and his first combat assignment was with No 3 Naval Wing flying Sopwith two-seaters (1½-Strutters) on bombing and recce missions. A posting to No 3 Naval Squadron on Pups followed before he joined the newly formed 10 Naval to command 'B' Flight. His first Triplane victory came on 28 April 1917—his fifth victory in all.

His Black Flight was so-named for two reasons. First, its Triplanes had black-painted engine cowlings, wheels and tailfins, and each machine had a 'black' name painted on the fuselage—*Black Maria* (Collishaw), *Black Sheep* (G. E. Nash), *Black Roger* (E. V. Reid), *Black Death* (J. E. Sharman) and *Black Prince*, (W. M. Alexander). Collishaw was to claim 33 victories with the Triplane, Nash six, Reid nineteen, Sharman seven and Alexander ten. In addition, J. A. Page claimed seven. Unfortunately, Page, Sharman and Reid were all killed, and Nash was made a prisoner of war.

Nash was brought down by Jasta 11's Karl Allmenröder on 25 June, the German's 29th victory. On the 27th he was himself brought down and killed. After the war, Ray Collishaw thought that he may have been responsible for downing Allmenröder, the belief made plausible due to Nash's being told by one of his guards that the great ace had been killed by the black-nosed Triplanes. However, it is now thought that the Albatros fell to ground fire, and in fact the time of its fall does not tie in with Collishaw's combat. Many years ago Ray Collishaw explained to me how that fight occurred:

The air war in the Ypres Sector became a contest of attrition. Any British aspirations were vested in the hopes of USA aircraft production,* while a vast German offensive would start before any American strength could materialise. I emphasise these points to indicate that indecisive combats were common on the Ypres Front in the summer of 1917. What happened on 27 June was that I led my Flight of No. 10 Naval Squadron over the lines at about 15,000 feet and I found that we suddenly found ourselves between two hostile formations, one below and one above; a kind of meat in the sandwich. We flew on in this way for some time.

The RNAS used the Pup and the Sopwith Triplane, but both suffered from poor armament with just a single gun. However, the Triplane was a useful fighter, and it gave a good account of itself in 1917.

Looking like a cross between Hannibal Lecter and something from the *Planet of the Apes*, Captain P. G. Taylor, MC, of No 66 Squadron boards his Pup, his face well protected from the cold, and wearing some whale-oil grease for the parts still exposed.

I know now that the German unit was flying in two Kettes (sub-flights), one above us and the other below, all three formations were climbing hard, so the three formations sustained their relative positions. I knew that we were in a dangerous position because if the upper flight attacked us, we should almost certainly get involved with the lower formation. I decided, therefore, to get out of the picture, by diving to escape to the westward, but as we did so, I prepared to try to shoot-up the lower group on the way. So I made a signal to my companions to attack.

When I got to about 1,000 feet above the lower formation, I opened fire at long range on the leading Albatros. I had hardly begun to fire, before I felt the impact of bullets on my Triplane—the upper flight had dived too— so I took violent evasive action and got out of the fight fast. As I fired at my target, I had noticed that it immediately moved in a peculiar manner, but I thought nothing of this at the time, as it seemed simply violent avoiding action which was in common us at the time.

Years later I was in touch with G. W. Groos of Jasta 11 who told me that one Sopwith Triplane fired on his flight from extreme long range and no one in flight seemed affected, when suddenly he saw Allmenröder's Albatros behave in a peculiar manner. At the outset it simply dived, then resumed a horizontal flight, but soon it went out of control. Groos and the others followed their leader down until he crashed [near Zillebeke].

With regard to the RNAS, Collishaw was at pains to explain their set-up in relation to the RFC, and an interesting fact about headstones to fallen naval airmen:

---

* In fact, the United States had no massive aircraft industry with which to fill the air with aeroplanes, and its air service had to rely totally on aircraft supplied by Britain and France. The US did, however, produce Liberty engines in numbers.

The highest operational unit was the Wing Captain's Command, which was considered equivalent to that of a battleship command. Wing Captains were allowed by the Admiralty to name squadrons in any way they preferred. Sometimes Group Captains commanded as many as five or six stations with squadrons, with numbered Flights and some squadrons identified by lettered Flights. Consequently, some historians have been confused in research. When 8 Naval went to the RFC on the Somme in October 1916, it was a lettered squadron, with numbered Flights. The RFC complained, and as a result the whole RNAS was re-organised to have consecutively numbered squadrons and lettered Flights.

While the RFC/RAF used a system of relieving pilots to Home service for a rest after eight or nine months of active duty, the RNAS and the German Jastas had no such system. It was left to the COs to decide when a pilot [or observer] was unable to go on. After a period of ardent work on a 'hot' front, a unit was sent to a 'quiet' sector for a rest.

The record of the Naval Fighter Squadrons has often been neglected by historians. RFC historians have ignored them on the grounds that they did not belong to the RFC, and Naval historians avoided them because they did not conduct their operations with the Fleet.

As the Naval Fighter Squadrons were under RFC operational control and they were called upon to do exactly the same as RFC squadrons, they were, to all intents and purposes, RFC squadrons. There is a curiosity about this—while all RFC and RAF grave headstones bear large 'wings' upon them, RNAS headstones bear only a 'fouled anchor' and no 'wings'. The 'fouled anchor' was never the symbol of the RNAS, and the use of this symbol, in my opinion, is especially inappropriate on RNAS graves of airmen killed while working with the Army.

A Rare Sight

On 27 July 1917, Captain P. G. Taylor of No 66 Squadron recorded an amazing sight not often seen in the skies over France. Taylor became an experienced airmen, winning the Military Cross in the First World War and the George Cross in 1935 during his pioneering flights in the world of civil aviation, for which he was knighted. Taylor noted that patrols of Pups from his own No 66 Squadron, S.E.5s of No 56 Squadron, Spad VIIs of No 19 Squadron and Sopwith Triplanes of the RNAS, met above Roulers from 18,000 feet down to 10,000 feet. Below them, R.E.8 Corps aircraft were busily circling above the front, as if waiting for enemy aircraft to pounce. Taylor thought that it must have looked a fantastic sight from the ground, and although the soldiers might expect to see the more regular small scout patrols each day, nothing like this armada had ever been seen before.

German fighters did rise to the challenge, but, because they were completely overwhelmed by the numbers, any fighting that did occur cost them a few machines, and those which decided to flee earthwards were harried by chasing S.E.5s. Few Germans reached as high as 16,000 feet this day, so the top RFC squadron could only watch the events below. As the armada began to disperse, four German fighters did fly in from the north and take a long-distance crack at the top squadron—No 66 and its Pups—but they did not close and, being now short of fuel, the Pups had to fly home.

Taylor was of the opinion that large formations would be far better than small, individual patrol formations, but nothing changed. No doubt there was a problem with being able to put sufficient numbers in the air at the same time, and, in consequence, there would be periods during the day when cover would be depleted or lost altogether, while aircraft were on the ground refuelling. The Germans, as far as the RFC and RNAS were concerned, were using larger formations, no doubt their grouping of Staffeln creating this impression, but for the foreseeable future the British would have to remain in small Flight patrols and hope another small patrol was nearby and be able to help out if needed.

EIGHT

War in the Air, 1917

THE SUMMER of 1917 saw the beginning of intensive air operations. During April that year the RFC has suffered enormous casualties on account of obsolete Allied aeroplanes being overwhelmed by the new and enthusiastic German Jasta pilots equipped with superior Albatros scouts, but by the summer the balance was being redressed with the arrival of the Sopwith Camel and the increase in the number of S.E.5a squadrons. The French fighter force was now being equipped with the improved Spad XIII, although while the French also had Nieuport 27s, these showed little improvement over the Types 17 and 23. The only new machine on the German side was the Pfalz D.III, which started to appear at the front in the autumn.

The Pfalz was a pleasant enough looking aeroplane, not that different in appearance from the Albatros scout, except for its tail. It, too, had 'vee'-struts between the upper and lower wings, and was streamlined in appearance. Its lower wing was broader than that of the Albatros and Nieuport, but the aircraft was still powered by the ubiquitous Mercedes 160 hp engine although the Pfalz's speed was not as high as that of the Albatros. It was first issued to Bavarian Jastas in the autumn of 1917, and, in general, the Jastas used a mix of Albatros and Pfalz scouts. Despite most pilots preferring the Albatros if given a choice, several aces flew the Pfalz with success, finding that it answered well to the controls. Unlike the Albatros, it did not last past the early summer of 1918, once the Fokker D.VII began to arrive.

Another aircraft introduced by the Germans later in 1917 was the Fokker Dr.I Triplane, a machine which was to become synonymous with First World War flying, made so by the famed Red Baron, Manfred von Richthofen, once he chose it to equip most of his Jagdesgeschwader with it. At first, however, there were only two prototypes in service, known by their early designation F.I. These two were flown to Jasta 11's base at Marckebeeke at the end of August: one for the exclusive use of von Richthofen and Kurt Wolff, Jasta 11's Staffelführer; the other went to the leader of Jasta 10, Werner Voss.

Von Richthofen had recently secured his 59th victory, but his 60th was scored while in the new Triplane in combat for the first time, on 1 September. Leading Albatros D.Vs to the front, he found a British R.E.8 two-seater, and it is obvious that upon his approach the two British airmen were faced with a quandary. As far as they could see, they were being approached by a Sopwith Triplane, this being the only three-winged aeroplane they were aware of—although, perversely, the Sopwith Triplane had all but disappeared from the front, having been replaced by the Camel. Von Richthofen closed to shooting range, seeing the observer, not wanting to shoot down a Naval fighter, make no move to engage him. Perhaps, he thought, the Naval pilot was

Not dissimilar at first glance to the Albatros was the sleeker Pfalz D.III Scout. Some pilots liked this aeroplane more than the Albatros, but, although in service for a long period, it did not enjoy the success of its rival. This is a Pfalz D.IIIa from Jasta 8 in 1918, with distinctive markings.

The Fokker Triplane has become synonymous with the first air war. This machine was flown by Manfred von Richthofen on 21 April 1918, the day he was brought down by ground fire over the Somme valley.

playing a game: surely he could not fail to identify his R.E.8! Richthofen's fire ended any further thoughts by the British observer, who died in a hail of bullets. His pilot, wounded, got his crippled R.E.8 down but was taken prisoner.*

It was not long before the two Fokker Triplanes saw further action, and no doubt Allied pilots reported more Triplanes than the one, or at most two, that they encountered. Such was the speed at which they could turn, often in and out of cloud, that some combat reports recorded as many as four or five Triplanes mixed in with the usual Albatros scouts. A No 45 Squadron Camel pilot even claimed two Triplanes shot down in one fight, on an occasion when only one Triplane was in action—and was *not* shot down!

After gaining his 61st victory, von Richthofen went on leave, his Triplane being taken over by Wolff. Meantime, Werner Voss had

---

* There was also the occasion when a German two-seater shot down a German Triplane owing to the same sort of misidentification. Josef Lautenschlager of Jasta 11 was flying along in his new aircraft on 29 October, but the two-seater crew, thinking it was a Sopwith Triplane, came up behind him and shot him down.

started to score with his Dr.I. Voss by this time had 38 victories, and number 39 came on 3 September 1917—a Camel of No 45 Squadron. His 40th 'kill', a Pup, came on the 5th of the month, followed by a French Caudron later that day. Another on the 6th (an F.E.2d) was followed by two Camels of 70 Squadron on the 10th, a third 'kill' this day was a French Spad. Victory number 46 fell on the 11th, and another Camel that evening made it 47. His 48th and last came on the 23rd—a D.H.4 bomber.

Voss was an exceptionally gifted fighter pilot. From Krefeld, he was born in April 1897 and had seen service as a hussar on the Eastern Front prior to joining the air service. He was an instructor and an observer, and he did not join the war until being posted to Jasta 2 in November 1916. He soon began to make a name for himself, and despite missing 'Bloody April'—he was on leave to celebrate his Blue Max award at the time—by late May he was given command of Jasta 5. In August, with his score at 35, he became leader of Jasta 10 in JG I.

With 48 victories, and with leave looming after the activities of the morning of the 23rd, Voss was keen (it has to be assumed) to raise his score to 50 before returning to Germany. His two brothers were visiting his airfield in order that all three could return home. Voss flew out with two companions, but soon left them and continued on alone. He had

The RFC used the Spad VII in France, and the French the VII and later the Spad XIII (pictured). The Spad proved a good, solid fighter for the French and later the Americans. (Bruce/Leslie Collection)

This S.E.5a was flown by No 60 Squadron in 1917. During the combats with Werner Voss on 23 September, it was flown by R. L. Chidlaw-Roberts. It was brought down by Jasta 18 on 5 October 1917. Oddly enough, it had earlier been with No 56 Squadron, and in combats L. M. Barlow had claimed seven victories.

a fight with some S.E.5as of No 60 Squadron, shooting up two, then had a running fight with S.E.5as of McCudden's Flight of No 56 Squadron. Despite opportunities to fly back to base, Voss took on the S.E.5a machines repeatedly, putting holes in several before his own Triplane was finally hit in either the engine or the fuel line, he perhaps also having been mortally wounded himself. With his engine off he was forced to go down. His machine was hit again, and the gallant Voss crashed to his death at Plum Farm, near Frenzenberg.

Like McCudden, Voss was able to survive on lone patrols, although by this time the tactic was rapidly falling out of favour because, in the main, of the increasing numbers of aircraft. The lone pilot had to spend much more time scouring the sky for hostile machines, and it was far too dangerous to chase and stalk an opponent, bearing in mind the ever-present danger of being stalked himself. Voss had survived in the midst of his last combat for some time, thanks to his skill and to a very manoeuvrable aircraft, but, in the end, numbers were against him.

Ray Collishaw gained much success with the Triplane with 10 Naval Squadron. He is shown here, left, by a Sopwith Camel, whose pilot, Art Whealy, a Canadian like Collishaw, was also successful on Pups, Triplanes, and then on Camels with No 203 Squadron.

However, ten victories in nine combats showed how well this new fighter could perform with an experienced pilot in the cockpit.

The S.E.5a , which replaced the earlier S.E.5, brought a better machine to the Western Front. The 5a had its aileron controls improved by a shortening of the levers on them. This, together with a wingspan reduced by shortening the rear spars, improved lateral control. The introduction in the S.E.5a of a 200hp Hispano-Suiza engine led to large-scale production of the aircraft, which continued in action for the rest of the war. The earlier S.E.5 had a 150hp H-S engine. It is no secret that Albert Ball had not liked the S.E.5 because of its poor lateral control and, having been allowed his personal Nieuport Scout, flew the latter whenever possible. Unfortunately he was in an S.E.5 when he was killed, losing control in cloud.

Rotary Engines

In the First World War, both sides had aeroplanes with air-cooled rotary engines, as well as in-line, water-cooled types. The rotary engine is not always understood by the layman: it was not just a stationary engine which rotated a propeller, the whole engine went round *together with* the propeller. Thus it can be understood that, with a large weight turning in front of the aeroplane, the torque produced was quite considerable, and could be used to advantage. With the crankshaft bolted to the machine and engine case, the propeller rotated around the pistons, giving the configuration a good power-to-weight ratio.

The RNAS, in particular, was well versed in rotary engines, having had the Pup, Triplane and now the Camel to fight with. I return to my correspondence with Ray Collishaw in the late 1960s:

After the war I met hundreds of First War fighter pilots. By talking to them, I realised that they had not been taught to know that a rotary engined fighter turned more readily to the right because of the centrifugal force and torque of the rotary engine. The Naval fighter pilots, because of their long RNAS experience with them, were well aware of it, and we all knew the importance of doing our utmost to engage German pilots in right-hand waltzing matches. On the other hand, the German and RFC pilots (except Camel boys) liked turning to the left because of their stationary engines. In combat I had often seen the expression of despair on the face of an adversary, as he perceived that my rotary engined aircraft was gradually drawing on to his tail!

Head-on Tactics

It often happened that hostile pilots met head-on. Each opposing pilot would keep his aircraft aimed directly at the other and as soon as one opened fire, the other did so too. The hostile on-coming tracer would appear to be aimed directly for one's eyes. One cowered as low as possible and at the last dangerous second one feared collision. There was no rule of the road, whether up or down, to the right or left seemed equally dangerous. Escaping collision, each opposing pilot was beset by the urgent need of turning about rapidly lest the opponent get on his tail. The usual consequence was that a second head-on encounter ensued.

The Sopwith Camel

The Fokker Triplane is one of the first aeroplanes laymen think of from the First World War, together with the Camel. The Camel continued the run of rotary-engined designs by the Sopwith company, and, as agility in combat was at last being seen as paramount, Sopwiths massed all the weight at the front—engine, guns, pilot, petrol tank—so that the machine's centre of gravity was well forward. Moreover, the torque of the turning engine, as Collishaw said, helped the Camel turn swiftly to the right. Camel pilots knew that they must never dog-fight a Fokker Triplane because, for, because of its greater wing area, it had a lower wing loading and could easily turn inside them. It must have been the same for German pilots in their heavy Albatros scouts: they would not to try to out-turn a Camel in a right-hand turning match.

Not that the Camel lacked vices. It was not a forgiving aeroplane to the inexperienced. When he was a retired Air Chief Marshal, Sir Leslie Hollinghurst, who had won his DFC flying Sopwith Dolphins in 1918, told me in one of our chats that he knew all about the Camel's bad habits. In early 1918 he was at Kenley at No 7 Aircraft Acceptence Park, and somewhere 'up north' a lot of embryo pilots were being killed in what were thought to be unnecessary accidents. 'Holly' had flown a lot of Camels in England, so he was sent to investigate.

Many of the new pilots, having flown gentle and more forgiving aircraft such as Pups or Avros while training, were sent off in Camels prior to being posted to France. Once airborne and attempting a loop, they were spinning out at the top and diving into the ground before they could recover. Hollinghurst quickly saw what was happening. The youngsters were merely going into a gentle dive, as they had on their Pups, throttling back and pulling back the stick. Once nearly upside down, where the Pup would curve over and complete the manoeuvre, the Camel's powerful torque was sending the machine into a violent spin. He quickly taught the Camel boys—and reminded their instructors—to 'fly' the Camel through this manoeuvre and not try to let the machine do it by itself.

Norman Macmillan, MC, who flew Strutters and Camels with No 45 Squadron (all the Strutter squadrons in the RFC changed over to Camels in late 1917), described his first flight in a Camel:

> The Pup [had been] smooth and stable, mellow like old wine. The Camel was a buzzing hornet, a wild thing, burning in the air like raw spirit fires the throat. This fierce little beast answered readily to intelligent handling, but was utterly remorseless against brutal or ignorant treatment. Possessed of a sensitive elevator control, she reacted swiftly to slight fore and aft stick movement. I spun her and she fell earthwards in a mad whirl.
>
> Her fuselage was short. She was tail heavy, so that one had to press the stick forward in normal flight because there was no tailplane adjustment. Her rudder was too small. The gyroscopic action of the rotary engine in her light wood-and-wire framework forced her nose down in a right-hand turn. To

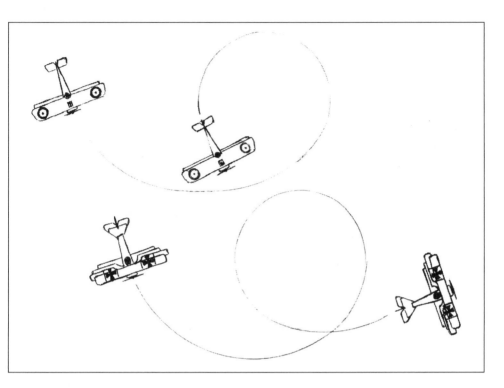

Know your opponent. All aircraft are different in some respect, and, as pilots on both sides discovered, the later powerful rotary-engined aircraft, such as the Fokker Triplane and the Sopwith Camel, were both able to turn exceptionally quickly. By late 1917 and into 1918, dive-and-zoom tactics were becoming better established than even the tight turning battle, and trying to turn with these two rotary fighters was a route to disaster. Mick Mannock told his pilots never to try to dog-fight a Triplane in a turning battle, as it would get behind the S.E.5 (or Camel) every time. Dive-and-zoom was the only tactic that was safe. If the initial attack failed, it was best to climb rapidly and select another moment to attack. The Triplane, and the Camel, were both better at low level, and if they attempted to climb after an opponent, their ability to fight on equal terms diminished. Both the Triplane and, especially, the Camel had all their main weight up front, and the torque of the turning engine helped the aeroplanes to turn quickly in the direction of their movement.

make swift right-hand turns without losing height one had to apply left rudder the instant the manoeuvre began and push on full rudder before full bank. Then the Camel turned very fast, far more swiftly than to the left. It was mainly on this ability that she won her fame in fights, for the heavier stationary-engined German scouts could not turn as quickly and, when they were engaged at close quarters, the Camel could make three turns to their two in a right-hand circle, in spite of her relative inferiority in climb and speed at even moderate altitudes. But let the ham-fisted or inexperienced pilot pull the stick just a little too far back while turning all out, and the Camel would flick quickly into a spin, which was the pitfall of many a novice and, could be a death-trap at low heights.

Leonard 'Titch' Rochford, DSC, DFC, flying Pups and Camels with Nos 3 Naval/203 Squadron RAF, recorded his feelings on the Camel too:

> I flew the Camel around for about half an hour, carried out some flick rolls and side loops and liked it very much. It was a complete contrast to the Pup, which was docile and stable with its 80hp Le Rhône engine and dihedral on both top and bottom planes. The Camel had a 150hp Bentley rotary engine and dihedral only on the bottom plane. It was an unstable machine, and the powerful engine gave it a vicious kick to the right as soon as it was airborne which had to be corrected by using a lot of left rudder.
>
> However, no aeroplane could be manoeuvred so quickly, and that was its great advantage in combat. During the several hundred hours I flew the Camel in France, I never met a German fighter which could outclimb me, though some of them were faster on the level and in a dive. None could out-manoeuvre the Sopwith Camel.

Len Rochford, one of the nicest and most modest men I ever met, claimed 29 victories between May 1917 and the war's end, all but three in a Camel. He came from Enfield, and after learning to fly he joined the RNAS in May 1916, aged nineteen.

In combat, the Camel was a pugnacious fighter, and with aggressive pilots that got in close, success was almost assured. Rochford himself told me that his personal tactic was to get in close before firing:

> My own tactics no doubt differed from those of other formation leaders, but I considered them to be the best if the objective was maximum success with minimal losses.
>
> Immediately after take-off we formed up and headed towards the line at our best rate of climb. Whilst still climbing along the line, all pilots maintained a thorough search of the sky, especially above and below to the east, so as to spot an E.A. as soon as possible. If these were sighted, I made certain that we were above and, ideally, up-sun to them. Clouds, too, were used as cover from which to stalk the enemy. This positioning was important before initiating an attack, which was made as a steep dive by the whole Flight.
>
> Fire was opened at about 100 yards' range and continued, in bursts, until it was necessary to break away, left or right, and regain height and formation. In the case of a single two-seater target, if the first attacker missed, a following member of the Flight would tackle it, and so on.
>
> On E.A. in numbers a formation attack was made, each pilot selecting a target amongst them. Following the initial engagement, the Flight would climb and re-form without delay, ready for further attacks on any E.A. still about.

The famed Sopwith Camel came to the front in mid-1917 and was still operating at the war's end. This machine, F6240/'X', was flown by No 201 Squadron. (Bruce/Leslie Collection)

> I always tried to avoid prolonged involvement in 'dog-fights', there being no sense in relinquishing the advantages of superior height. Nor did I favour headlong charges by the formation into that of an enemy—particularly if they were in greater numbers.

The Camel was also good at low level, and because of this it was used a great deal for ground strafing. Attacking ground targets was something which had developed at around the time of the Battle of Cambrai, in November 1917. With air supremacy over the battle areas, it was possible to send in fighter aircraft to bomb and strafe German troops, transport and other targets, either in the front line or a few miles inland. This tactic became the bane of the German soldiery, and was something the RFC, and later the RAF, used extensively over the remaining year of the Firtst World War.

The low-flying missions offered more than a little excitement. Things flashed into view, were fired upon, and were gone in an instant. If there were an artillery barrage in progress, the pilots had first to be briefed where the barrage targets were, together with the maximum heights of the flight of the shells. These gave the pilots aerial 'tunnels' through which to fly and attack ground targets, although any attempt to fly out through the shell-walled sides of the tunnels spelt severe danger. How pilots in the heat of all this could even begin to focus on where the barrage tunnels were is unclear—and some were obviously brought down by 'friendly fire'.

The Germans flew ground attacks too, and to some effect, with specially formed units equipped with armoured aeroplanes. These units were at first called Schutzstaffeln (protective squadrons) but were later known as Schlachtstaffeln (battle squadrons), and generally flew two-seaters such as the Halberstadt CL.II (later CL.IV) or Hannover CL.III.* Initially these Staffeln were used as protection for other two-seaters, leaving the single-seater Jasta pilots free to hunt rather than be tied to any form of close escort. German soldiers in the trenches were having a bad time, thanks to increasing ground attack sorties flown by the RFC.

The cockpits for pilot and observer were close together so that the two men could communicate easily, pointing out hostile aircraft or ground targets. They were particularly effective during the Cambrai battle, so much so that a Court of Inquiry was convened to examine why the Germans had been so successful in counter-attacking during that battle. Part of the answer was the sudden appearance of German two-seaters flying close-support missions, often below 100 feet. As well as guns, these aeroplanes carried trays of grenades, dropped by the observer into trenches or any other target that seemed worthy of such attention.

The Schlachtstaffel was but a small unit, no more than six aircraft and more often than not only four. During assaults by German troops, the aircraft would be given specific targets, gun positions or strongpoints, and they were not encouraged to attack anything else. The crews would fly ahead of the attacking infantry to help blast a path through, and, other than by rifle or machine-gun fire from the Allied trenches, combating these strafing aircraft was far from easy.

Eduard Wolfgang Zorer, following service on the Eastern Front with FA 54, moved to the Western Front to command a Kampfstaffel, bringing with him his own special ideas for attacking Allied ground positions in the front line. He recorded:

---

*The 'L' in 'CL' stood for *leicht* (light), to differentiate such aircraft from the usual heavy C-type reconnaissance machines.

A Halberstadt CL.III used for ground attacks and trench strafing. This machine is from Fliegerabteilung 25 The pilot has a forward-firing machine gun, the observer a Parabellum. Note the line of flares by the observer's cockpit, ready for instant use.

I trained my Staffel in methods to use against enemy infantry, later artillery and other targets, and I led them in three types of engagements—frontal assault, attacking along a line, and assaulting a broad area, wherein the basic principle was to fly close together, with all aircraft [pilots] unquestioningly and relentlessly following the leading aircraft through its movements at altitude and by flare signals from the beginning of the battle until it was broken off. Black, white and red streamers on the end of the wings and tail of the aircraft were our recognition sign, and, at the sight of them, our infantry were to display white panels that would enable us up above to determine the course of the most advanced lines.

Zorer made an assault on British lines during a battle between Gavrelle and Rouex, his pilot being Vizefeldwebel Schleiffer:

We were at about 600 metres' altitude. We made one pass along the Front in order to orient ourselves precisely in terms of the hard-pitched battle going on. In all my life I had never seen such a murderous fire of all calibres.

Up here we were threatened by death every second by shells that flew right by us—first one side, then the other—with such turbulence that we were almost drawn into the abyss below.

In response to the green and red flares that I fired, the infantrymen laid out their white panels. So, with their help, at 0640 hours, I was able to determine the general course of our most advanced lines.

About this time two British fighter aircraft appeared on this side of the line. They thought they would catch us unawares, but we were on our guard and so there was no surprise. At the same time, two German aeroplanes showed themselves: an artillery spotter with his Schützhäschen (protective young hare, as escort aircraft were called). This Englishmen quickly disappeared.

Close to 0650, a wonderful sight presented itself: the barrage ceased. Down below, which had been such a raging hell, there was life in the shellholes and dug-outs. We went over ever lower to about 20 metres above the ground. Soldiers sprang up, individually and in groups and moved forward. I could clearly recognise individual infantrymen. Whenever Schleiffer dropped down close to them, I leaned out of the aeroplane and yelled as loud as I could: '*Feste Druff!*' (Give it to them!) and roared '*Hurra!*' at them. They waved back at me.

At 0655 things were also active in the British trenches. soon I saw the Tommies with their 'dish helmets'. Now Schleiffer with his fixed machine gun and I with my movable machine gun alternately began to shoot at those fellows. He fired forward through the propeller arc and I fired over the side. The British went back, our troops went forward. After 500 rounds we let up on the enemy. But, gradually, the situation for us became ever less pleasant and ever more dangerous. Round after round from rifles and machine guns whistled by our ears. Then a machine-gun shot smashed into the fuselage behind my seat and ricocheted off the ammunition drum of my gun with a loud *clank*.

Our oil line broke and covered us both with hot oil, thus requiring us to break away and make an emergency landing. . . oil poured out at a dreadful rate. It was a difficult piece of work for Schleiffer to get us back to the airfield at Douai but he did it. The last drop of oil was used up as he set the aircraft down.

Another machine used in this assault role was the armoured Junkers J.I, which appeared at the front in late 1917, its crews liking the armour provided for their protection against small-arms fire. As well as attacking ground targets, the J.I was also used for contact patrols, for obvious reasons: contact with the enemy usually meant bullets striking the aircraft!

Very few Allied combat reports mention specific actions against low-flying Schlasta machines, because, I suspect, they were in and out of the battle areas quickly, and not many British pilots wanted to be at low level in a battle area unless they were themselves ground-strafing. In order to try and combat them, or, at least, to show willing, the RFC in 1917 used Advanced Landing Grounds (ALGs).

Knowing that the German two-seaters could nip in unobserved by fighter patrols beyond the lines, shoot up trenches, etc., and be gone in a few minutes, the ALGs were established close behind the front lines. The few fighters they accommodated would take off immediately any low-flying German machines were either seen or reported by telephone. Nieuport Scouts were used with some success, but, as the soldiers found, they could not be everywhere, and the RFC was unpopular with soldiers who had been shot up by enemy aircraft with no sign of help from their flying brethren. Balloons were always vulnerable to sudden assaults, and the ALG-based pilots were used against these intrusions as well.

Mick Mannock, of No 40 Squadron, was relatively unknown in early August 1917, but he was certainly a force within the squadron. Pilots who used the unit's forward landing ground at Mazingarbe, about seven miles due east from their base at Bruay, were usually volunteers, so one can assume that it was the more 'press-on' types who used it. We know from one pilot's diary, and subsequent book, that among those using the ALG at this stage were Mannock, Captain A. W. Keen, J. H. Tudhope, G. L. 'Zulu' Lloyd, A. E. Godfrey, R. N. Hall and the book's author, W. 'Mac' MacLanachan.* All were to become aces.

Often the pilots would land at Mazingarbe after a routine patrol, knowing they were fairly free unless a call for another 'show' came from Bruay. They could indulge themselves a little, while on the look-out for any German aircraft which suddenly appeared over the front. With the trenches at this period only a matter of a few miles away, they could easily observe the sky above the lines and take off at a moment's notice. Otherwise they flew patrols up and down the lines, at between 4,000 and 8,000 feet, watching for German two-seaters, or looking towards the ALG to see if the ground crews had laid out a signal panel warning them of hostile aircraft in the vicinity.

During the afternoon of 12 August, MacLanachan heard shouting while he was in a tent telephoning base. Running outside, he saw

---

* *Fighter Pilot*, by 'McScotch'.

Mannock hurriedly taking off in his Nieuport, and a couple of minutes later he spotted him about a mile away to the south-east, chasing an Albatros scout. It seemed as though the German pilot were heading for the Allied balloon lines and had been seen by the men on the ALG. Both aircraft were at 500 feet, Mannock close behind the Albatros, which was faster than the Nieuport and should have got away. However, Mannock was firing each time the German pilot held a straight course for a second or two, forcing the German to take evasive action and thereby slowing down his progress.

The German then appeared to realise this was not getting him anywhere and turned to face the Nieuport, but Mannock pulled up into a zoom and a final burst sent the Albatros down to crash-land near the trenches, though still on the British side. The pilot, Leutnant Joachim von Bertrab, of Jasta 30, had been wounded in one arm and a leg, but he survived to become a prisoner. He had five victories, none of which was a balloon, although he had achieved an impressive four victories in one day back on 6 April.

Mannock's tactic of forcing von Bertrab to take evasive action rather than fly straight and level, and possibly making his escape, is in direct contrast to the pearls of wisdom dispensed by other experienced pilots to newly arrived novices. They would probably be told not to fire early, as it indicated to their opponent that they were inexperienced and firing excitedly rather than being cool and closing the range before opening up. While undoubtedly both ploys worked, it is easy to see that tactics—any tactics—only produce results if applied in the correct situation.

Balloon Strafes

On the face of it, kite balloons seem ideal targets—fat, juicy and tied to the ground on the end of a cable. However, that is a truly false impression. They were highly dangerous, surrounded by machine guns and light AA guns, and, being a few miles behind the front line, needed to be attacked with care and some cunning. Whenever balloons were up, with the observers in the wicker baskets dangling beneath them, directing artillery or merely observing movements deep in occupied territory, aircraft patrols were always nearby to intercept would-be attackers.

As the war progressed, there were three types of fighter pilots concerned with balloons. There were those who, despite the dangers, seemed to be mesmerised by them and took every opportunity to attack them. Many were successful and ran up impressive scores of balloons destroyed, although several had their luck run out. The Belgian pilot Willy Coppens claimed 37 victories, of which 35 were balloons.

The top scorer on the German side was Fritz Röth, who 'killed' over 20 balloons out of a total victory list of 28. Then there were those who were specifically ordered to attack them, on account of a particular offensive starting and the need to 'blind' the enemy. Lastly, there were those who never attacked balloons! Of these, some were obviously lucky never to be requested to make an attack. Philip Fullard, an ace with No 1 Squadron, told a friend of mine that he disliked attacking them as the risk was not worth it.

Again reading William MacLanachan's book, there are an interesting few pages on specific 'balloon strafes' mounted by No 40 Squadron. These were ordered by RFC or Brigade HQs prior to an offensive, the need being to sweep the sky of as many of the German balloons in the area—if not all of them. If they were not destroyed, damaging them sufficiently to put them out of action for repairs, or just keeping them down, was as important. Several squadrons had to mount these 'balloon strafes' from time to time, and they often feature in the unit's folklore as momentous events.

No 40 Squadron flew to Mazingarbe during the morning of 9 August, and the pilots found that the planned attack had been better prepared than had a previous attack back on 7 May, when the squadron had sent seven Nieuports out over the lines at 20 feet while British artillery put up a barrage against the German trenches, during which time twelve other scouts went over higher up in order to draw attention away from the low flying attackers. On that day, seven German balloons were destroyed, three burning in the air, two more being set alight as they neared the ground, and two more destroyed while on the ground. One Flight Commander had failed to return, but the others had faired only a little better. All six remaining Nieuports had been shot about, although their pilots survived. Two pilots crashed at base, one crashed just inside British lines, while another crashed at Savy airfield.

Mannock claimed one of the balloons, his first victory. He did not score against a balloon again.

MacLanachan does not say why this second balloon attack was better than the first; indeed, he had not yet joined the Squadron when the 7 May sortie was mounted. He does tell us, however, of the plan for 9 August. He says that a measure of safety was offered to the Nieuport pilots by the artillery. Batteries were to bombard the German front line and the support trenches in order to keep the Germans in their dug-outs, while leaving gaps of around 200 yards through which the pilots could fly.

The attack was planned for 9 a.m.; the barrage was to start ten minutes earlier and end at 9.05. The pilots were given the option of flying out through the 'safety' gaps, or of waiting till 9.06 when the gunfire ceased. MacLanachan himself had no desire to meet a shell in mid-air, although most of the others elected to head along the gaps.

From Mazingarbe, ground observers, or others, like MacLanachan, waiting for the end of the barrage, watched as the five Nieuports headed towards the shellfire, wending their way between the explosions. As it ended, MacLanachan set off. He had been allocated the balloon at the southernmost end of the balloon line. Sergeant L. A. Herbert had been assigned to attack the northernmost balloon, and as 'Mac' became airborne he saw this balloon ignite and go down. 'Mac' was at the trenches within minutes and raced over them at around 10 feet, but already he was surrounded by ground fire.

He began taking violent evasive action, to put off rifle fire and so as not to give experienced machine-gunners the opportunity to get a bead on his aircraft. The further he went, the less the firing, as he got away from the front line. Gaining a little height, he levelled out around 50 feet once he was three to four miles inside German territory, but already his target balloon was being hauled down by the winch operators. This was going to make his job easier: it was coming down to his level, so he would not have to climb to it. Deciding to attack when the balloon was only 200–300 feet up, he also saw that, if he attacked from the east, the men at the two-gun emplacements he had spotted to the west of the balloon would be in danger of hitting their own balloon if they fired at him. 'Mac', therefore, flew about a mile to the east of them—but then saw a column of soldiers on a road.

They made no immediate sign of scattering, and 'Mac' was undecided what to do, so he zoomed up and then dived on them, aiming for a bunch of mounted troops at the head of the column. The sound of his diving engine stampeded the horses and sent several across nearby fields, having unseated their riders.

By this time the balloon was almost down, so he went straight for it. Knowing that his bullets would 'drop' slightly after firing, he aimed towards the top of the balloon, so that his fall of shot would splatter all over it. He sat fascinated as the Buckingham ammunition (it was the first time he had used it) sent smoke streamers into the fabric. As he turned he was suddenly exposed to ground fire, but as he looked back he was disappointed to see that the balloon had not exploded as he expected.

He turned and came down again, firing once more into the gas-bag, and again there were no satisfying flames or explosion. Changing the Lewis drum, he attacked for a third time, but now he was using non-incendiary bullets. The balloon was looking a bit limp, and some wisps of smoke were coming from one end of it. Heading away, 'Mac' saw another balloon still up, but only at 200 feet, so he went for it, but again there was no obvious result. Surrounded by exploding AA shells, he headed for home, happy that, if not destroyed, both balloons had been badly holed and would be out of action until repaired.

When he landed back at Bruay, with several staff officers waiting and looking round, MacLanachan saw that everyone else had got back safely from the raid. All five Nieuports had been hit and damaged, one of the pilots having also flown into a German telephone cable and returning with much of it wound round his propeller. Two others, like MacLanachan, had seen enemy soldiers and shot them up. Officially, the Squadron had destroyed one balloon; three others had been seen to be smoking, and the other two had certainly been hit and damaged to some degree. Aircraft from the 5th Brigade had also attacked German balloons, and one had been shot down in flames.

Very often the experience of attacking a balloon made some pilots loath to repeat it. MacLanachan refers to an interesting fact, noting that no pilot was ever expected to undertake a second 'balloon strafe'—at least, not as far as No 40 Squadron was concerned—and other attacks would be undertaken by the junior pilots. New pilots did not know of the dangers of these 'strafes', which led the senior pilots to chasten some of the more boisterous new boys with a threat along the lines of 'What you need is a "balloon strafe" to knock the stuffing out of you.' Apparently participation in one was regarded as a true baptism of fire.

We shall meet some of the more persistent 'balloon-busters' in another chapter.

Dicta Richthofen

Baron von Richthofen put together some of his thoughts whilst leading JG I, and it is understood that these were distributed to several senior air staff officers and to commanders of other Jagdesgeschwader and Jagdgruppen. Extracts from his paper follow:

Geschwader Flights

During a period of very busy English aerial activity, it is necessary to work with a large group: I am then forced to start out with a Geschwader of 30 to 40 aircraft. (The reason for this being the inferiority of the German fighter aircraft or the strength of the enemy activity.)

The formation in such a large Geschwader is as follows: The Geschwader commander flies lowest and in front, Staffel 1 to the left, Staffel 2 to the right, Staffel 3 100 metres above the commander, Staffel 4 at the same height as Staffel 3, 150 metres behind the commander.

Each Staffel follows its Staffel leader, and these follow the commander. Before taking off, I discuss my intentions, such as initial direction, with my pilots. This discussion before take-off is at least as important as the one on return.

Greater preparation is necessary for a flight with a full Geschwader than with a Staffel. That is why it is essential for a Geschwader flight to be announced in advance. The night before, I announce the Geschwader should be ready to start at 7 o'clock the next morning. By 'ready to start', I mean ready to fly, with each pilot beside or inside his aircraft, not somewhere else without his flying kit. Because I cannot know whether there will be enemy activity at 7 o'clock . . . it is possible that the whole Geschwader must wait for several hours at this state of readiness.

The start is ordered . . . Each Staffel starts by itself, with the leader last. He gathers his Staffel, at a low altitude (100 metres) over a specified point to right or left of the previously announced commander's flight line. Then the commander takes off and immediately takes the direction he has stated. The commander flies slowly until the Staffel leaders have occupied their prescribed positions. In order that the Staffeln are not confused, it is best to give each its own colours. The aircraft commander should also be painted in very

Werner Voss, left, in conversation with the leader of JG I, Manfred von Richthofen.

conspicuous colours. During assembly, the commander must not deviate. If possible he should also fly slowly towards the front line. When he is convinced that the Staffeln have closed up and that no aircraft is lagging behind, he can gradually begin to exploit the performance of his own aircraft.

The height at which the commander flies is also the height at which the Geschwader flies. It is absolutely wrong for one pilot to fly 200 metres higher or 50 metres lower. In such a large formation (30–40 aeroplanes), the position of the Staffel leader must be maintained during the whole flight.

When an enemy is sighted, the Geschwader commander will increase his speed. This instant must be recognised by every individual in the Geschwader so that the very strong formation is not pulled apart. If the commander dives, then the whole group follows at the same time. Tight spirals and large wide turns should be avoided.

A deputy leader should be designated before the flight in case the commander needs to drop out through unforeseen circumstances. A pistol flare signal will signify the transfer of leadership to his replacement.

The aim of strong Geschwader flights is to destroy enemy squadrons. In this case, attacks on single pilots by the commander are ineffective. For this reason, strong Geschwader flights are only worthwhile when good weather brings the expectation of much enemy air activity. The most favourable circumstances occur when you can place yourself between a disrupted enemy squadron and the front. Thus, you cut off its escape, overtake it and force it to fight.*

A close attack guarantees success. If the commander has decided to attack, he flies towards the main body of the enemy. Immediately before he attacks he must slow down to allow the formation, which may have been spread out by speed or manoeuvres, to gather itself once more. Each pilot should note the number of enemy from the first sighting. From the moment the attack begins, everyone should know where all of the enemy aircraft are.

The commander must not concentrate on stray enemy planes but should always attack the main body; stray fliers will be destroyed by the planes that follow. Until this time, no one from the formation should pass the commander. Speed is to be regulated by throttling back and not by manoeuvre. But, from the moment the commander dives on the enemy squadron, each pilot should be intent on being the first to engage the enemy.

The enemy squadron should be ripped apart by the impact of the first attack and through the absolute determination of each individual to get into battle. If this has succeeded, then the shooting down of any enemy is only a single battle. The danger now exists that single fighters may hinder each other and that, because of this, many an Englishman will be given the chance to escape in the turmoil of battle. Therefore, it should be that only those

---

* This is why a Geschwader did not fly or fight as a complete unit on every occasion, and more often than not sorties were flown in just Jasta strength. Only when 'situations' occurred—usually over active battle areas—did the Geschwader fly in strength.

nearest to an opponent should shoot. If two or more are at a similar range from the enemy (100 metres) then they should wait until the first attacker is thwarted by a jammed gun or the like and turns away, or leave to find a new opponent.

The Attack

I distinguish between attacks on squadrons and on single aircraft. The latter is the simplest. I wait for artillery observation machines which usually fly up and down on the other side of the lines at not too great an altitude. I spot five, six or ten such planes all at once. I observe their altitude and course, whether they have high flying, well armed protection or not, then I fly back away from the front to return to the front at a little higher altitude than the enemy aircraft I intend to attack, having kept the enemy continually in view. The most favourable moment for attack is when such an observer comes from the other side and flies towards the front. Then I dive out of the sun at him, taking into consideration the wind direction. Whoever reaches the enemy first has the privilege to shoot. The whole flight goes down with him. So-called 'cover' at great altitude is a cloak for cowardice. If the first attacker has gun trouble, then it is the turn of the second or the third and so on; two must never fire at the same time.*

If the enemy pilot was alert and the surprise did not succeed, he will in most cases seek the lowest altitudes in dives and manoeuvres. To follow him, then, is usually not successful because I can never hit a manoeuvring opponent. Also, there is no practical value in just driving him away, for five minutes later he can continue his activities. I hold that it is better in this case to withdraw and to fly back towards the front later and to repeat the manoeuvre. I have often brought an English observation machine down with my third attack.†

A formation battle on this side of the lines is often more successful, because an enemy can be forced to land. Formation fights on the other side are the most difficult, especially with an east wind. Then the commander must not stick rigidly to his plan, for he will face great losses. As long as I can remain offensive, I can engage in squadron battle also on the other side [of the lines].

The leader should not pursue a scattered squadron, but should position himself between the enemy and the front, and climb above them so that he can cut off the enemy's retreat. If the enemy squadron breaks up and disperses, there is danger that some will be lost to sight. It is the responsibility of the formation leader to ensure that this does not happen. When I approach an enemy, I count the individual aircraft. Thus I avoid being surprised at the

---

* It is strange how von Richthofen appears to discount the value of leaving aircraft above as cover in case of a surprise attack from unseen fighters.
† This is an interesting admission by the Baron—that he could not hit a twisting, turning aircraft; and he does not see the value in having driven off the observation machine, which has therefore been removed from its assigned task. Even though he may later have the luck to down the machine if it returns, the soldiers on the ground will be happy that the British crew is—if only for a short time—prevented from directing artillery fire down on them.

moment of attack. During the battle the leader should not lose sight of his own flights or the enemy squadron. To see clearly is the pre-requisite and the principal requirement of the Flight leader.*

The One to One Battle

Every formation battle dissolves into individual combat. The subject 'Aerial Battle Technique' can be explained with one sentence, namely: 'I approach the enemy from behind to within 50 metres, I aim carefully, fire, and the enemy falls.' These were the words used in explanation by Boelcke when I asked him his trick. Now I know that this is the whole secret of aerial victory.

One does not need to be a clever pilot or a crack shot, one only needs the courage to fly in close to the enemy before opening fire. I only see one difference between single and two-seaters. Whether the two-seater is an RE8 or a Bristol Fighter, or the single-seater is an SE5 or a Nieuport, is totally immaterial.

The two-seater is attacked with great speed from behind in exactly the direction it is flying. The machine gun guard of the alert observer can only be avoided if you stay calm and incapacitate him with your first shots. If the enemy manoeuvres, I take care never to pass over him. A longer manoeuvring fight with a powerful, agile two-seater is the most difficult. I shoot only when the enemy machine is banking. However, I may try to unsettle him by firing warning shots (phosphorus tracer). I regard a frontal attack on a two-seater as most dangerous. In the first place, one rarely hits the enemy and can hardly ever completely incapacitate him.

Further, if I have passed under the two-seater and wish to bank, I come within range of the observer's gun and, in manoeuvring to place myself in the direction of his flight, I offer his observer the best target.

If attacked by a two-seater from the front, one does not need to flee but can try to make a sudden U-turn under the enemy plane. If the observer did not see you, you are readily able to shoot at him from underneath. When, however, he has paid attention and your U-turn brings you into his view, then it is often best not to continue within his range, but to turn away and attack him anew.

In an individual combat against a single-seater, it is easiest to surprise him from behind. If I am alone with an enemy on this side of the lines, only an ammunition jam or engine trouble can prevent me from shooting him down. The simplest [method], which succeeds very often, is to surprise a single-seater from behind. If [the pilot] is vigilant, he will immediately begin to bank. Then it depends on [my] making tighter curves and to remain above him.

If the battle takes place on this side of the lines or on the other side with a favourable wind, such a manoeuvring fight will end with me forcing the enemy [pilot] towards the ground. He must then decide either to land, or to

---

* On 21 April 1918, von Richthofen did lose sight of his men, did, in part, pursue a scattered squadron—or, at least, one Camel—deep into enemy territory, and did not take full account of the wind direction. These circumstances led to his death.

risk flying straight ahead, in order to escape to his side of the lines. If he does the latter, I am sitting behind an enemy flying straight forward and can shoot him down with ease.*

When I am attacked by a single-seater from above, in principle I never reduce speed, but make all my turns and dives with full throttle. I bank towards the opponent and seek, by climbing in the turn, to get above him. In doing this, I must never allow the enemy to get behind me. When I have overtaken him, the course of the battle is different. A single-seater can safely be attacked from the front. Nevertheless, I believe that, because you are in range for only a brief time, shots fired head-on rarely hit.

---

* As in the case of Hawker.

NINE

The Lessons Thus Far

AIR FIGHTING really come of age during 1917. Airmen of both sides had learnt a good deal about the environment in which they lived, fought and sometimes died. In an amazingly short period of time, not only had the aeroplane become a reality, but a powerful weapon of war—although in many books about the First World War the aeroplane hardly gets a mention. Nevertheless, it would be a very obtuse soldier who did not acknowledge the constant sight of airmen above him during his period in the trenches.

I remember talking once to Tyrell Hawker, the brother of Lanoe Hawker, VC, who had been both in and behind the trenches with the artillery but did not serve in the RFC. He obviously understood more about the war in the air via his brother, but had no desire to transfer to aviation. As he saw it, the soldier's lot may not have been a happy one, but at least he did not have to 'go over the top' every day—unlike the aeroplanes flying above and beyond his trench and observation post, who *did* have to!

Many soldiers, on both sides, left what they described as the squalid, rat-infested, dank and dangerous world of the trenches to become observers or pilots. Perhaps seeing scores, if not hundreds, of their comrades mown down by machine-gun fire as they struggled through the mud of No Man's Land was seen as the quickest way to a short life. The aviator's life looked somewhat more glamorous, and the fighting must have seemed more dignified—and with more chance of survival. However, many found to their cost that air fighting gave no more assurance of survival than the ground war, and numbers would-be aviators quickly returned to their regiments after perhaps one or two flights as an observer—especially, perhaps, if they had had the experience of being shot up by an enemy fighter. Others did not get the chance to return, falling in flames, or hurtling down from a great height in a shattered aeroplane with no hope of survival whatsoever. Yet the hardy ones stayed on. Some lived for a long time, and even survived the war: the law of averages dictated that a percentage *had* to survive.

By mid-1917 at least, the air war had in many ways become as static as the ground war. Attacks and offensives did little to break through the opposition's lines, and hundreds—thousands—died trying to gain a few yards of mud. With the ground troops going nowhere fast, the air war remained equally stagnant above them. Nevertheless, the generals continued to insist on photographs of enemy positions and the RFC and RNAS continued to attack supply dumps, lines of communication and camps in the rear areas with bombers, all of which needed escorting. In addition, fighter patrols still went out daily to keep the hostile fighters away from the recce and bombing squadrons. Close fighter escort was coming in, but it was no guarantee of survival if determined German fighter pilots got through the British or French scouts. The only real thing that changed was the equipment. Each side was not just fighting an air war, it was fighting a war for air supremacy, and this required better and greater numbers of aircraft.

The number of Jasta formations had increased since the start of the year. Jasta 41 had been formed in June 1917; thus there were now 40 Jastas on the Western Front (Jasta 25 was in Macedonia). The RFC and RNAS now had totally dedicated aircraft for each of its fighter units, although the Germans continued to have a mix of machines—at this period Albatros and Pfalz scouts, with a smattering of Fokker Triplanes. However, the Triplanes were having some structural problems and were quickly withdrawn, although they returned in the new year of 1918.

At least the aircraft engines were now far more reliable than had been the case during the first two years of the war. There was less risk of a pilot being forced down because of engine trouble than hitherto. However, anti-aircraft fire had increased enormously, and although most pilots tended to ignore it, it only took one lucky shell to smash an aircraft and end its crew's lives. With AA fire, the Allies' shell burst produced white smoke and the Germans' black, so this helped identification. Exploding AA shells attracted attention and brought the single-seaters to the honey-pot like flies. Sometimes the AA gunners fired at aircraft in order to attract fighters to a target as much as trying to hit them. In the British messes, AA fire was known as 'Archie', so named because of a popular music-hall song of the day, one line of which was: 'Archibald, certainly not!' The inference here was that 'Archie' would certainly not hit them—a belief held to be true until it actually happened.

Artillery observation and direction was now down to a fine art, and, if not disturbed by enemy fighters, experienced Corps crews could direct heavy gunfire on to a target in a short space of time. Aerial cameras had improved too, bringing crisp, clear images of enemy positions rapidly to the generals. Yet all the while the fighter pilots of both sides fought valiantly to interfere with the work of these crews, and each one stopped meant less death and mayhem on the ground.

The RFC and RNAS were still flying an offensive war, the Germans a mainly defensive one. The principal British aircraft were the S.E.5a, Camel, F.E.2d (with Bristol Fighters soon to take over the F.E.'s day role) and Spads, plus a few Nieuports in units that had not yet re-equipped with S.E.5s. Day bombers were now the DeHavilland D.H.4 in the RFC; the French, not having a really good bomber in mid-1917, carryied on with some of their earlier Caudrons and Farmans, plus the Letord types which were also used for reconnaissance. New types were on their way, particularly the Breguet XIV for bombing and the Salmson 2A2 for Corps work.

The British already had a new Corps machine which had started to arrive in early 1917—the Armstrong-Whitworth F.K.8, known as the 'Big Ack'. By the end of the year four squadrons were operating with this aircraft. Meanwhile, the R.E.8 still battled on as a recce and photo machine, and would do so until the war's end.

The aircraft which had got off to a bad start in April 1917, with No 48 Squadron, the Bristol F.2A fighter, was now rapidly taking over the role of fighter-recce in Nos 11, 20 and 22 Squadrons on the Western Front. The initial error was to defend against fighter attack by bunching up and hoping the observers would be able to fend off the enemy. Once it was realised that this two-seat fighter could combat successfully all types of German fighters just by dog-fighting them, things changed and the Bristol Fighter caused a considerable number of German casualties. It was highly manoeuvrable, and, with the pilot having a forward firing machine gun, and his observer behind him with one, sometimes two, Lewis guns, both crewmen were able to concentrate on separate opponents. Usually the limiting factor in having one or two Lewis guns behind was the strength of the observer to manoeuvre them—and two ammunition drums—about on the Scarff mounting. This mounting was fitted to most rear cockpit gun positions, and if it carried two guns it was known by the RFC as 'Huntley & Palmer' after the biscuit company.

With the Bristols taking over from the F.E.2ds, the last of RFC's 'pusher' types to operate in daylight was being ousted. The F.E.s were now relegated to night bombing. Despite their antiquated appearance, the F.E. two-seaters had given sterling service in the RFC, and No 20 Squadron, in particular, had produced a number of high-scoring aces, as well as a large score by the unit overall—though not without heavy casualties. Among the ace pilots was Henry G. E. Luchford, from Bromley in Kent, a former bank clerk. He joined No 20 Squadron in May 1917, and he and his observers began scoring in mid-June. By 17 August they had been credited with eleven victories, four destroyed and seven 'out of control'. Transferring to the Bristol Fighter, Luchford raised his score to 24 (thirteen destroyed and eleven 'out of control') and won the MC and Bar. However, on 2 December he was shot down and killed by Walter von Bülow-Bothkamp of Jasta 36, although his observer that day survived as a prisoner.

The most successful F.E.2 pilot was Frederick J. H. Thayre, a Londoner born on 20 October 1893. He gained his first success while flying a B.E.2 in March 1916, his observer downing a German scout. Moving to No 20 Squadron, he had several observers, but the one who shared most of his 'kills' was Francis R. Cubbon, who also came from London, born on 26 November 1892. Pre-war Cubbon had lived in India. Thayre increased his score to twenty (eighteen destroyed, two 'out of control') by 7 June 1917, at which time Cubbon's own score was 21. Both received the MC and Bar, but were killed on 7 June following a direct hit by anti-aircraft gunfire. 'Archibald, certainly . . . !'

(Right) The big F.E.2d. This machine, from No 20 Squadron, has three machine guns, two used by the observer to fire forward, and back over the top wing, with another fixed gun for the pilot. Note, too, the camera on the left side of the nacelle. The crew are Lts F. D. Stevens and W. C. Cambray, MC, summer 1917.

The reader is reminded that two-seater crews shared their victories no matter if they were downed by a front gun or the observer's guns. Most F.E.s at this stage did have a fixed, forward-firing gun for use by the pilot, although most 'kills' were made either by the observer's front gun or by the rear-firing one as described earlier. The feeling was that if the pilot scored the 'kill', it was because the observer was guarding the tail; if the observer alone scored, the pilot was holding the aircraft in a good position.

The F.E.s in particular were famous for forming a defensive circle if attacked by hostile scouts—at least, when circumstances permitted. If they were scattered before they could form up, they had to fight their way out of trouble the best they could, but, if they managed to close-up, each observer could give cover to the machine circling ahead of him, knowing that th rear of his own machine was likewise being protected. As this occurred, the pilots steadily headed towards the lines.

It was in one such fight on 6 July that Manfred von Richthofen had been hit and wounded in the head. He had chased the F.E.s just that bit too long and one observer's fire drilled a furrow across the top of his skull. For several moments he was blinded, but his sight returned in time for him to make a forced landing without further injury. It happened while his Jagdgeschwader was just starting to get into its stride. JG I was taken over by Kurt von Doring, leader of the group's Jasta 4, while von Richthofen recovered. Von Richthofen, of course, did return to operational flying and continued his run of successes, but he was never the same man again, the wound having affected him more than he cared to admit. He had suddenly found himself vulnerable— and it was a sobering experience.

On the German side, the basic two-seater reconnaissance C-type machines such as the Albatros, LVG, DFW and Rumpler continued their work. So similar did they look to Allied airmen that, more often than not, they were collectively reported as either Aviatiks (often seen in 1915–16) or Albatros types. The DFW C.V was the most prolific two-seater in the war and was used for recce and photographic work as well as bombing. After several Rumpler types had been produced, the type C.IV appeared at the end of 1916 and had good climb and speed at high altitudes so was employed for long-range recce sorties, using its height performance as its main defence against Allied fighters.

The Rumpler C.VII—which was a C.VI with a 240hp Maybach super-charged engine—could reach around 24,000 feet and had oxygen generators as well as electrically heated suits for the crew. It carried a Görz electrically operated camera, and it dispensed with the pilot's forward machine gun to aid performance.

Only a few pilots had any real success against these high-flying machines. McCudden was one, and to help his S.E.'s performance he 'tweaked' its engine, reduced wing dihedral and used a captured German spinner on his propeller to reduce wind resistance. On 23 December he downed four two-seaters during the day, two LVGs and two Rumplers; three of these aircraft fell inside Allied lines. (Generally, his patrol area was between Arras and Cambrai, but if he failed to find any 'trade' he was quite happy to poach further south inside French air space.) Having shot down one LVG at 11.25 a.m., he headed south and came across a French Spad, whose pilot was obviously wondering why this British S.E.5a was poaching. As McCudden gained more and more height, so the Frenchman was forced to remain at 14,000 feet. Then McCudden spotted a Rumpler C.VII high over Péronne at around 18,200 feet. The German crew saw him and rose further, but McCudden's S.E.5a was still climbing fairly well. McCudden knew the Rumpler was a good climber, and at 20,000 feet its heavily cambered wings were extremely efficient, whereas the S.E.5a, with its flat wing section, although fast, was just about at its ceiling.

As McCudden approached, however, the German crew began to run for it. Closing in, McCudden got himself into an attacking position, and although the Rumpler was fast, he was able to keep up with it. The German pilot swerved slightly in order to let his gunner get a burst at the S.E.5a, which was now right behind his tail, in the German's blind spot. In doing so, the Rumpler's forward speed lessened slightly and it began to lose height. In this way, McCudden chased it down from 18,000 to 8,000 feet. McCudden had fired as his sights came to bear, and finally the Rumpler's right-hand wings ripped off, the S.E.5a very nearly flying into them. The wreckage fell at Contescourt, west of St Quentin at 12.20. It was McCudden's 30th victory.

Falling Aces

Of course, by 1917 the fighter aces were becoming household celebrities. Hero-worship in whatever form can be a good thing, whether it is the support of a football club or of a military formation. Support encourages progress and a keeness to do well. So, too, with the airmen of the First World War, and particularly the fighter pilots. It is unfortunate that other airmen, doing jobs just as vital—bombing, reconnaissance, artillery observation—did not receive the same degree of public acclaim, but there it is. It should also be remembered that it was mainly these poor souls who became the victories for the aces.

Germany and France actively encouraged the public adulation of their heroes, not least by media coverage. Newspaper photographs, and postcards, were readily available, and they were treated just like film stars later in the century. The British never officially allowed this, although they could not stop a certain degree of information being obtained by the media and published. Each time an airman was decorated by his King, he was then photographed emerging from Buckingham Palace after the investiture. He soon had his story displayed in the newspapers or aviation magazines; and once the hero became known, his further exploits were eagerly awaited by the adoring public. Citations for awards such as the VC, the DSO, the MC and, later, the DFC that appeared in the *London Gazette* also described the airmen's exploits, although specific squadron identities were not revealed.

One problem with all this publicity was that should he fall, the celebrity's loss was keenly felt, not only by his family, his friends in the squadron and his friends and colleagues in the service, but with the public too. In 1917 many well-known aces were shot down, and in the autumn a number of prominent aces died. Albert Ball, in May, is a case in point.

On 11 September four aces went down. The amazing Georges Guynemer failed to return from a morning patrol over the Front. Despite his vast experience and 53 official victories, plus 35 'probables' (i.e. 88 'victories' in British terms), his victor is understood to have been a much less experienced fighter pilot, Leutnant Kurt Wissemann of Jasta 3. The German had no idea at the moment of his triumph whom he had shot down. As far as he was concerned, it was just a French Spad.

It was only three days later, once the French finally released the sad news of Guynemer's fall near Poelcapelle, that the Germans searched their records to see who might have shot down a French Spad in the area mentioned. Guynemer had fallen in the middle of a heavily shelled battle area and his body had simply been lost. So keenly was his loss felt that French schoolchildren were told that he had flown so high he was unable to come down.

Wissemann came from Elberfeld, born 20 March 1893 and had earlier been through the observer mill, then pilot training prior, to joining Jasta 3. His first victory, a Bristol Fighter, came on 6 July 1917, followed by a Camel, a Nieuport and a Spad. Guynemer's Spad XIII was the German's fifth 'kill', but, although he had time for some reflected glory as the victor over the great French ace, this was short-lived as he too fell in combat to S.E.5as of No 56 Squadron before the month was out.

The second ace to fall on 11 September was flying a Camel of No 45 Squadron. A patrol had a fight with Werner Voss' Jasta 10 on the 11th, and he shot down Oscar McMaking, a six-victory ace, for his 47th 'kill'. Thus we have the position reversed, a high-scoring ace downing a minor one. It has to be remembered here that it was mostly the inexperienced, or the unlucky, who fell victims to the big aces in the First World War—and, for that matter, in the Second: very rarely did high-scoring aces shoot each other down. There were exceptions, such as Georg von Hantelmann, about whom we shall read later.

No 1 Squadron, still flying Nieuport Scouts in September, lost two aces on the 11th, one being Louis Jenkin, MC, with 22 victories, and another William S. Mansell, in another patrol, who had five victories. Mansell's aircraft received a direct hit by an AA shell, so his was a case of his luck running out. Jenkin's patrol got into a scrap with seven German fighters and two two-seaters and Jenkin himself failed to get home. He may have been downed by Oberleutnant Otto Schmidt, leader of Jasta 29, and have thus become his eighth victory of an eventual twenty at least, although Jenkin was last seen chasing a two-seater.

Kurt Wolff, the 33-victory ace with von Richthofen's Circus, had only returned to Jasta 11 on this same 11 September, having recovered from a hand wound, just after those two new Triplanes had arrived.

Lt W. W. Rogers, MC, of No 1 Squadron, in his Nieuport Scout, with a good view of the Lewis gun, and also the Aldis telescopic gun sight.

He test-flew one and liked it, and on the 15th he was out leading his men in it. They ran into Sopwith Camels of No 10 Naval Squadron, who later reported fighting not only five Albatros Scouts, but *four* Triplanes! In the fight, Wolff obviously showed his fighting prowess by appearing to his enemy to be in four places at once, but, in the end, Flight Lieutenant N. M. MacGregor, a twenty-one-year-old from London, got in a telling burst which sent the Triplane spinning down into cloud.

MacGregor only claimed an 'out of control' victory, but in this instance the German fighter had continued down with either a dead or dying Wolff at the controls, to crash into the ground north of Wervicq. It was the Londoner's fifth victory of an eventual seven, and the Triplane was the first shot down by the Allies, there being only two (as far as is known) on the Western Front.

Another big loss was that of the mercurial Werner Voss on 23 September, as mentioned in the previous chapter. Then, on the 27th, the acting leader of Jasta 37 was brought down and taken prisoner-of-war. He was Oberleutnant Hans Waldhausen, a Bavarian and former artilleryman. After a period on two-seaters he had transferred to fighters, but he only joined Jasta 37 towards the end of July. He was made acting leader on 26 September, by which time he had opened his score and scored three victories—two aircraft and a balloon—plus another aircraft unconfirmed.*

On that fateful 27 September he flew out in the late afternoon, heading for the British balloon lines. At 5.05 p.m. he flamed a balloon south-west of Roulette, and five minutes later attacked and shot down an R.E.8 over Farbus Wood. Just over an hour later he dived on another British balloon at Neuville-St-Vaast, and destroyed this as well. However, he had been too long over the British lines and had attracted two experienced fighter pilots, one RFC and the other RNAS.

Mannock's pal in No 40 Squadron, J. H. Tudhope in a Nieuport, and Flight Commander C. D. Booker, with 8 Naval Squadron, caught him near Souchez and shot him down. Waldhausen force-landed and was taken prisoner, his very brief career at an end, although he had doubled his score to six on his last flight. The shared 'kill' was Tudhope's second of an eventual ten, and Booker's 23rd of an eventual 29. It was also Charles Booker's first Camel victory, all but one of his previous successes having been achieved on the Sopwith Triplane.

It seems plain from his combat report that John Tudhope did not think much of Booker's attack or involvement, and even thought his Camel was a Nieuport. Again, this victory was by a pilot using the unit's ALG at Mazingarbe:

> At 6-50 pm I was sitting in my machine on the Advanced Landing Ground when I observed an Albatros Scout under AA fire approaching one of our balloons.

---

* Oddly enough, Waldhausen became known(exactly when is unclear) as the 'Eagle of Lens', much as Immelmann had been called the 'Eagle of Lille'. Why this should be is a mystery to this author (as Immelmann's sobriquet is), for his three victories had been achieved over Fresnes, Cagnicourt and Béthune, not Lens. Even Jasta 37's base at Phalempin was well to the east of Lens.

I immediately started the engine and took off, heading straight for the EA, and when about 1,000 feet up observed EA firing into the balloon. EA passed over and west of balloon before turning, by which time I was directly between EA and the lines.

I then attacked and fired a burst of about 30 rounds at very close range into EA, which dived and manoeuvred but was unable to put any distance between himself and [my] Nieuport.

I fired two more bursts, almost crashing into EA on the second. EA immediately turned west and went down very steeply with engine stopped and Nieuport above. EA went straight down and crashed alongside the light railway station at Souchez. Nieuport came right down and circled round EA, which was immediately surrounded by troops.

During engagement a second Nieuport approached from the east and fired a few rounds at long range. Shots were also observed being fired, apparently from the ground.

Types of Fighter Patrols

Tudhope noted on his report that he had been on an H.A. (Hostile Aircraft) patrol. In this particular case it meant a 'scramble' (to use a Second World War tern) to intercept specific aircraft either seen from the ground or reported by front-line troops or observation posts by telephone. By late 1917 observers on the ground were able to intercept radio/Morse signals, so Wireless Interception Patrols were instigated. Maurice Newnham, of No 65 Squadron, explained to me:

A Flight of scouts, usually rotary engined, for quick starting, were detailed for the job of 'wireless interruption', on each Army front. A special wireless station established on or near the aerodrome intercepted messages sent from hostile machines and immediately informed the Flight by telephone.

Exploding 'Archie' usually supplies the height at which the Hun was flying. At the airfield the I.O. [intelligence officer] sounds a klaxon horn, the mechanics start engines, while the pilot leader obtains the location of the Hun from the Orderly Room, then rushes to his machine. Once in the air and nearing the area where the Hun is flying, if the AA gunners are working well, three white puffs of exploding shells will indicate by way of an arrowpoint where the two-seater is. The rest is up to the leader and his two companions.

There were a number of abbreviations for the various patrols undertaken by RFC fighter pilots. O.P. was the most common, which stood for 'Offensive Patrol'. 'Line Patrols' were just that, patrols along the front lines, carried out to keep an eye open for German aircraft operating over the front, particularly artillery observation aircraft.

149

They were usually flown by new pilots or newly arrived squadrons, so as to gain experience of the front without going beyond the lines and into obvious danger. Later there were H.O.P.s, or 'High Offensive Patrols'—patrols at height, usually to protect other patrolling aircraft lower down from any sudden attacks from above.

These patrols were usually supposed to be of around two hours' duration, unless an action split up the Flight, or fuel and ammunition ran short. It was a long time if not engaged, and more often than not they ended after about an hour and a half. The first twenty minutes or so was spent gaining height behind the Allied lines, as there was no future in crossing the trenches where exposure to AA and ground fire should be avoided. Then after an hour, often in cold conditions, patrols would tend to drift westwards, and the last 10–15 minutes would be used in descending towards base airfields.

D.O.P.s were 'Distant Offensive Patrols', and these were specifically patrols flown some way into German-held territory, or 'Hun-land', as it was often referred to. These patrols would often go as deep as 10–15 miles over the lines and needed to be led by experienced commanders. Pilots liked experienced leaders, so long as that experience was accompanied by caution.

In the main, the D.O.P.s were not well liked, and most pilots preferred not to engage enemy aircraft way over the lines, unless the circumstances were in the RFC pilots' favour. For the Sopwith Pup pilots, this was not below 17,000 feet, where they could generally outfly the Albatros Scouts. This was due to the Pup's low wing loading: it could manoeuvre without stalling, unlike the heavier Albatros. If they did spot German aircraft below this altitude, it was far better to try and entice them up to the Pup's height, rather than surrender their own height advantage by diving to attack. If this ploy failed, however, they could dive, fire, then zoom back to height rather than join in a dog-fight.

By and large, many squadrons could not see the point of a D.O.P.— unless it were to help cover a bombing raid, or a deep photographic reconnaissance mission. The pilots saw no reason to 'trail their coats' in such a fashion merely in the hope of engaging hostile aircraft. It would be the same for the Luftwaffe in 1940, its Me109 fighters being ignored by the RAF Spitfires and Hurricanes unless the Germans were

The Sopwith Pup was a delight to fly, and although it could just about hold its own against the opposition, it took an experienced pilot to coax it to do so. It carried a single Vickers gun on the top of the cowling.

escorting bombers. Similarly, in 1941-42 the RAF, when flying sweeps over northern France, were often ignored by Luftwaffe fighters. The RAF sent small formations of bombers escorted by massed fighter Wings, again in the hope that the German fighter pilots would react and be drawn out.

While RFC HQ may have believed that these aggressive D.O.Ps produced more combats, in fact they did not, for the real fighting in the air was to be found over or just behind the lines, the Germans reacting to RFC and French Corps machines working there.

In the periods between ground battles, squadrons usually settled down to a fairly regular routine, daily patrols being flown except when bad weather prevented them—'dud' days, as they were called. Pilots waking to find heavy rain or fog gratefully turned over and went back to sleep. RFC squadrons had three Flights, A, B and C, with six pilots in each. In a busy period each Flight might fly one patrol per day; during quiet periods, two Flights would operate, leaving one on rest. Thus A Flight might fly a morning, or dawn patrol, and B Flight an evening patrol. C Flight, on rest, then took the early patrol the following day and 'A Flight' the late patrol, while 'B Flight' took a rest. RFC Flight patrols were often in fives, so that one pilot could be away on leave. Not that all resting pilots took the day off: several 'press-on' types would make lone patrols or ask permission to have a go at a balloon. Later in the war, squadron establishments increased slightly, giving each Flight at least one more pilot.

French fighter squadrons also flew in small numbers—often just two or three aircraft—as they generally operated much nearer the lines. Their successful aces were usually protected by wingmen who, like those in British and German units, had first crack at a target aeroplane before any dog-fight started. However, many French aces also flew alone and deep into German territory, which is why so many had 'probable' victories: confirmation was difficult. Nevertheless, the time of the lone hunter was fast disappearing: it had become too dangerous.

With the coming of the Jagdesgeschwader and the Jagdgruppen, it had become noticeable that larger formations of German fighters were being met, and so patrol sizes on the Allied side also had to be larger. Some D.O.P.s were of squadron strength. The problem, however, was that large groups of aeroplanes just could not be tactically handled in combat. Wing wobbling, hand signals, or flares were only of use before a combat. Once a large fight started, aircraft tended to expand the area of battle upwards and to the flanks, each pilot who knew what he was doing trying to gain height and space. The latter was a consideration in order to avoid collision with another aircraft, or even to reduce the chance of accidentally being hit by friendly or hostile fire.

Real in-fighting tended to be between small groups of aircraft, a quick, fierce action taking place—often lethal to a couple of pilots, especially if an ace managed to single out a novice, where a personal one-on-one duel usually ended quickly. Arthur Gould Lee, MC, who flew with No 46 Squadron in 1917, recorded in his book *Open Cockpit**—and emphasised it to me whilst talking in his London home—that, at the start of an action, a British patrol would be reasonably tidy, in loose formation, and if the aircraft dived on enemy aircraft cohesion would still be maintained. But then, once firing

---

* Jarrolds, 1969.

commenced, everyone would begin wheeling about. Almost at the same time the leaders would lose tactical unity and it was every man for himself. Pilots would react to every change of situation in the battle, where the ferocious pace and intensity meant that it was all over in a few minutes. Bill Cambray of No 20 Squadron explained his method of hand signals used between him and his pilot:

We practised a great deal together, as it was essential to use sign language in the air. We developed this to quite a fine art. Some of the signs we used were these: (1) For six Huns in formation a long way off: look at one's pilot, shake a fist ('Hun'), raise six fingers, point to direction and hold arms wide apart. (2) Four friendly aircraft close to us: make circles with hand ('RFC'), show four fingers and bring hands close together. (3) Huns getting closer: shake a fist, point to direction, bring hands together and pretend to be scared. (4) One of our own formation lagging behind: tap one's chest ('ours'), show one finger, point to throttle, and indicate pulling it back. (5) The laggard regains formation: tap one's chest, show one finger, indicate pushing throttle forward, give 'thumbs-up'.

The usual perch for the observer was on the side of the cockpit, always on the watch above and to the rear. As leader of a patrol my pilot would instruct other pilots in the formation of three, five or eight, to keep close—'but not too damned close, for fear of collision'. The enemy usually collected a formation of six, then perhaps an additional eight, and when there were about 20 of theirs to five of ours they would come close in to attack. I would thereupon fire a red Very light, which told our formation we were going to fight.

We would then go round and round in a big circle, each pilot following the tail of the man in front, and always making the whole circle approach gradually closer to our own lines. Should a Hun dive to attack, the observer of one machine in the circle would fire his top gun and the observer of the next F.E. would use his front gun, so that at any given time the attacker would have two guns firing at him.

A close understanding between pilot and observer was essential. On one occasion I was with a new—but good—pilot who had not previously been in a fight. We were flying in a formation of only three aircraft when we became engaged in a brief but rather exciting encounter. A Hun dived down from our rear and I could see his tracer bullets going under us as I stood up to firing over the tail. I signalled to the pilot to throw the machine about to get rid of him, but to my surprise, he only did a simple aerodrome-style turn. The Hun climbed again and made another attack, and this time I was fortunate enough to hit him and see him going down out of control while we did a second aerodrome turn. On returning to the aerodrome I asked my pilot in no uncertain terms why he had not thrown the machine all over the place. 'I was afraid I'd chuck you out,' he answered. I replied that it was my job to stay in.

A very minor incident, perhaps, but one illustrating the necessity of close co-operation.

Follow Your Leader

A pilot in Gould Lee's No 46 Squadron was Eric Yorath Hughes, who was born in July 1894 and hailed from Bridgend in South Wales. Following service in the Royal Field Artillery in France and Egypt, 'Taffy' Hughes joined the RFC and, on becoming a pilot, was posted to No 46 in June 1917. In 1968 he recalled for me his first war patrol:

> The morning of my arrival at 46, my Flight Commander, Captain Macdonald, asked me what flying I had done, and when I told him eighteen hours in all, including my duel at Netheravon, he said, 'My God, is that all? Well never mind, we are going on a line patrol, and you just fly on my right, stick by me, and, if we run into any Huns, don't turn and fire your gun, just turn and stay with me.'
>
> Sure enough we did run into some Huns, and before I knew what was happening I was alone and rather frightened. I didn't know where I was or how to read a compass, but remembered to turn 'where the golden sun sinks in the west' so I knew home was in the west, when suddenly I heard *ack-ack-ack-ack-ack*, and, turning my head round, saw two Huns on my tail, both firing at me.
>
> I had never been so terrified in all my life. I remember murmuring, 'Oh, God. Oh, Christ' repeatedly, putting my nose down with full engine and not having enough sense to even kick my rudder. I should have been cold meat, but for some unknown reason they left me and I eventually landed so far over our side of the lines that I must have been very near the English Channel!
>
> I expected a good ticking off when I got back to the Squadron, but got nothing of the sort, and was just told how lucky I had been, that I had to learn by experience and that it had been a lesson to me.

'Taffy' Hughes went on to gain five victories by the end of 1917, by which time he had become a Flight Commander flying Camels in No 3 Squadron, returning home in February 1918. In the Second World War he was in Training Command, receiving the AFC, and became a Wing Commander.

Kenneth M. St C. C. G. Leask was a retired Air Vice-Marshal with a CB when I was in correspondence with him in the late 1960s. In the Great War he had a fine fighting record which had brought him the MC and Bar. From the Devonshire Regiment and the Machine Gun Corps, he had joined the RFC in 1916, flown Corps aircraft with

No 42 Squadron and finally managed to get on to scouts as 1916 ended.

His first fighter unit was No 41 Squadron, equipped with F.E.8 pushers. He was greeted with the comment that if he ever got into a spin in the F.E.8, he would never come out of it. Well, as he was pleased to say, later he did—and got out. After a period of instructing at home he became senior Flight Commander with No 84 Squadron, flying S.E.5as and returning to France in September 1917. He fought through the autumn battles, including Cambrai and all its ground strafing, and in the final weeks of 1917 he was based at Izel-le-Hameau, west of Arras:

> During the period we were at Izel we had numerous combats with Hun formations, and it was quite normal to be outnumbered by at least two to one, and in consequence we suffered losses, chiefly due to inexperience and failure to keep formation. Usually what happened was that, in the excitement of the moment and in the eagerness to get a Hun, the young pilot would forget sticking to his leader and go down after an enemy. This was what the Germans wanted, because they had another machine detailed to cover their chap who was being chased, with the inevitable result that our machine was easy prey.
>
> On one occasion, having maintained my height, I found myself being given the works by six Triplanes, which were more manoeuvrable than the SE, and they came down from the sun. I got a real thrashing. I had two main spars shot about, my gravity tank in the centre section was holed and petrol was spraying back over my head. One of their bullets in the group had been a phosphorus one, which had set the fabric smouldering a few inches from the leaking tank. My machine was full of holes—even the axle was shot through—but I had a charmed life which stood me in good stead on many occasions. In this scrap we accounted for two of the Huns but they got two of us.
>
> When we moved to Flez I once had to lead wing formations of some 20 or more fighters, and we got into enormous dog-fights with casualties on both sides, and in several of them I saw the horror of aeroplanes in flames diving or spinning earthwards.
>
> One day we went over in squadron strength together with a squadron of Camels as a high altitude escort to No 5 RNAS Squadron's D.H.4s, bombing Busigny aerodrome. We were at 18,000 feet and had the advantage over the Huns, who came up in swarms—about 50—to attack the bombers. We swooped down and attacked with good results, and the thing developed into an enormous dog-fight. We were a good twenty miles over, and I had made one successful attack, when to my horror my engine started to cut out and fade, generally behaving erratically.

155

Realising I had carb. trouble, I glided out of the fight, fortunately not being spotted by any Huns. I was lucky not to be attacked, as I should have had to start weaving about, losing valuable height, and unable to stretch my glide across the lines. Luckily the S.E.'s low wing loading gave us a small gliding angle, and, provided the wind was not too bad, we could glide about one mile for each 1,000 feet of altitude lost.

Graeme Leask was credited with eight victories with the squadron and remained in the RAF after the war. He retired to Buckinghamshire, and very sadly he and his wife were killed in a car accident in April 1974, both aged 77.

Henry Samson Wolff was a small man, but he had a big heart and was always ready for a scrap. In 1917–18 he flew with No 40 Squadron, alongside such men as Mannock and MacLanachan. He was only nineteen years old in 1917, having left school the previous year, and went to France with just eight hours of solo flying time in his log-book. Shortly afterwards, on 23 September, he filled a vacancy in No 40 Squadron. Back in 1970, he recalled for me one of his first real fights just over a month after joining the squadron, on 31 October:

We saw two Huns east of Lens as soon as we crossed the lines. We then proceeded north, where we spotted one solitary Hun two-seater and dived to attack, but twelve Albatros Scouts came for us. A fight apparently ensued whilst I was attacking the two-seater. There were three of us, Mac MacLanachan and R. E. Bion.

Just before take off, Mac called me aside and said that, whatever happens, stick close to him and do not break formation. I carried this out to the letter. In doing so I did not realise this two-seater was a decoy, and in concentrating on getting the two-seater I was fired on by the Albatri [sic] and did not realise I was in a real 'party scrap'.

I saw the two-seater go down out of control after my attack and then joined up with Mac, who was never far away from me, and then we made for base. When I landed I found I had several shots through my top plane but a few inches from my reserve petrol tank and realised my narrow escape. Mac came over to me and asked what I thought of the scrap, to which I replied, 'What scrap?' He told me to look at my top wing, but I said that I had stuck with him and had only left for a second or two in order to attack the two-seater, and hadn't seen any other aircraft in the sky.

Later on in the Mess, Mick Mannock accused Mac of being a murderer for leading such a young lad on to a decoy, which, as a decoy, must have stood out a mile. This was, of course, said as a joke as he and Mac were great pals.

It should be realised that fights in the air took place over a period of a few minutes, and one always followed the adage 'He who fights and flies away, lives to fight another day.' Mac, of course, was stunting and twisting in order to get me away from a veritable hornet's nest. It certainly taught me a lesson, and to look around more before diving in. It spoke well of the S.E.5 to have stood up to so much aerobatics.

The decoy tactic has been mentioned before, and this author does not subscribe to German single or two-seater crews actually flying such sorties—not in that pure sense anyway. After all, as we can see in Wolf's report, the two-seater may well have been shot down, and none of the three Nieuports was knocked out. It is easy to see why the Germans *seemed* to use this tactic if one had been on the receiving end of a sudden attack while diving on another hostile aircraft. The simple truth is that fighter patrols of both sides were flying about above any Corps-type aircraft in order to be on hand if they were assaulted. It was probably also more acceptable to report a nasty decoy than admit having missed seeing the danger above before going down!

However, Captain G. W. Murlis-Green *did* use decoy tactics on the Salonika Front, as one of his pilots, Gerald Gibbs, remembered. He recorded that Murlis-Green sometimes asked for volunteers to act as 'bait' for him, and, Gibbs says, they were delighted to do so! They would then cruise in a B.E.2c at around 8,000 feet a few miles over the lines, while he would sit in the sun a couple of thousand feet above. Sometimes a German aircraft would approach to take the bait, and the men in the B.E. would rapidly dive for the lines. Happily, Murlis-Green never let anyone down, even though he did not always get the German. He called his men his 'Tigers', but, as Gibbs recalled, they were in reality frightened little rabbits. Probably the sunnier weather over northern Greece helped crews spot approaching danger rather more easily than in the cloudier skies over the Western Front.

Murlis-Green had a long and distinguished war, winning the DSO and Bar, the MC and two Bars, the French and Belgian Croix de Guerre and the Serbian Order of the White Eagle. His modest score of eight victories—which included claims whilst on B.E.12s and a Spad, plus a final night 'kill' in a Camel over south-east England in December 1917—does not do justice to his skill. Had he flown a better fighter than the converted B.E.2, and fought on a more active front, his score would undoubtedly been higher.

★ ★ ★

During routine patrols over the Western Front, British squadrons would be assigned an approximate altitudes at which to fly in order to co-ordinate their efforts with other patrols, thus keeping a fairly tight defence over the front lines. Thus it might be that S.E.5as would be patrolling at one height, with Spads lower down and Pups below them. Some patrols regularly flew towards such 'hot spots' as Douai, where several German fighter airfields were known to be located, in the hope of provoking the enemy to take off and have a fight. Sometimes the Germans obliged, but unless they thought they could gain some advantage, or unless British Corps aircraft were up and working, they more often stayed on the ground. RFC fighters on their own did not pose any danger to German soldiers, unless they happened to be ground-strafing. One can read statements by the Allied airmen to the effect that the Germans were often reluctant to engage in a scrap, but it was their system—their tactics. Rarely did they engage while at a disadvantage, and although the RFC in particular thought this rather cowardly—unsporting, in fact!—in reality it was a good tactic. It was far better to have the odds on your side. There was no use in downing one British or French machine if you were going to lose two or three of your own.

Tactics were obviously discussed on the squadrons, but it is always difficult to predict that a particular manoeuvre will be possible in a forthcoming action. In combat reports there is hardly a mention of any pilot going into a tactical routine, probably because it was taken for granted that he had done so, or, perhaps because, once an action was joined, each pilot merely did his own thing, with his own degree of expertise—or lack of it. The leader, of course, would have doubtless initiated the first attack, but one often reads in combat reports of a pilot, seeing a hostile aircraft, just winging over and attacking it on his own.

Once an attack had been signalled by the Flight leader, the whole pack would engage the enemy, but after the first pass it was usually every man for himself. From then on the priority would be to fire at any enemy machine seen attacking another member of the patrol. All the while there appeared to be a not unnatural tendency for the British fighters to try and drift to the west—wind permitting—and if a fight broke up and the Flight were able to re-form around its leaders there was the hope that the patrol could continue. If, on the other hand, the Flight was attacked first, after the initial parry, it would be a case of getting into a dog-fight with the nearest hostile machine. On many occasions this was not possible, for the attackers, from either side, tended to dive and zoom, trying to regain height—which was all important in staying alive.

Identification in the Air

For the British, after any scrap, the quickest way to find one's leader was to look for the machine with a pennant flying from each wing strut—always assuming he had not been shot down in the fight. The deputy leader usually carried a single streamer attached to his rudder. If both had been shot down or had disappeared, it was best to give up and go home. Surprisingly, there are countless reports in which a pilot, finding himself alone, dusts himself off and continues the patrol. This says much for the spirit of Trenchard's offensive doctrine, though less for common sense.

In 1917, No 40 Squadron Flight leaders carried three pennants, one on each wing strut and another from the rudder, while deputy leaders carried just a single streamer on the tail. New pilots would follow these leaders, but were always ordered, if they became lost or separated, to fly west until they located the trenches, then make for base. New pilots invariably flew at the rear of formations, and again the rule was that if the group were attacked, they should try to dive beneath the other aircraft, not wait to be shot down. Nor should they lag behind—that was almost certain death.

On the German side, pennants or streamers were also used. Von Tutschek, the leader of Jasta 12, had two black-and-white pennants attached to the lower wings of his Albatros and later his Triplane. Others tended to distinguish themselves through the colouring of their aircraft. Von Richthofen, when leader of both Jasta 11 and JG I, had a very visible red colouring on parts of his aircraft, and although others also had areas painted red, his was the most prominent. During offensives he used an all-red machine for even greater visibility, in the air and on the ground. He needed people on the ground to identify him on the occasions he brought down an Allied aircraft which crashed into the battle area and therefore was not so easily confirmed

159

by a leisurely inspection of the wreckage or the capture of the occupants.

Other German leaders exhibited equally good examples of identification, whether it be the bright yellow engine cowling of Werner Voss's Triplane or the white winged-sword on Rudolf Berthold's fighters as leader of Jasta 14. Large letters, numbers or some easily identifiable emblem were used—anything that might help was employed.

The French also used colour. In 1916 several aces doped their aircraft with broad red, white and blue bands. Other escadrilles had large letters, often bright red, or numbers: Maxime Lenoir had the letters 'MAX' in red, white and blue, large on his fuselage. Lenoir had eleven victories in 1915–16, mostly with N 23, but was killed in October 1916. Jacques Leps of Spa 81—twelve victories—had the name 'L'HOUZARD' painted in large white letters along one side of the fuselage of his Spad in 1917, in reference to his former service with a Hussar Regiment. On the other side was painted, in equally large white letters, 'BERCHENY', referring to the Hungarian founder of the regiment during the 1700s.

The British frowned on any flamboyant markings on their aircraft, not wanting the camouflage effect to be negated, or more likely, to curb the more extrovert pilots! Occasionally a Flight leader might get away with a red or blue cowling round his rotary engine, or perhaps a coloured fin, forward of the rudder. The RNAS Camel pilots were able to decorate their Camels with colour at one period. 10 Naval painted large white and black horizontal lines on the front of their machines to denote A Flight, red and white for B Flight, and blue and white for C Flight. 9 Naval (later 209) had red cowlings, wheel covers and rudders.

Thus by mid to late 1917 there was a high degree of sophistication in the way operations were being flown. The main drawback was the lack of any really good communication between pilots. Wing-waggling and flares were all very well, but there was no guarantee that everyone saw them, or even interpreted them correctly. It was often just a case of spotting the enemy, checking as much as one was able the sky above and nearby, and, if it seemed clear, attack from the sun—if it was shining! German two-seaters were quick to turn and head eastwards if they saw danger, so while this may have stopped the crews from doing their work, there was much less chance of Allied pilots getting close enough to open fire on them. German single-seaters, too, were quick to fly off, especially if their tactical situation were unfavourable. As far as they were concerned, there was always tomorrow.

TEN

The Aces Speak

AS ALREADY mentioned, a number of successful fighter pilots on both sides had either been asked for or volunteered their personal views on air combat for the benefit of those airmen arriving at the front. In June 1917 the French ace Albert Deullin, whose score at this time had already run into double figures, set out his combat doctrine. Much was thought of it, not least by the embryo United States Air Service: they adopted it within their training manual, and so it was undoubtedly read by most of the arriving USAS pilots completing their training in France.

Albert Deullin was 27 and had been in the military since 1912, as a Dragoon NCO. Commissioned in 1915, he moved to aviation, firstly as a reconnaissance pilot and then with Escadrille N 3 as a *chasseur*. He received the Croix de Guerre (with fourteen Palmes) and later the Légion d'Honneur. By early 1917 he was commanding Spa 73, and in 1918 would lead Groupe de Combat 19, ending the war with twenty personal victories and five 'probables'. I have not included his words in full, but the following comes from his narrative as recorded in the USAS training manual:

Pursuit Work in a Single-Seater
by Capitaine Albert Deullin

The single-seater pursuit pilot should be a combination of, and unite all the indispensable qualities of, a pilot and of a machine gunner.

AS A PILOT, he should be, before everything else, skillful in maneuvring. He can never practice too much in aerial acrobatics; the short turn without change of height, climbing and descending in spirals, nose spins, '*renversements*', '*retournements*', looping the loop, short climbs at a very steep angle (the '*chandelle*'—a maneuver executed, when a plane has acquired an excessive speed in a dive, by pulling the plane into an angle greater than the best climbing angle. By using full motor [power], a very steep ascent may thus be made until the machine begins to lose its speed, when a more normal angle is adopted. The height which can be gained in this manner will of course depend upon the machine and the amount of excess speed at the beginning of the ascent), dives and so on are the beginning of his period of instruction. He will only be ready for the '*chasse*' when he can execute then with precision relative to an adversary who maneuvers likewise.

GENERAL PRINCIPLES. The single-seater only shoots in its own axis and in the '*chasse*' can only fire on his opponent in certain well determined positions and consequently maneuvers to a place in his field of fire an enemy who is seeking to get out of it. This is only part of the difficulty—it is necessary at the same time and under pain of running a terrible risk, to keep himself in the dead angles of the adversary. There lies practically the entire difficulty. Certain pilots neglect this principle and are soon beaten. The bold stroke succeeds sometimes, but generally those who use it are riddled and often brought down. I need only cite as proof of this the *Boche* single-seaters who dive like lost souls on our R.4s [large Caudron reconnaissance machines] and who regularly get themselves shot up. In this same respect I may mention Adjutant (later Sous-Lieutenant) Dorme, who has brought down, up to the present time, 18 *Boches* officially, fought more than 100 combats and has received in all three bullets in his machine. My conclusions therefore are:

The single-seater is badly protected from the rear, it has in this direction neither eyes nor machine gun. Always when he is making an attack in front, the pilot of the single-seater should watch out for a surprise from the rear. Before attacking, scrutinize the neighborhood most carefully. The sky is clear, watch out, it will not be perhaps for more than ten seconds. Never forget than an aeroplane soaring vertically above your head is very hard to see and that you will often overlook it. During the entire attack, look out for this second-contingent opponent, constantly throw a glance to the rear, calculate if you have time to press your attack home before being attacked yourself; consider after your own maneuver that of a second enemy. In brief, never forget the old principle, 'Attack ahead while looking to the rear.' (The importance of this advice cannot be over-emphasized and, in spite of all that can be said, it is the fundamental principle which is most constantly overlooked.) It can be said, without fear of contradiction, that the overwhelming majority of pilots brought down by other single-seaters are surprised from the rear, and this is usually when their sole attention is concentrated upon a Hun whom they themselves are trying to attack. Especially the new pilot in his first combats will be so taken up with the one idea of bringing down the machine that he sees before him that he will

Albert Deullin of Spa 3 and CO of Spa 73, who contributed a paper on tactics which the American Air Service incorporated into its pilot training programme.

entirely forget that there is any danger to himself other than such as may come from this one adversary. As a matter of fact, this is much the lesser danger. Not only do new pilots forget the all important principle, but even the experienced ones. Of the latter, with the exception of those who are shot down by the machine gunner of a two-seater, the last flights are usually those in which they are taken by surprise. A skillful pilot can usually extricate himself even when greatly outnumbered, if only he can see the enemy before they get to close range. It is the 'sitting shot' which is fatal. Once this has missed, even at point blank range, a skillfully maneuvered single-seater is an extremely difficult target to hit.

Any number of things combine to make other machines difficult to see in the air, the sun, mist, clouds and the protective silver [light?] colouring of the [aeroplane's] under-sides. Anyone who has ever shot ducks can appreciate this difficulty and will recall the many times when, after he has searched the sky in every direction without seeing so much as a speck on the horizon, he looks down for what seems but an instant and is startled by the rustle of wings over his decoys. The same thing applies to machines in the air, where they come from nobody knows but suddenly there they are. It is for this reason that the oldest and wisest pilots consider it foolish for a man to get to the lines by himself, not matter how great his skill and experience. 'To attack from ahead while watching to the rear,' is a fundamental principle, but if sufficient attention is paid to the attack ahead to make it successful, it is impossible at the same time to see everyone in the rear. Suppose a pilot sees a single enemy machine 3,000 feet below him and apparently entirely alone and dives on its tail unknowing that perhaps, 1,500 feet below him and behind his intended victim, [there] were four other enemy machines which a combination of mist, their camouflaged upper surfaces, and the fact that they were [obscured] under his lower wings, caused him to overlook. His attack takes him below and in front of these others, who in turn dive on his tail, with the exception of one who stays behind to watch their rear. As the first machine steadies himself to shoot, these second attackers have a comparatively easy shot, and the knowledge of their own security greatly increases their accuracy. The ultimate result is that the man who thought he was going to spring a surprise is somewhat surprised himself, if he knows anything at all, when six machine guns open up 50 yards in his rear. If he himself had a companion whose duty it was to stay above him and watch the rear, he might at least have been warned of the danger in time.

The attacker, however, should never rely entirely on his rear guard, but should always also watch his own rear. In addition to this, when a pilot does find himself alone on the lines and wishes to make an attack, realizing the danger of surprise, he will, before he attacks, spend several seconds in making an extra careful scrutiny for the second-contingent enemy. He then attacks, only to find that these several additional seconds were just what the Hun needed to give him a head start to escape.

The Germans fully realize the importance of this principle of surprise and their single-seaters practically always fly in groups. The tactics of these groups are based largely on the same principle, and I have personally seen several first-class French pilots brought down by the following maneuver. Suppose a half dozen Hun single-seaters are flying in a group when two or three French machines approach from above and maneuver as if preparing to attack. Several Huns will detach themselves from the rear of the patrol and make a circle to the rear, while at the same time climbing. Just as the French machines begin to dive, the leading Huns start into a dive also as though their one thought was to escape. This encourages the Frenchman and leads him on. Those who have turned to the rear may not have noticed and it is extremely difficult to keep track of a number of planes maneuvering under you own wings. He realizes that he must attack at once or the enemy will escape, and consequently gives attention to getting on the tail of one of them. The Hun ahead goes into a spiral for instance, thus making an impossible target, and knows as well that his friends above will not allow him to be followed very far. Each second the Frenchman thinks that 200 yards more will give him that shot he is working for, but in the meantime, he passes below the Huns who turned to the rear. As he steadies himself to shoot, they who are in turn on his tail do likewise. The Frenchman's companions may be too busy with a Hun of their own to keep track of him, and one more pilot is added to the list of 'missing.'

DISTANCE OF COMBAT. The single-seater should profit by its speed, its manageability and its small size to fight the shortest possible distance. The corresponding speeds of its opponents, impossible to calculate and constantly varying, make illusory an exact correction. The only sure shot for him who wishes to bring down some *Boche* is the shot at point blank range. The great majority of successful fights are fought at distances varying from 300 to 30 feet. (It would seem, so far as I have been able to learn, that again the majority of these fights have been fought at under 150 feet and that this principle of getting to very close quarters has been used by all the most successful French and British pilots.)

THE ATTACK. At these short distances, the difficulties of shooting are very much simplified. The science of the pursuit pilot lies especially in the maneuvers of the approach. These are entirely different according to whether the enemy is a single, two- or three-seater. One single rule is common to all—try always to effect surprise by placing yourself in the blind spots of the enemy and making use of the mist, the clouds, and the sun.

SINGLE-SEATER. At attack upon a solitary single-seater is much the easiest. For an old hand in a very good machine, it is practically without danger. The average of French single-seaters (pilots and machines) is clearly superior to the average of those opposed to them. It is sufficient to approach the enemy with the entire confidence; the result will not be in doubt. Seek always to surprise him (mist, sun and so on). You may also seek to place yourself vertically above your opponent, who catches sight of you very seldom in this position. The approach from below and dead ahead, or three-quarters ahead and above, is equally good. Suppose the approach has succeeded, it is necessary to place yourself in a shooting position. Execute a *renversement* (in the case of the approach from the front and above it will be a *retournement*) or a dive so as to place yourself at some yards behind and below the enemy, at the same time avoiding being blown about by the back draft [slipstream], and shoot. This principle applies to the attack on all types of machines (except the 'Gotha,' which has appeared upon the front since these notes were written. This machine has a trap [-door] in the bottom of the fuselage permitting the rear gunner to cover the blind spot which usually exists below the tail). The back draft is almost always easy to avoid. It is sufficient to dive fairly far behind the enemy (about 100 to 150 yards), to cover the last yards of approach about 25 yards below him, and to put yourself in a firing position by pulling your machine into a climbing angle.

Suppose the enemy sees you. If he catches sight of you when you are far off and begins to maneuver, it is advisable, before approaching him, to make sure of a slight advantage of height which will enable you to carry our your maneuver, at the same time remaining outside his field of fire.

He runs or accepts combat. If he runs, dive behind him. If he accepts, maneuvering begins. Each tries to place himself behind his opponent. Here is where skill and a keen eye come in.

When the *Boche* feels he is up against a better man, he tries to escape by diving. This is his ruin. If he dives straight you can shoot at him as at a target. If he executes zig-zags, you can stay behind him and take him each time at the chord of his curve. His one chance of safety is either a nose spin or a descent in *renversements*. Some of these excel at times.

The 180 hp Spad will outfly the Albatros [scout] on the level or in a dive at a small angle with the motor on, but in a steep dive an Albatros with its heavy motor will go at least as fast as any other machine. The same comparison would seem to be true of the 200 hp Spad, except that its superiority is more marked and it will also out-climb an Albatros. In combat the best results will be obtained by using full motor at all times except of course when it is necessary to shut it down to do a *renversement*, a dive and so on. In maneuvering against a single-seater, the principle thing to do is to get above him, and to do this it is obvious that the more motor the better.

TWO-SEATER. An attack upon a two-seater is a more delicate matter. One finds oneself against a slower machine, less manageable, but possessing an enormous field of fire. The gunner with his swivel, has only two dead angles: (1) ahead and (2) under the fuselage and under the tail, as well as behind the tail in the axis of the fuselage (rudder and elevators). The shot face to face and from below is not to be recommended. The added speeds of the two machines makes accuracy almost a nullity. In addition to this, the pilot and gunner are protected by the motor. A good shooting position will be found behind the tail and slightly below. But one must get there, and here again is where the cunning of the pursuit pilot comes in. Try always surprise (sun, mist and so on). From ahead and below one is almost sure of not being seen, and the same is true of three-quarters above and slightly above. (The reason the three-quarters position is recommended when one is above, is to keep out of the field of fire of the pilot's guns.) In these two situations execute a *renversement* (or *retournement*, according to whether you are below or above) upon arriving at the vertical of the *Boche*, and place yourself under the tail. Do not forget that at this moment the two machines are going in opposite directions and that hence the two speeds are added. Therefore begin the *renversement* about 200 yards before arriving at the vertical, otherwise you will always be too late.

I repeat that a machine very seldom sees another machine soaring above it and considerably higher. An excellent scheme is to fly high (from 14,000 to 16,000 feet) fairly far on the other side of the lines (from four to five miles). The *Boche* is not on his guard, sees the sky clear before him and comes on unsuspectingly below you towards the trenches. Let him pass well by, then dive with the greatest possible speed and a long way behind him (about 1,000 yards), level out slightly below him in the blind spot of his tail and make use of the speed which you have acquired in diving to cover the distance in a few seconds. The surprise has succeeded. Shoot at point blank range. Get very close before shooting at all, and then use the utmost care in aiming the first shots. Do not throw away the great advantage of having a steady target by too great haste with the first shots. If you miss him you will probably never get as good a chance again. There is nothing that stirs a pilot into action so quickly, and causes him to perform acrobatics of which he never before believed himself capable, as hearing a machine gun behind him and seeing a bullet go past his head or through a wing. The same thing of course applies to attacks upon all kinds of machines. Be at all times ready to shoot on the instant should he see you, but if he does not, do not be tempted to shoot until you are very close and sure you have it [your sights] on him.

Both the gun and ammunition are improving, and the machine now carrying two guns shooting through the propeller instead of one, as on the 180 hp Spad [Spad VII], is a great advantage. I think it safe to say that the type of Vickers used on the 180 hp Spad, shooting French ammunition, jammed or required re-cocking by hand in order to eject a defective cartridge in the majority of combats. It was certainly unusual to be able to fire 200 shots without trouble of some kind. This difficulty is not so bad as it was, but it is still something to be taken very much into consideration.

As a general rule, any adversary who does not alter course as you approach, does not see you. He dives or accepts combat. If he dives steeply, he usually prevents his gunner from shooting and it is easy to follow him.

If he accepts combat, he will more often endeavor to present to you his left flank rear in a three-quarters position, the best position for his gunner. Do not persist under these conditions. The risk is too great except if one is close enough to quickly pass to the right and then again to the left and so on, turning each time that the *Boche* gunner changes his gun from one side of his machine to the other.

It is the attack from three-quarters in the rear which I wish to emphasize, because it is tempting, and a number of inexperienced pilots allow themselves to be caught by it. I warn against it because it is too risky. It has only two chances of success: (1) for a remarkably sure shot to bring down his opponent with his first shots and from a long distance, and (2) for a remarkable maneuver [a pilot] who can approach, while at the same time fluttering about, allowing the machine gunner to use up in vain his cartridges and profiting by the moment when the *Boche* is re-loading his gun to approach and bring him down. If your opponent opens fire far off and shoots without stopping during your maneuvers, he is a frightened man who shoots recklessly and will soon be short of ammunition. If he shoots calmly and with short bursts of fire, he is a man who knows his business, and it is well to beware of him.

Suppose the two-seater is above you when you catch sight of it. This will often afford an excellent chance of climbing up under his tail without being seen, all the time watching him carefully and trying to keep in his blind spot. If, however, he sees you, the best method of coming to close quarters would seem to be to follow him at 300 or 400 yards, turning as he turns and never coming close enough to give him a reasonable shot while you are still climbing. If you come within the danger zone while you a climbing, you will remain there much longer than usual before coming to close quarters. It would seem therefore better to first climb up to at least slightly below the Hun, so as to be able to go in on the level at normal flying speed and thus cover the last 200 yards more quickly. There will probably not be time to climb up above him and dive down.

ATTACK UPON MACHINES IN A GROUP. It would be foolhardy to dive into the midst of a group of enemy two-seaters if they stay in formation and one is flanking the other. One must try to separate them and make use of the confusion to attack those who [become separated]. You [could] remain some distance above the group and wait for a false move (it often happens that, in turning, one of the machines turns in the wrong direction or even simply too late and becomes separated by some hundreds of yards from his comrades). That is the moment to make use of.

Are you well supplied with ammunition? You may often open fire from a distance and sprinkle successively each enemy machine. Then more often the *Boches* takes fright and makes the fatal false maneuver which will give you a chance to fall on a solitary machine and shoot him down before his companions can come to his assistance. Is it a brush with single-seaters? Attack always the highest one, the others are less dangerous.

Deullin later updated in part his narrative, which was dated November 1917, to take into account the ever-changing combat scene above the trenches. In general terms, Deullin felt that for a while the Germans appeared demoralised and rarely joined combat. Whether this had anything to do with the fact that German units badly mauled on the British front often came south to the 'quieter' French sectors, were only required to show a presence and were to engage only if the advantage was with them, is unclear. However, the French noted that any approach by French aircraft was almost certain to result in German aircraft heading away east rapidly. Deullin later noted that things began to improve for the Germans and that they appeared to become less disorganised. His thoughts continued:

ATTACK UPON SINGLE-SEATERS. The finest fight, and that which requires the greatest skill and experience, is the encounter with single-seaters. When the leader of the patrol has seen the enemy and has resolved to attack, he gives his pilots the signal 'attention' by rocking his wings, and begins to maneuver about his adversary. The maneuver is long and more or less difficult. One must be sure of the advantage of height, of the sun. In most of the *Boche* patrols, a solitary machine keeps about 1,000 yards higher than his comrades, ready to dive treacherously upon the enemy that the main body has enticed in. He must be discovered. One must climb up to his height and shoot him down, or force him down to the level of his comrades.

The fight develops in accordance with the principles of combat among single-seaters, with the difference that the attack under the tail becomes almost impossible. The Albatroses generally execute circles, each protecting the rear of his comrade. One of them is attacked. He dives and draws the enemy [a Frenchman] who is on his tail under the fire of his companion, who is following him. One should never allow oneself to follow the Albatros who dives into the middle of the formation. One should always, even if it makes you miss a good chance, keep above the highest enemy and attack only the last one by diving either from the rear or head-on without ever reducing the motor, so as to always maintain an excess of speed and power, which will enable you to make a steep climb and regain your commanding height.

CONTROL OF MANEUVERS. The control of maneuvers in use by Groupe de Combat 12 [Les Cigognes] has, up to the present, given complete satisfaction. Before starting, the leader indicates his deputy, should one be necessary, and assigns to each pilot his place and the part he is to play. He gives a meeting place [rendezvous] at a certain height above a given point. The machines circle about to the left of the meeting place, and the first one to see the leader, closes up on him to the assigned position and distance. The patrol acts like a ball of snow and grows quickly. As soon as it is in order, the leader rocks his wings and starts for the lines at low speed. The only way to keep the patrol grouped together is to fly at about 200 rpm less than the maximum.

During the flight, the leader watches his group constantly and slows down or speeds up as may be necessary, waiting for those who are behind. He avoids stunts and sudden changes of direction as much as possible. He watches his surroundings constantly, and especially the rear of his group, so as to avoid surprises.

CODE OF SIGNALS. The signals of command or warning have been simplified in the extreme. The rocking of wings from side to side indicates 'Attention, enemy approaches.' A second rocking, 'Attack.' During the mix-up, a rocking of wings means, 'I am forced to go back. Do not bother about me.'

In the course of a flight, if a pilot sees an enemy whom the leader appears not to see, he comes to his height and warns him by rocking his wings. Under no circumstances should he either attack first or leave the patrol to attack by himself. In aviation more than anything else, sticking together is difficult and requires the finest discipline.

Albert Deullin was killed testing a prototype aeroplane at Villacoublay in May 1923.

★   ★   ★

In the Karl Bodenschatz diaries published in 1935,* the author recorded reports by Staffel leaders of JG I (the Richthofen Geschwader) requested by the Commanding General of the Air Service, General Hermann von der Lieth-Thomsen, on the Allied aircraft and airmen his pilots were facing in the late summer of 1917. Oberleutnant Oskar Freiherr von Boenigk, Acting Commander of Jasta 4, who would end the war with 26 victories, wrote—after listing the aircraft the Geschwader was fighting—the following:

> Almost all of the single-seaters have a fixed machine gun. Recently, SEs have appeared with 200 hp Hispano-Suiza engines which possess very good climbing capabilities and speed.
>
> Promising the most success is an attack on a single-seater squadron from above and behind, during which you mustn't push out over the enemy machine. The best defence against an enemy single-seater attack from above and behind is to climb steeply in a sharp turn, but only if the enemy does not have machines too superior to our own aircraft. In such a case, allowing yourself to go into a spin is the most advisable.
>
> The attack on two-seaters best takes place from the front and above or from behind and below. In a dog-fight with a two-seater, always try not to climb above him, but rather stay below and behind him.

Leutnant Hans Adam was leading Jasta 6 at this period. Adam's total victory score was fast approaching twenty, and in fact he scored 21 before he fell in combat on 6 November 1917. He was also 31 years old, and was married with two children. His report quoted:

> 1. Attacks on single-seater Sopwith Pups and Sopwith Camels, from above towards the rear, or from above obliquely towards the front, can be carried out almost without any counter-action. Technically, both are inferior to the Albatros 'D' machine.
>
> 2. SE5a. Attack as in paragraph one. Technically, about equal to the Albatros 'D' machine; superior to the average 'D' machine in dog-fights at higher altitudes. They themselves frequently attack from behind, in a dogfight, as well.
>
> 3. Spad, 140 hp. Inferior to the Albatros 'D' machine. Spad 200 hp: superior to the Albatros 'D' machine in climbing capability and manoeuvrability.
>
> 4. [Sopwith] Triplane of more recent construction (same length wings) is very manoeuvrable, good in a dog-fight, tolerates the steepest dives, is not better than the Albatros 'D'.

Jagd in Flanderns Himmel

Leutnant Hans Adam, leader of Jasta 6. His death in action on 15 November 1917 precluded him receiving the Pour le Mérite, despite having 21 victories, but he was made a knight by the Bavarian award of the Military Max-Joseph Order.

5. Nieuport single-seater, exceptionally manoeuvrable, always defends itself by diving, is otherwise inferior to our 'D' machines in every respect.

In general: Attacking from below advisable only if first burst of fire will hit for certain. When enemy single-seaters approach at a higher altitude, they are almost impossible to climb over, since during an attack they usually don't push down low enough for us to dog-fight and possibly climb above them. When the enemy single-seater attacks, many times he fires too early, so upon hearing the first shots, turning and flying under the attackers is [*sic*] still possible. If the attacker has a rotary engine, defence by means of a right-hand turn is advisable because machines with rotary engines perform poorly in right-hand turns, and less possibility of being hit exists.

Two-seaters and multi-seaters: De Havilland 4. Attack from the rear and from the same altitude if you are close enough to be able to hit with the first burst of fire. Otherwise, do not close in any more. This type is just about as fast as an Albatros 'D' in a climb. If possible, attack first from in front and above and then from the rear immediately afterwards, in order to make the observer turn the gun in the gun turret [*sic*]. If the De Havilland is at the same altitude and must still be approached from further away, then the attack is almost always without hope of success. Usually operates at an altitude of over 5,000 metres.

Jasta 10 had just recently (23 September) lost its mercurial leader, Werner Voss. His Jasta submitted the following report, which was the last thing he wrote prior to his death in action:

All English single-seaters are superior to the German fighter aircraft in climb, handling, and dive capabilities, and most of them are also superior in speed. Only the Sopwith Pup is slower.

You should not, under any circumstances, attack formations of Sopwiths, which fly higher, on the other side of the enemy lines for you must then start the fight under unfavourable circumstances from the outset.

Of the two-seaters, the FEs can be particularly dangerous in air combat; they band together in a circle.

Vickers and FE squadrons respectively must be attacked together as a unit. Only then does the possibility of successfully dealing with them present itself.

Most fighter pilots do not like attacking the FE directly from the front, but this very method of attack is the most advantageous for us against the FE since the enemy has the least protection in front, while our fighter pilots have good protection because of the engine. With this last type of attack, it is absolutely essential for the fighter pilot to keep himself below the enemy aeroplane and not fly over the latter, under any circumstances.

Finally, Leutnant Gisbert-Wilhelm Groos, acting leader of Jasta 11—who had six victories to date and would survive the war with seven 'kills', wrote the following shortly before he was badly wounded (though he returned to the Jasta in July 1918):

The combat method of the enemy single-seater is always the same and doesn't depend on the type itself. The enemy single-seaters swoop into German squadrons from overhead, usually coming out of the sun (even in the mornings). With the sun at their backs, they attack just as readily from the front or the rear. If the Englishman does not have visible success after the first attack, he then climbs sharply, and, after a short time, tries a renewed, surprise attack.

The English flights do not usually attack together as a unit, so the few brave ones get caught up in a dog-fight where they are then overcome by the numerical superiority of the German

Lt A. P. F. Rhys Davids, DSO, MC, who shot down Werner Voss, leader of Jasta 10, on 23 September 1917 in a classic dog-fight of the First World War.

Josef Mai, a successful pilot with Jasta 5. He scored 30 victories in air combat between August 1917 and September 1918, winning the Blue Max.

single-seaters. If the German single-seater has found an opportunity to attack the English single-seater from above, the latter then seeks to evade his attacker by continuous tailspins and turns. However, as soon as he notices that the German is close, he turns suddenly and attacks from the front and below, attempting thereby to climb over his opponent, which he often succeeds in doing, owing to his fine machines.

★ ★ ★

Whatever the tactics adopted, whatever the experience, there was still no defence for that moment of carelessness, or the moment a pilot just did not see a hostile machine sneaking up on him. Josef Mai, from Berlin, gained 30 victories with Jasta 5 between August 1917 and September 1918. His second confirmed victory was a D.H.5 scout which he shot down near Selvigny, but, despite his inexperience, luck was certainly with him on this 25 August 1917, as he later wrote:

> In the morning we were asked to serve as escorts. Between 7.15 and 7.55 a.m. we fired at the enemy artillery positions near Boussoy. We were attacked by four Sopwith [*sic*] single seaters. One of these I was able to chase behind our lines and shot him down at 7.25 a.m. near Selvigny. Pilot, Captain de Bush, dead. The *Kiste*★ collapsed in the air.

In fact, Mai had been returning to his Jasta's airfield and had spotted the D.H.5 with two streamers, denoting, he thought, a squadron

★ Literally 'box'—German aviation slang for an aeroplane.

leader. To him the pilot seemed preoccupied with his map and did not detect the Albatros approach. Captain J. S. deL.Bush, of No 41 Squadron, was found with seven bullets in his back.

Mai, despite his 30 victories, failed to have another fifteen claims verified. Usually if there was a dispute over a 'kill', or if two or more pilots had helped in downing an Allied machine, a roll of the dice decided who was given credit for the victory.

ELEVEN

The Winds of Change

THE AIR WAR was to change dramatically and constantly during the last year of the Great War. It was almost as if everything that had gone before was about to culminate in a climax. For the Germans, one thing was ominously clear: although the United States of America had come into the war in April 1917, it was only now that this 'mighty giant' was looming on the horizon, and time was running out to defeat Britain and France.

The US Army had been moblised and the US Navy prepared, but the small air service, although keen and able, did have one serious problem: it had no front-line aircraft of its own. There was no shortage of American aviators already in the war. The pre-April 1917 volunteers who had been flying with the Lafayette Escadrille—officially Escadrille N 124 of the French Air Service—had already captured the imagination of Americans at home. Others, wishing to join them, had to be content with being members of the Lafayette Flying Corps, and to be assigned to other French units, as N 124 could only accommodate so many members at one time. Others still had travelled to Canada and joined the Royal Flying Corps and had been scattered amongst various RFC squadrons.

Those who had gone the 'long route' by joining the US Signal Service (the USAS was part of the Signal Service) and, having been accepted, then trained as aviators, were only now starting their journeys to France, where the US Expeditionary Force was building its strength alongside the French, preparing for battle. During late 1917 and early

1918, Americans with the French and British were being encouraged to transfer to the US Air Service and to bring their experience with them. Some did; others remained with the British. Meanwhile, a number of US aviators were assigned to various RFC units in France for combat experience.

Once in France, the American Air Service was given aircraft by the French. For the pursuit squadrons there was the Nieuport 28 fighter, a machine, curiously, rejected by the French themselves. The embryo bombing and reconnaissance squadrons were issued with French Salmson and Bregeut two-seaters, and with British D.H.4s.

The only thing in the German's favour was that its war with Russia had ended with the Revolution, releasing thousands of troops from the Eastern Front who were now heading for France. The British and French, thankful for the arrival of fresh troops from across the Atlantic, were, however, only too aware that 'fresh' also meant 'unblooded', and that the New Year of 1918 would certainly bring a massive offensive by the Germans once its more experienced Eastern Front troops were prepared.

In the air, too, the Germans were increasing their fighter strength: the coming months would see a doubling of the approximately 40 fighting Jastas. Indeed, this had been achieved as early as February, although not all units were complete Jagdstaffeln, many being neither fully equipped nor fully manned. Many of the new Jastas were formed around an experienced pilot from an existing Jasta, who was allowed to take one or two pilots with him. From these nuclei, units could be formed by posting in newly trained pilots from the Jastaschulen. Generally, pilot numbers continued to be well below the establishment of Allied squadrons, and a number of the new Jastas rarely had more than eight or nine pilots at best. Nevertheless, they were keen to get to grips with the 'Tommies' and the Frenchmen, and even the Americans. For the new pilots, despite the fall of a large number of well-respected and much-decorated German aces, the chance of glory and reward was seductive.

In addition, there were a number of KEST (Kampfeinsitzerstaffel) units in being, used for home defence. These fighter units had a small number of pilots, often supplemented with experienced fighter pilots on a temporary rest period from the front, based near towns or industrial centres on the western fringes of Germany. With the British and French occasionally flying bombing raids into western Germany, and, in 1918, the Independent Air Force D.H.4 and D.H.9 bombers also flying similar raids, plus night raids by Handley Page O/400s, these KEST pilots were kept busy.

Further Jagdesgeschwaders

The success of Richthofen's JG I encouraged the German Air Force High Command to form two more Jagdesgeschwader, JG II and JG III, in February 1918. This grouping of two, three or four fighter Staffeln had become popular—not just the permanent grouping JG I but also the non-permanent Jagdgruppen (JGr). Again, these were, in the main, administrative formations, but they were banded together for specific actions in specific locations and battle zones, and some merit had been found in them. Some of these Jagdgruppen only lasted for a few weeks, others only a few days, but, flying together, they had at least helped to overwhelm the increasing numbers of Allied aircraft.

JG II was commanded by Hauptmann Adolf von Tutschek, formerly commanding Jasta 12, and his new command consisted of Jastas 12, 13, 15 and 19. Von Tutschek had by this date achieved 23 victories and won the Pour le Mérite, although he had been badly wounded on 11 August—shot down by the same Charles Booker who had assisted in downing of Hans Waldhausen on 27 September 1917.

Many experienced German fighter pilots were only reserve officers (Leutnants der Reserve), commissioned for war service only, and it had been deemed that, like Manfred von Richthofen, only regular officers could command a Jagdesgeschwader. Even so, although von Tutschek was both experienced and held a regular commission, he had not been in combat for six months.

JG III was given to Oberleutnant Bruno Loerzer, an equally experienced fighter pilot with 22 victories, and another holder of the Pour le Mérite. He came from Berlin, born on 22 January 1891. Like so many First World War aviators, he came to flying from the Army and had been a two-seater pilot in 1915, his observer at that time being none other than Hermann Göring. Loerzer had moved on to monoplane fighters by 1916 and gained his first two 'kills' with KEK Jametz. He flew with the early Jastas, and was then given command of Jasta 26 in

January 1917. His Blue Max had been awarded just over a week prior to his taking command of JG III.

The German Jastas still had a collection of diverse aircraft. At this stage the Albatros D.V and D.Va were still the most widely used, along with Pfalz D.IIIa and Fokker Dr.I Triplanes, although in the main the latter were grouped together, one reason being they were rotary-engined as opposed to having water-cooled in-line engines.

On the Allied Side

Fighter aircraft with the RFC and RNAS in the late winter of 1917/18 were principally Camels and S.E.5as, No 1 and then No 29 Squadrons being the last RFC units to change their Nieuport Scouts for the S.E.s. The RFC used the D.H.5 fighter for a fleeting period in the autumn of 1917, but this was an unpopular machine. It had only equipped five squadrons (Nos 24, 32, 41, 64 and 68 AFC) for a few months, its most successful exponent being Arthur Coningham, a future Air Marshal and Knight of the Realm.

Coningham was born in Brisbane, Australia, but had spent his early life in New Zealand, having served with that country's forces in Somaliland and Egypt at the start of the war. Typhoid in 1916 almost put paid to his military career, but he survived to join the RFC in England and was posted to No 32 Squadron early in 1917, gaining one victory flying the D.H.2 pusher. Once D.H.5s arrived, he became a Flight Commander, and in July 1917 he gained nine further victories before being wounded, winning not only the MC but also the DSO. 'Mary' Coningham (there are several theories about his nickname) later commanded an S.E.5a squadron in 1918, won the DFC and brought his score to fourteen. In the Second World War he commanded the Desert Air Force and later the 2nd TAF in Europe.

The D.H.5, despite its arrival in 1917, still only had a single machine gun. The good forward view created by the back-stagger of the top wing had, not surprisingly, been achieved at the cost of a poor view to the rear, especially upwards—the direction from which enemy attacks would come. No 32 Squadron's early experiences involved several crashes, but later the aeroplane's ability to dive steeply and recover quickly meant that its pilots found themselves being assigned more and more to ground-attack sorties.

179

Tommy Rose, later a famous post-war pilot, flew D.H.5s with No 64 Squadron, and then S.E.5as. In 1967 he told me:

The fact that 64 Squadron did not achieve the glamour of some others was due to our position in the line and the fact that it was initially equipped with the DH5. Once the change over to SE5as was completed, we started to have some success. Edmund Tempest, who was one of our flight commanders, was the brother of Wulstan Tempest, who shot down the Potters Bar Zeppelin. He was the greatest patrol leader I had ever known. I was in his Flight initially, and I am certain that if the opportunities had come his way he would have been known as one of the best.

Jimmy Slater was the opposite type. If an 'Archie' burst was close, he would loop round it. If one of his Flight habitually left the patrol with 'engine trouble' he would follow him down, firing his guns at him, etc., etc.

At Cambrai in late 1917 the Squadron did low strafing with the DH5s, and for this job they were eminently suitable. The flocks of magpies which came out of Bourlon Wood will be ever remembered in this connection.

In the event, Edmund Tempest and James A. Slater did well. Tempest claimed one victory with the D.H.5 and sixteen more with the S.E.5a. Born on 30 October 1894 and from Pontefract, he had been with Nos 6, 29 and 15 Squadrons prior to No 64, and had received the MC and DFC. Slater was born on 27 November 1896 and he too had served in other squadrons, as an observer with No 18 Squadron and then as a pilot with No 1. Whilst with the latter unit he downed two German aircraft. In No 64 Squadron he claimed a third with a D.H.5. Then, flying S.E.5as, he brought his score to 24 by the end of May 1918, and received the MC and Bar, and the DFC. Ending the war as in instructor, he was killed in a flying accident the day before his 29th birthday in 1925. By late autumn 1917 all D.H.5s had been replaced by S.E.5as.

The Sopwith Triplanes and Pups, too, had all gone by now, the RNAS using only Camels. The RFC still had two Spad squadrons, Nos 19 and 23, although both were about to change to Sopwith Dolphins. Two-seater fighters were now just Bristol F.2b fighters, the F.E.2s and Sopwith 1½-Strutters having been discarded.

The Sopwith Dolphin was a complete departure from Sopwith's rotary-engined scouts, having a Hispano-Suiza in-line, water-cooled engine. After the experience with the recent D.H.5, it was surprising to some pilots that the Dolphin had a similar back-stagger to its top wing, although the design actually put the pilot's head above the top wing, which gave a good all-round view. Twin Vickers guns were supplemented with one, sometimes two Lewis guns fitted to the top wing cross-members just above the Vickers, although in practice most pilots discarded them eventually, if sometimes retaining just one. Experiments with two further Lewis guns fixed to the upper surfaces of both lower wings, fired by pulling a cord from the cockpit (the bullets passed clear of the propeller blades) was an innovation, although they could not be re-loaded in the air.

The Dolphin had a good performance at height, and for a period was used to help combat the high-flying Rumpler two-seaters. As an experiment, No 87 Squadron, one of four Dolphin squadrons which would see action in 1918 (the others being Nos 19, 23 and 79), fitted an oxygen tank behind the pilot's seat, with a tube connecting to a crude face-mask. Testing it on the ground, a bullet was fired into the tank. The resulting explosion ended the experiment, the pilots deciding that the risk of anoxia was far outweighed by the risk of a hit in the tank from a German aircraft.

Operation 'Michael'

The long-awaited German attack came on 21 March 1918 along a broad front from north of Arras to just south of La Fère. The German 2nd, 17th and 18th Armies forged forward following a terrific barrage, and by the 24th it had pushed the British back more than ten miles; two days later some sections of the line had gone back 15–20 miles. By April the German advance had passed Montdidier and Noyon on the southern French front, and beyond Serre and Moreuil on the British front. The major centre and town of Amiens was within sight, and there seemed an imminent danger that Paris might finally be reached.

Naturally, much air fighting took place over the front, by both sides, Corps aircraft tried desperately to direct artillery fire upon advancing German troops, contact patrols tried to locate forward elements of the Germans and retreating British troops, and bombing attacks were made on both front-line troops and strongpoints, as well as the German supply lines.

For their part, the German fighters were battling against every type of operation the RFC, RNAS and French Air Service could mount,

The Sopwith Dolphin arrived in France in the spring of 1918. It carried twin Vickers guns and was designed to carry two Lewis guns on its cockpit frame, although often this was reduced to one, and later none. No 87 Squadron experimented with two Lewis guns, one on each lower wing as in this photograph. With all six guns in place, it was the first multi-gun fighter in history.

while its own ground-support two-seaters were operating with devastating success all along the advance. As well as fighter patrols, the RFC in particular were once more throwing their scouts in to bomb and strafe the German troops, pilots flying several sorties a day. The only limiting factor was the time spent refuelling and rearming. The 25lb Cooper bombs were used in their hundreds, Camels and other machines carrying four such weapons beneath the fuselage.

During these ground battles in March, and those which followed in April, the RFC—which had become the Royal Air Force on 1 April, by merging with the RNAS—did much to stem the tide of field-grey uniforms of the German Army. Graeme Leask of No 84 Squadron, whom we met earlier, was nearing the end of his period in France as the German March offensive began:

> The Huns started their big offensive on 21 March; it was a foggy day. On the 22nd is was also foggy and we left Flez as Germans were approaching, but we flew low bombing raids in the afternoon. This went on three or four times a day on free-lance sorties till I left the squadron, flying from Champien, near Roye, then from Vert Galand. On 31 March I had a forced

landing on the way home from patrol during which we had scrapped nine Huns. I got down at Bertangles airfield with an empty radiator due to a broken water pipe.

On 1 April, I had my last day with the Squadron, and I had three forced landings that day. First, on 24's aerodrome and when I took off again, the engine again cut out, but I managed to get down. Took off with another kite, but after 70 minutes over the lines the engine seized up, but I got down at Boves.

It is essential to mention the importance of markmanship, without which there would be no victories. Without boasting, I was a crack shot with a rifle or MG and had been since school, where I won shooting cups three times running. I shot down two EAs on our side of the lines; one was a DFW and the pilot was hit twice in the head and five times in the body. The other was a scout shot down during the Battle of Cambrai at 1,000 feet. My Vickers gun jammed after three rounds, but the pilot went straight down and landed. I was firing at an angle and must have hit some vital part of his engine. We did not get the machine back as the battle was raging to and fro, but it was confirmed by two members of the patrol and also by ground troops.

Lawrence P. Coombes had been a pilot with 10 Naval Squadron (which had become No 210 Squadron RAF on 1 April), and in early 1972 he recalled for me a couple of incidents during this difficult period, which was not helped by the weather.

The Germans began a big offensive near Ypres, and the Portugese, who held the line there, gave up when the Germans attacked, retreating in disorder. A big salient formed at this point of weakness, and the front was in such a state of flux [that] nobody knew where it was and we had to be careful to distinguish friend from foe when ground strafing. The weather was bad— low cloud and mist—so we were sent to ground-trafe and drop 25lb bombs on any targets we could find. [Battle of the Lys.]

On 9 April, my 19th birthday, I went out on low bombing and trench-strafing. It was misty with clouds at 1,000 feet. I dropped my bombs on a bridge over a canal and fired on troops on roads. Then I was heavily machine-gunned from the ground. Turning home, an aeroplane turned up in the mist and passed close to one side. I saw the black crosses; it was a two-seater DFW. I turned on his tail and fired at very close range. I saw a fire start behind the pilot's seat, the machine went down in a steep dive and crashed, burning fiercely. It was seen and confirmed by three members of my squadron.

That evening we had to move the squadron from Treizennes, which was now very close to the advancing enemy, and landed at Liettres aerodrome. No 8—208—Squadron, also Bentley Camels, were not so lucky. Their aerodrome was covered by ground fog, and though the personnel escaped by road, the Squadron Commander, Chris Draper DSC, refused to risk his pilots taking off in the thick mist. They set fire to the aircraft and we saw the ring of machines burning as we flew over in the clear air above.

On 11 April I was on another low bombing patrol. After dropping bombs on some barges and firing at transport vehicles, I was flying at 300 feet when I was shot up from the ground. The engine stopped and I prepared to force-land as I felt petrol soaking the seat of my pants. I realised that the main pressure petrol tank on which the pilot sat was holed so I switched to the gravity tank and the engine picked up. When I got back, it was found that, besides the petrol tank, two cylinders had been pierced. It was a miracle that the engine kept going.

Coombes, who had been born in India, joined the RNAS in July 1917, and this victory on 9 April was his second of an eventual fifteen, which brought him the DFC. Post war he became an engineer at Farnborough, and in 1927 he was the Technical Officer with the British Schneider Trophy Team. Just prior to the Second World War he went to Australia to establish an aeronautical research laboratory for the Australian Government, and later still was an adviser to the United Nations. He died in Melbourne in 1988.

Draper, CO of No 208 Squadron, had been faced with a desperate choice and in the end decided that destroying his unit's Camels was the only solution. The airfield was La Gorgue, and, in all, sixteen machines were burnt. Draper was an ace, having gained four victories on Strutters with 3 Naval Wing in late 1916 and a further four with 6 and 8 Naval Squadrons, flying Camels. His ninth and final victory came on 8 May.

Von Richthofen Falls

Baron von Richthofen and his JG I were well to the fore during these March and April offensives, supporting ground troops and endeavouring to ward off British Corps aircraft. In his all-red Triplane—totally red so as to be perfectly identified by his men over the fluid battle areas— he brought his score to 80 on 20 April 1918. There were strong rumours that he was to be rested from front-line action because of his importance and already long service. He had now doubled the score of his mentor, Oswald Boelcke, and one has to wonder if he perhaps saw the chance to increase his own victory tally to 100 before being forced to call it a day.

He still led his four Jastas from the front. The tactic of the leader having first crack at the enemy, supported by his men, still produced results, and there was no reason to change it. The Fokker Triplanes were still performing well, but von Richthofen was, nevertheless, looking forward to seeing the new Fokker D.VII arrive at the front. He had flown a prototype in Berlin, and he had already written several letters to friends in high places, saying that their early arrival was much anticipated.

On 21 April 1918 he received orders to try to clear the air east of Amiens, over the Somme valley, so that photo-recce two-seaters could attempt to locate a gun battery situated somewhere on the far side of the Morlancourt Ridge. These guns were threatening the build-up of German troops in and around Le Hamel and so needed to be found and dealt with by German artillery.

Sopwith Camels of No 209 Squadron RAF, on patrol over the area that morning in squadron strength, had had a fight with two German two-seaters and the three Camel Flights had been separated. Two Australian R.E.8 machines had become embroiled with von Richthofen, who was leading Jasta 11, since the Jasta commander had had his Triplane hit and damaged, forcing him to break off and go home. In the meantime, as the fight ended, the Baron was having trouble with his Spandau machine guns: one had jammed, and the other had suffered a split firing pin.

Probably, if the task assigned to him had been less important, he too would have returned to base, but he did not, and a short while later he ran into the main group of Camels. A fight began, and because the wind this day was blowing east to west rather than the usual west to east, the battling aircraft slowly drifted nearer to the front lines. The Baron then saw one Camel break off and head for home, and he took the chance of going after it. No doubt misjudging his location and not appreciating the wind direction, he was not aware that he was about to cross into Allied territory, still with one gun out of action and the other firing only intermittently. The Camel, flown by a novice, went low over the Somme, desperately trying to evade fire from the pursuer and get far enough over the lines for the German to give up and fly back.

However, Richthofen did not break away, and his gun trouble was making it difficult to nail the jinking Camel ahead of him. By this time the action had been spotted by Captain Roy Brown of No 209, who broke from the main fight and went down after the two aircraft. Unable to make a direct attack on the Triplane, he positioned himself with the sun behind him and the mist of the Somme under him, to take a long shot at the German in the hope of putting him off his attack on the other Camel. This worked to a point, and as Brown then had to turn to avoid the high ground of the Morlancourt Ridge, he lost sight of the two machines as both zipped over it. As the Baron headed over the Ridge, he most probably saw ahead of him the very guns everyone was trying to find, but as his remaining gun had now quit too he left the jinking Camel and turned to head east, finally realising his mistake of getting too far into hostile territory.

By this time countless rifles and machine guns on the ground were blazing away at the red machine, and as he headed back a single bullet hit him in the right side, deflected off of his spine, ripped through his aorta and just exited the left side of his chest, the bullet stopping short and not exiting his flying jacket. Mortally wounded, he endeavoured to make a hurried force landing—and almost succeeded. With his wheels ripped off, he came to a stop in a field in front of the local brickworks, and moments later died of his wound. That wound would have given him 12–20 seconds of life after being hit, and Brown's long-distance shot had been around one to two minutes earlier.

Although Brown was later credited with the Baron's end, he only claimed it because others had deduced that the Triplane had gone down following his attack—which was not strictly accurate. It was Brown's tenth victory, and although he received a Bar to his DSC, he was virtually at the finish of a long combat tour, and by the end of the month he was sent on rest.

The Baron's fall was, naturally, not only a blow to his men, to the High Command and to the German air service in general, but a demoralising event for the German public too. JG I was taken over by the leader of Jasta 6, Willi Reinhard, who had twelve victories at this time and who had previously been leader of Jasta 11, both within JG I. Reinhard brought his score to twenty by mid-June but was then killed in a test flight in Berlin on 3 July. His replacement as leader of JG I, who was required to be another regular officer, was Hermann Göring, the leader of Jasta 27, part of Loerzer's JG III. Göring had 21 victories, but would only gain one more, despite leading JG I for the rest of the war.

Bristol Fighters

The two-seat Bristol Fighters were really coming into their own by early 1918. A good crew was generally able to match any opposition, and scores among these crews were on the increase. One pilot in No 22 Squadron stood out during Febuary and March—Sergeant E. J. Elton, who won the DCM, MM and Italian Bronze Medal. He and his various observers accounted for sixteen German aircraft between 26 February and 29 March, ten with his front gun and six with the rear. Born on Christmas Day 1893 and from Dorset, he had begun his RFC career as a mechanic, actually helping to design and build the gun mounting on Lanoe Hawker's Bristol Scout back in 1915.

Like several First World War pilots, two-seater and single-seater, who suddenly appeared on the scene of action, Elton burned brightly

This Bristol Fighter has extra armament, with a movable Lewis gun on the top wing for the pilot, as well as his own fixed Vickers firing through the propeller. The observer has twin Lewis guns. These latter weapons were heavier to use than the single gun, and an airman needed that extra muscle to be effective. The pilot of this machine is Sgt E. J. Elton, DCM, MM, who claimed sixteen victories in 32 days in early 1918, flying with No 22 Squadron.

like a meteor for a short period and then disappeared. In his case he survived the war, while others ended their short careers in death or injury. All but three of his victories were in multiples: 2–2–1–2–2–2–1– 1–3. Quite obviously, some of these Bristol Fighter actions produced more claims than actual losses, mainly due to the complexities of multi-crewed aircraft. Several pairs of eyes saw different angles and situations, and all felt they were responsible for aircraft falling or bursting into flames. This is not to detract from their prowess and bravery while in a furious dogfight, but a balance needs to be struck in dealing with the number of claims.

Alfred C. Atkey, a Canadian from Saskatchewan who was born on 16 August 1894, was another hugely successful 'Brisfit' pilot, although his early victories—nine in number—were gained whilst flying a D.H.4 bomber with No 18 Squadron RFC between February and April 1918. Moving to Bristols with No 22 Squadron, he and his observers racked up another 29 victories between 7 May and 2 June! They also had multiple 'kills': 5–3–2–2–1–2–3–1–1–3–2–2–2. If they could down such numbers, the RAF need only have employed Bristol F.2b crews to fight the air war! Perhaps significantly, around two-thirds were 'out of control' claims, but Atkey nevertheless received the MC, and of his D.H.4 days it was said that he handled the bomber like a Sopwith Pup.

Bristol Fighter formations. Several different flying formations were tried in the F.2b squadrons which flew in France during 1917–18. An extension of the standard escort system was the 'Three Pair'—six aircraft in two pairs, each pair 50ft apart and 50ft astern of the next pair, staggered off to one side or the other, the leader of the second and third pair immediately behind the second machine of the preceding pair, although each succeeding pair would be slightly higher than the one in front. The 'Diamond' was for twelve aircraft, each in a diamond-four formation, again with 50ft between each aircraft. Each leader of a Diamond would fly at its apex, and each 'four' flew slightly higher than the group in front. The 'Brigade' (top diagram) was for five aircraft. Nos 1 and 2 machines flew in line abreast, 100yds apart, with a three-man 'vee' formation behind. Used effectively in photography missions, the No 3 aircraft, which was the leader of the rear 'vee', carried the camera, flew a little lower than his two wingmen, and thus had protection from ahead and behind. The 'Vee' (centre and bottom diagrams) was simply either a pyramid of, say, six aircraft, the leader with two wingmen immediately behind and slightly above, with the last three in line abreast behind them, again slightly above. If it were a nine-man patrol, the leader at the head would have a box of four machines immediately behind him, with, behind them, a four-man section in line abreast. If this formation were increased to a squadron strength of twelve, the last three would 'sit' up above and slightly to the rear in order to guard against surprise attacks. The 'Vee' was the most commonly used formation. With a full squadron of aircraft, the main formation might operate in three tight, three-man 'Vees', while a 'guard Vee' of three aircraft would fly higher and to the rear, on the opposite side to the sun.

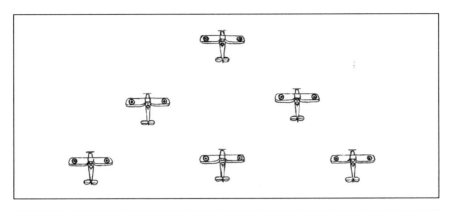

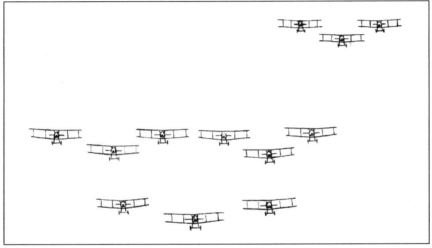

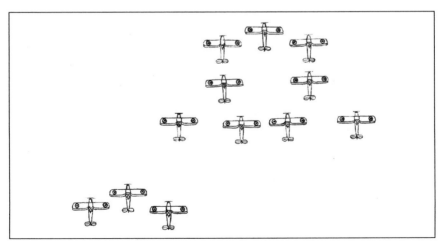

Atkey's main observer was C. G. Gass, MC, from London, who was born in April 1898. After Army service he tranferred into the RFC in 1917. Apart from Atkey, Gass flew with other pilots and his victory score,shared with his pilots, was 39 by mid-August 1918, at which time he was rested. In the late 1960s I corresponded with Charles Gass, and he told me that

Pilots used to be awarded their 'wings' after many hours' flying solo, no matter where they were at the time. We observers had our training in England, but then had to do 15 hours [of] what was known in those days as 'war flying', in other words, over the lines. The CO then recommended you to Air Ministry as being efficient. If they agreed, you were then awarded your observer's wing, and this meant that from that date you received an extra eight shillings [40 pence—although this bears no relation to the monetary values of today] per day, known as flying pay. Pilots also received this. If by any chance you were grounded for any length of time, this pay was stopped. We had to have so many flying hours per month to qualify for the eight shillings—I forget the exact number. This restriction applied wherever one was stationed. As you can well imagine, a great number of observers had 'gone west' before they had completed the qualifying time, and even if they had been taken prisoner, they never received their brevet. There was a saying in those days that if you survived three weeks of war flying you had a reasonable chance of lasting for quite a while. This was very true, as in my case.

Atkey was a Canadian, but what a pilot! What a man! He had no fear, but there was an uncanny communication between us. I always seemed to sense what he was going to do, and he had the same feeling about me. On one patrol the end of our top plane was hit by shrapnel and crumpled, and the result was that although the machine still flew straight, the other wing dipped, so we were flying one wing low. Atkey just turned round to me and said get out on the wing to balance the machine up, and this I did, and all he had to fly the Bristol Fighter was elevator and rudder controls, but he got us home with me standing on the wing and nearly frozen to death.

By the spring of 1918 we were finding it very difficult to get near any German aircraft in the air. As soon as they saw us they used to stick their noses down and beat it, except for Richthofen's Circus, who seemed willing to fight. We met them several times. Our CO, Major McKelvie, decided that instead of flying as a squadron or in Flights of five, we would fly in pairs with a chance of getting near to some Huns. This proved successful.

On the evening of 7 May, two Bristols took off on an Offensive Patrol, Atkey and I in one, John Gurdon and John Thornton in the other. At 18,000 feet, between Arras and Lille, I spotted seven German Pfalz Scouts about 2,000 feet below us. I pointed them out to Atkey and down we went among them. This was the mistake of my life, because I had not seen two more formations of seven following them up. This became known as the famous battle of two against twenty in the RAF, [and] the artist Joseph Simpson produced a drawing that was published in the *Sphere*. Atkey and I were in aircraft 'E', Gurdon in 'D'.

The scrap must have lasted about half an hour, Atkey got three Huns and I got two, while Gurdon got two and Thornton one—eight in all. The fight had been seen by the infantry in the trenches and by the artillery, so all our victims were confirmed. Our two machines were shot up quite a bit, and Gurdon had to make a forced landing in a hospital ground near Arras. We had not a round of ammunition left between us.

During the fight one of the Germans tried to do a climbing turn on to our tail, and came so close I just pressed my trigger in fright. I must have got tracer into his petrol tank as he burst into flames. As he dropped he pushed back his goggles, half raised himself out of his cockpit and saluted me. What a man!

While this was, no doubt, a very gallant and prolonged fight, there are simply no German casualties—certainly no fatalities—to support these eight victories. Obviously several German fighters were seen to spin or dive away after being either hit, or just fired at, but while some may well have force-landed, of the two German fighter pilots killed this day, one was flying a Triplane, shot down by an S.E.5a, and the other went down on the French front. These sorts of actions were much like those fought by American B-17 and B-24 bombers in the Second World War over Germany, where many gunners would be firing at an FW 190 or a Me 109 which, if it went down, might be claimed by up to a dozen or more airmen, each convinced it was *his* burst that did the damage.

In the early 1970s I met Ernest Hardcastle, DFC, who had been an observer with No 20 Squadron in 1918, and his pilot, Victor Groom, DFC, a future Air Chief Marshal. It was a unique experience. Ernest Hardcastle recalled one incident for me:

Eric Sugden was, like myself, a Yorkshireman—perhaps why I remember him so well. I do have 5 June 1918 down in my diary, and on this date Groom and I did two OPs, one in the afternoon and the other in the evening, when Sugden and his observer were taken prisoner. I remember it as if it were yesterday. Sugden, being a new boy, was flying what we called 'tail-arse Charlie'. Unfortunately, the newest pilot to join the Squadron was always given the oldest machine—that is why he was always placed right in the rear of the Flight, so that he could be protected and warned of approaching enemy aircraft.

We were carrying bombs this day, and had ourselves dropped our bomb on Armentières, and this was about as far as we dare go over German territory as we were taxed on petrol consumption and had to get back. The Germans knew these facts and often waited until we had turned round and were on our way home, and this is what happened this day.

Sugden, for some unknown reason, didn't turn with us, and shortly afterwards I saw him gliding down into Hunland. Just don't ask me why he kept his 112lb bomb on board—he was told to release it as soon as ever possible on being warned of approaching enemy aircraft. We had seen the enemy fighters coming round the back of us, and I fired the usual red Very light in the direction of Jerry. Naturally Jerry concentrated on Sugden and did not follow us at all.

In fact, No 20 Squadron lost two machines on this sortie, both being brought down by a pilots of Jasta 52.

Victory claims for Bristol Fighter crews were a little different from those for single-seater fighters, as August Iaccaci, an American, explained to a pal of mine back in 1966 August and Paul Iaccaci (later spelt Jaccaci) were unique in that they were two brothers from New York who began pilot training together, were both posted to No 20 Squadron on the same day, both won the DFC and both scored seventeen victories. August was three years younger than Paul:

The Bristol Fighter was primarily a fighter plane apart from its other duties. The man in the rear cockpit was not really an observer, he was a gunner. The thing that made the Bristol Fighter such an effective fighting plane was [that] in addition to its compactness, manoeuvrability, performance, and its wonderful Rolls-Royce engine . . . a first rate pilot and gunner could engage several enemy planes on an equal basis, firing effectively in several directions through positioning the plane rapidly to take advantage of the guns quickest to bring to bear—whereas the single-seater scouts could only shoot forward.

So it was a team effort of pilot and gunner. Sometimes we would hit an enemy aircraft with the front gun and finish it off with rear guns, or visa-versa. One time, on September 27, 1918, we got two enemy aircraft at once, one with the front gun and the other from the rear. My log-book shows mostly we got one, and not often I got one or Newland* got one.

So you can't rate a Bristol two-seater fighter pilot with a single-seater one, for the single-seater man did all his own kills, whereas the Bristol Fighter pilot and gunner both made kills. However, the official records always

---

* Sergeant A. Newland, DFM and Bar, shared in 22 victories with various pilots, including both the Iaccaci brothers. He was the only RAF airman to win a Bar to his DFM in the First World War.

By 1918 the Bristol Fighter was a veritable tiger in the air, and crews of this two-seater could easily see off the most ardent German fighter pilots. Nos 11, 20, 22, 48 and 62 were the foremost squadrons, and many observers, such Lt S. A. W, Knights, MC, from No 62 Squadron (left), seen here with his pilot Captain G. E. Gibbons, MC, DFC, used twin Lewis guns from the rear cockpit.

credited the Bristol Fighter pilot with all the enemy aircraft brought down, whether by the pilot or the gunner.

If there is a reason for this, it must have been that the pilot was held responsible for putting the plane in a position to destroy the enemy, whether by shooting forward with the front gun or shooting aft or sideways with the rear guns in the hands of the gunner. So I think the Bristol Fighter pilot's record should be classified separately from single-seater pilots for these reasons.

The . . . intense fighting in May and September 1918 was due to the German Circuses* trying to put us out of action. The casualties were extremely high on both sides, but the Bristol Fighters held off the Circuses and killed as many as we lost, and we never ceased to have one or more offensive patrols over the lines daily, weather permitting. There was a twenty-day period in August when the Huns would not engage us. We believe German squadrons were advised to give us a wide berth, and, in spite of our attempts, it was not possible to engage the enemy.

During that summer, five pilots from the American Air Service were sent to us to get experience on this type of plane. We lost all five flyers in action. They hadn't had enough experience and they were lost because they were green and up against the best German Circus flyers.

---

* Jagdgeschwader I, II, III and IV.

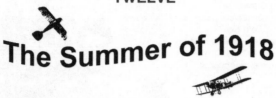

TWELVE

The Summer of 1918

T HE LONG-AWAITED Fokker D.VII biplanes began to arrive
in early May 1918. The first were collected from an aircraft park
by pilots of Jasta 10 (part of JG I), and for a short period the
Staffel flew a mixture of Triplanes, Albatros Scouts and D.VIIs.
Jasta 10 was commanded by Erich Löwenhardt, an ace with eighteen
victories thus far. Löwenhardt, born on 7 April 1897 the son of a
doctor, came from Breslau. After serving in the infantry on the
Eastern Front in 1914, the seventeen-year-old was wounded and then
moved to the Alpine Corps. He transferred to aviation, flew two-
seaters before becoming a fighter pilot, and joined Jasta 10 in March
1917.

The pilots who began operating the D.VII found it less manoeuvrable than the Triplane—which was to be expected—but much
faster. Its 160hp Mercedes engine had high compression for high-
altitude flying, so that, while it climbed slowly at low altitudes, it
became much faster in the climb at height. Löwenhardt first flew it in
combat on 9 May and downed a British S.E.5a for his nineteenth 'kill',
which was followed by a D.H.9 bomber on the 10th, another on the
15th, a Spad on the 16th, and then a Camel and a balloon on the 18th
and 20th. With his score passing the required twenty, he was awarded
the Pour le Mérite.

Meantime, all four Dolphin squadrons were now in France. Nos 19
and 23 had exchanged their French Spads for the new Sopwith
fighter, and Nos 79 and 87 Squadrons were both newly arrived. Nos 19

The Fokker D.VII. This machine was the most successful German fighter of the First World War, although it was gradually overwhelmed by the sheer weight of Allied aircraft pitted against it. Nevertheless, its pilots were still downing of British, French and American aircraft right up to the Armistice.

and 23 had both suffered losses during March and April, mostly in ground-attack sorties, but now all four were flying fighter patrols, though No 87 for a while operated against high-flying two-seater photo Rumplers.

Ground-attack sorties were now familiar to most fighter squadrons, especially the Camel units. They were flown not only in specific offensive support operations, but also in poor weather which curtailed high-flying patrols. Trenches would be attacked, or other targets of opportunity strafed and bombed behind the lines, making the German troops feel particularly vulnerable as they either moved up to the front or came out of the line for a brief rest. Lawrence Coombes of No 210 Squadron recorded one incident showing that it was not only the enemy that pilots had to be wary of:

> On 11 May a patrol of 24 British and Australian Camels did a High Offensive Patrol. We dropped 92 bombs on Armentières, setting fire to an ammunition dump. About eight EA dived on us and about 20 more attacked on our level.

There was a general dog-fight, one Australian Camel going down in flames while Captain W. M. Alexander of 210 got an EA in flames. I shot down an Albatros out of control.

Turning for home, we discovered that a ground mist had suddenly come up, covering a huge area of France. Nine of our Squadron, including myself, crashed trying to land in fields, one pilot being killed, and one seriously injured. Quite a number of Allied airmen were taken by surprise and suffered the same fate.

Coombes later flew with No 204 Training Depot Station at Eastchurch, in charge of a Camel training flight. While there he was sent on an instructors' course at Shoreham and discovered how little he knew about the finer points of flying, even though by that time he had nearly 500 flying hours recorded in his log-book. One of his last flights was in a captured Fokker D.VII, which he found very nice to fly and light on the controls.

Captain R. A. Little, DSO and Bar, DSC and Bar, was a former RNAS pilot and now a Flight Commander in the RAF, a fact he 'celebrated' on 1 April 1918 by shooting down his 39th German aircraft. He had flown Pups, Triplanes and Camels with 8 Naval, and just prior to the amalgamation of the two services had joined 3 Naval, under Ray Collishaw, which had become No 203 Squadron. In the Squadron was Ronald Sykes, from Stockton-on-Tees, who back in the late 1960s recalled for me two episodes in the spring of 1918 concerning Bob Little, who came from Melbourne, Australia:

Captain Little, after shooting down an enemy aircraft, had all his controls shot away and his Camel dived at high speed but rounded out at ground level and broke up. Little was thrown clear and fell into a very large, soft, manure heap. Although bruised and stiff, he blazed away with his revolver at the German machine which had followed him down. He got back to our Mess during the evening still wearing his sodden clothing!

On another occasion he pre-arranged that we should end a HOP by flying over a German AA battery near La Bassée at 7,000 feet, where he pretended to be hit and did a falling-leaf manoeuvre to ground level. He then pulled out and started to chase the German gunners round the field before finally hedge-hopping home.

Bob Little achieved 47 victories, but on 27 May 1918 he took off on a night flight to try and intercept German Gotha bombers. He found one in the beam of a searchlight, but as he closed in he was hit either by one of its gunners or from a shot from the ground. The bullet went through both thighs, forcing him to crash-land, where he bled to death before he could be rescued.

The Yanks Are Coming

Meanwhile the Americans were busy preparing for their participation in forthcoming battles along the French sector. The first Nieuport 28-equipped squadrons, the 94th, 95th and 103rd Aeros, were all activated in France during February 1918, although, incongruously, the first Nieuport 28s the pilots collected had not yet had their guns fitted, so patrols were flown well inside Allied lines, just for the experience!

The 94th was commanded by Raoul Lufbery, the hero of the Lafayette Escadrille, and its first two victories were scored on 14 April. Among its pilots was Edward Rickenbacker, who would survive the war as America's ace-of-aces. The 95th was commanded by Captain J. E. Miller, but prior to receiving its aircraft Miller led two other pilots in borrowed French Spads out on patrol on 9 March, where he was shot down and killed in a fight with two-seaters.

Then, on 19 May, the great Raoul Lufbery was killed. He took off to engage a German two-seat Rumpler, but the latter's observer got in a telling burst at the Major's Nieuport and set it on fire. Rather than suffer a slow and terrible death

Hero of the Lafayette Escadrille, Raoul Lufbery transferred to the USAS in late 1917, having scored sixteen official victories. Although he imparted much of his accumulated knowledge to the embryo American pilots, he was killed in action on 19 May 1918 before being able to lead them into combat.

by burning, Lufbery elected to jump from his stricken machine and fell to his death. He and other members of the Lafayette Flying Corps who died had the Lafayette Memorial in Paris erected in their honour.

The 103rd Aero had been created from the Lafayette Escadrille (N 124) and was commanded by a former American pilot in that formation, William Thaw, who would become an ace while leading the unit. Initially the 103rd remained under French control in Groupe de Chasse 21, but it moved to the Americans in April.

Once these and further squadrons had been activated in France, they were organised into Pursuit Groups, three in number, with two more arriving just too late to see combat. The 1st Group was formed in June and comprised the 27th, 94th, 95th and 147th Aeros. The 2nd Group, made up of the 13th, 22nd, 49th and 139th Aeros, was also formed in June, followed by the 3rd Group, consisting of the 93rd, 28th, 103rd (ex-1st Group) and 213th, in September.

The First Test

After the two great German offensives on the British front, Operation 'Michael' and then the Battle of the Lys which began on 5 April 1918— and in which the Allies had lost around 350,000 men during six weeks—the pressure continued. Despite failing in a decisive break-through, General Erich von Ludendorff struck a third blow on the Aisne sector in an attempt both to pin down the French and to draw their reserves away from the British front.

Forty-two divisions struck at the French on 27 May, taking the Chemin-des-Dames area, so that by 3 June the Germans had reached the Marne at Château-Thierry. The target was Paris, which now stood just 56 miles away. Helping to stem the advance were the American 2nd and 3rd Divisions, on hand to help ward off a fourth assault and to expand the salient in the Marne area and hoping to link up with the bulge in the Amiens line around the Somme.

Although only designed as a diversionary attack before striking again on the British front, the successful advance to the Marne, from Reims to Château-Thierry, gave Ludendorff several new possibilities. He therefore pressed on, but his force was beginning to be overstretched and the French and American Armies had managed to stem the advance.

These new Battles of the Aisne/Marne saw the Americans' first test—a test shared by the US airmen, who until now had seen only light action along the Toul sector. The 1st Pursuit Group and I Corps Observation Group, plus several French units, came under the command of Colonel William 'Billy' Mitchell, charged with the defence of the Château-Thierry area. Opposite them, with the German 7th Army, was JG I, commanded by Willi Reinhard, but soon to be taken over by Hermann Göring, together with Bruno Loerzer's JG III, plus other Jastas combined into Jagdgruppen. Rudolf Berthold's JG II, and two Jagdgruppen were in support of the German 3rd Army. The battle areas now had approximately 46 German Jastas along the front, with the mainly untried Americans facing them.

Quite often the lesser German Jastas were based on the French front, or others would come there for something of a breather. Until now it had been these German units that the early American fighter pilots had been up against. On the morning of 2 July, a patrol from the 27th Aero ran into some Fokker D.VIIs of Jasta 4 and 10 of JG I, led by Ernst Udet, who by this date had amassed 38 victories. In a desperate fight, two American Nieuport 28s went down, although the German pilots claimed four. The surviving Americans also claimed four Fokkers, but JG I had no pilot losses.

The observation squadrons came to the front with little experience, particularly of a moving and fluid battle zone, although the US 88th Squadron was commanded by Captain K. P. Littauer, who had a good deal of experience with the French, having been with the Lafayette Flying Corps for well over a year. It was men such as Littauer, who moved from the French or British air forces and took their knowledge and experience with them, who gave the young American airmen a better chance of survival. The Americans were facing tough opposition, for the German fighter pilots were being led in the air by some exceptionally gifted and experienced leaders.

The 96th Aero Squadron, based at Amanty to the south-west of Toul, was equipped with French Bregeut XIV bombers, and was commanded by Major Harry M. Brown. Brown asked Major Alex Gray, CO of the nearby RAF's No 55 Squadron, to come and visit so that he could try to invest some up-to-date knowledge of combat flying into his men. The 96th's first raid came on 12 June, several celebrities seeing them off, including Billy Mitchell, Colonel Dodd (a staff officer) and RAF General Sir Hugh Trenchard, commanding the RAF's Independent (Bomber) Force. All returned without any real mishap.

On 10 July, Brown led six crews out on a bombing raid despite strong winds and cloud. They became lost, and, not being able to identify for certain their target, had to turn for home. However, the wind was against them, blowing strongly from the east and making progress home almost impossible. Eventually all six aircraft were forced to put down behind the German lines, where the twelve men were taken into captivity. It was a salutary experience for the Americans.

During the rest of July. the US Aero fighter squadrons lost seventeen pilots killed, wounded or taken prisoner, mostly through air combat but with a few to ground fire. While the number may seem small, it was quite a large percentage of the USAS. August was no better. On the first day of that month Fokker D.VIIs brought down two crews from the US 1st Aero, with another observer wounded, while the 27th Aero had two fighter pilots killed and two taken prisoner by Fokker D.VIIs. Another pilot was killed in a crash at base. Two more pilots from the 95th Aero were lost on the 10th, and on the 11th the 88th lost two crews to Fokkers and three fighters also went down. The German Jastas were having several field days!

Despite the losses inflicted by the experienced German aces, there was always the exception. One was the loss of the German ace Carl Menckhoff, leader of Jasta 72, who had scored 39 victories by 25 July. In a fight with the 213rd Aero Squadron over Château-Thierry, Menckhoff came off second best against Walter L. Avery and was forced to come down inside Allied lines. Menckhoff, from Westphalia, was, at 35, older than most pilots, having been born in April 1883. His first twenty victories came against the British whilst flying with Jasta 3 as an NCO. Commissioned and awarded the Pour le Mérite, he took command of Jasta 72 in April 1918 and began operations on the French front. This Jasta achieved many victories without losses, and the first loss for some time turned out to be that of its Staffelführer. One can imagine his anger, even disbelief, at being told his victor was an American who was still learning his trade. Indeed, this was Avery's first of only two victories!

Georg von Hantelmann, of Jasta 15, ended the war with 25 victories, his victims including American aces David Putnam and Joe Wehner and French ace Maurice Boyou. This photograph was taken following his 20th 'kill', on 9 October 1918.

The fall of another ace, albeit a month earlier on 17 June, demonstrated another twist of fate. Kurt Erwin Wüsthoff, from Aachen and born on 27 January 1897, had learnt to fly when he was sixteen, but his age stopped him flying for his country until 1915, and even then it was over Bulgaria, Romania, Macedonia and Greece. In mid-1917 he was made an officer and moved to France, joining Jasta 4 in JG I. Between 15 June 1917 and 10 March 1918 he achieved 27 'kills' on the British front, including three balloons. Awarded the Blue Max, he became leader of Jasta 4 prior to a staff appointment with JG I on 16 March. Following this rest period, he was assigned to lead Jasta 15 on 15 June. The next day, without a Fokker of his own, he borrowed the skull-and-crossbone marked D.VII flown by Georg von Hantelmann. He was obviously a bit rusty from his enforced period away from daily action, and when his Staffel met several S.E.5as from No 24 Squadron he became separated from his men. Surrounded by a large number of experienced RAF air fighters, he was quickly brought down and taken prisoner.

Surviving a forced landing inside Allied lines, with little damage, von Hantelmann's DVII was well photographed. Initially it was thought that this was his personal mount. However, with just three victories thus far, von Hantelmann was still an unknown—but his moment was about to come.

Hantelmann brought down a very high number of top Allied aces during the summer of 1918, whilst being himself one of the youngest German aces, having been born in October 1898. Entering the Army in 1916, he was commissioned into the 17th Hussar Regiment—the Death's Head Hussars—which is why his aircraft carried a skull and crossbones on the fuselage. Unusually, he seems to have gone straight to a fighter Staffel rather than proceed via two-seaters, joining Jasta 18, which became Jasta 15 in March 1918.

His first victory was not confirmed, but during June 1918 he scored four 'kills' and in August two more. Having moved opposite the Americans, he quickly found his form during September, scoring an impressive twelve more victories, including three on the 14th. JG II were downing French and American aircraft at an alarming rate, and von Hantelmann shot down David Putnam on 12 September. Putnam came from Jamaica Plains, Massachusetts, and was a couple of months younger than von Hantelmann. A Harvard man, and a descendent of General Isaac Putnam of Revolutionary fame, he had joined the French Air Service in April 1917 and was assigned to the Lafayette Flying Corps.

He flew with French Escadrille Spa 94—the 'Spa' designation indicating that the unit flew Spads—but then was reassigned to MS 156, flying the Morane-Saulnier A1, a high-winged monoplane which equipped only two escadrilles in the First World War. Nevertheless, Putnam did exceptionally well on this unusual machine, downing four German aircraft confirmed, and a further eight unconfirmed. Moving on to Spa 38, he brought his official score to nine on 15 June, but then transferred to the USAS, taking acting command of the 139th Aero. Now with his American brothers, he brought his score to thirteen confirmed and sixteen unconfirmed. He fell as the eighth victory of von Hantelmann.

Putnam had written home: 'Mother, there is no question about the hereafter of men who give themselves in such a cause. If I am called

Maurice Boyou, of Spa 77, claimed 35 victories before meeting von Hantelmann in combat on 16 September 1918. Of his claims, 21 were balloons.

upon to make it, I shall go with a grin of satisfaction and a smile.' He had received the Médaille Militaire, the Croix de Guerre and the Légion d'Honneur from the French, and although recommended for the US Medal of Honor after his death, he only received the DSC, in 1919. His Légion d'Honneur was announced on Armistice Day, 11 November 1918.

The German ace and another Jasta 15 pilot fought and shot down two French Spads on the 16th, von Hantelmann's victim being the ace Maurice Jean-Paul Boyou, an outstanding fighter pilot with 35 'kills'. Despite this, he became the fourteenth victory for von Hantelmann south-west of Conflans. Boyou came from Algeria, and at 30 years old was much older than his contemporaries. Before the war he had been in the Army, and had captained the French rugby team. He flew with Escadrille 77, first with Nieuports and then with Spads. He had gained his first victory on 16 March 1917, his 35th on the day of his death. No fewer than 21 of his claims had been against balloons.

Von Hantelmann's next victim was Joe Wehner of the 27th Aero, shot down on 18 September, the day the American became an ace himself with two balloon 'kills'. Wehner was the sparring partner of Frank Luke Jr, about whom we shall read later. From Boston, he was two days away from his 23rd birthday when he was killed. He usually flew with Luke, protecting him as he attacked the German balloon lines, but had himself made one aircraft and three balloon 'kills' in two days of action, 15 and 16 September. He went down near Serronville, where he was buried.

Despite his high score, and having exceeded the magic number of twenty victories on 9 October—and increasing this to 25 by 4 November—his recommendation for the Pour le Mérite did not receive official sanction owing to the Kaiser's abdication as Germany collapsed. Von Hantelmann was murdered by Polish poachers whom he challenged on his estates in East Prussia on 7 September 1924, six years after his glory days on the Western Front.

Position, Position, Position

Whatever tactics these and other aces used, or developed, most would agree that positioning was important if one was to achieve anything in air combat. There were two types of fighter pilots in the First World War: those who spotted the enemy and went for him—'balls out, hair on fire!'—and those who waited until they got themselves, and their men, into what would be the best situation before making an attack, having also checked the sky above and around them for any nasty surprises. In one of my conversations with Sir Leslie Hollinghurst (No 87 Squadron in 1918), we spoke of one patrol leader in his unit, Captain H. J. Larkin DFC, CdG,, an Australian. 'Holly' said that, despite Joe Larkin's skill, especially making certain his Flight was in the best possible position to hurt the opposition, there was just a little sense of him 'not quite playing cricket', simply because he was so cold-blooded in his approach to battle!

★   ★   ★

I once met Sir Gerald Gibbs, and although I only spoke to him briefly, he did comment about positioning, and said I should read his book and take note of what he had written. I had had his book for some time, but re-read it once I got home, and made particular notice of what he had recorded. Although Sir Gerald had not fought on the Western Front, his ten victories had been achieved in Salonika, but still against German aircraft (for which he received the MC and two Bars), and his words are no less important.

Gibbs had been taught that a good climbing turn would put him in a winning position against another fighter, but he rarely carried this out. He would always tighten his turns as much as possible in order to get his guns to bear. Then a little top rudder would cause a stall, and his S.E.5a would make the first half-turn of a spin in the same direction as the circle but cut across it. Putting the stick forward would straighten the S.E., and then by pulling the stick right back his machine would sit momentarily on its tail, giving him the chance of a quick burst of fire upwards at his opponent as he flew past.

He was an advocate of positioning, in which he believed that the fight was either won or lost before it started. He also thought that the attacking pilot must have the determination to destroy, and take calculated risks to do so. In getting into position, the pilot must always keep a good look-out behind him. He found that the leather flying coats of good pilots were always nearly worn through across the backs by the continual rubbing against the seat and cockpit rim, as they checked against hostile aircraft trying to creep up on them. He had kept his coat all those years, and the tell-tale signs were still in evidence.

Sir Gerald felt, too, that the RAF pilots went in for more close in-fighting than did the Germans, who tended to dive, peck, and fly off. Probably this was because British aircraft generally had a tighter turning circle, even though they were inferior in some other respects. In the Second World War the Americans and British found that dive-and-zoom tactics were far better against light, more manoeuvrable Japanese fighters that could constantly out-turn the Allied machines.

Gibbs thought also that he was far more stupidly over-confident than courageous. If on occasions a German pilot managed to get in a burst at him, it was like sitting in front of a watering can in full pour, due to the fact that both sides used a good deal of tracer ammunition. However, he knew perfectly well he would never be hit: he was 21 years old and fireproof—and so, by inference, he knew it all!

America's Top Ace

The US fighter pilot who claimed the most victories was Edward Vernon Rickenbacker (formerly Rickenbacher), who came from Columbus, Ohio, and was born on 8 October 1890 of Swiss immigrants.

Eddie Rickenbacker scored his early victories in the Nieuport 28, with its unusual 'side-saddle' gun arrangement. His unit was the 94th Aero ('Hat in Ring') Squadron, as indicated by the emblem on the fuselage sides.

By the time he was in France with the 94th Aero Squadron, he was already worldly-wise in many respects, having already made a name for himself in motor racing. While visiting England in 1916 on behalf of his motor company, he was caught up in the war fever and joined the colours. He became General George Pershing's chauffeur, but later moved into aviation and became a fighter pilot.

His first tentative combats in the late spring of 1918 gained him six victories on the Nieuport 28, despite the aircraft's tendency to shed wing fabric in a dive— which was somewhat disconcerting—but then an ear infection put him in hospital. He did not return to the war until September 1918. However, flying Spads, he quickly returned to form, downing five aircraft and a balloon before the month was out, while in October he added a further three balloons and eleven aircraft, to bring his score to 26—or, to be accurate, 25, as one claim was not finally confirmed and made official until 1960. He received the DSC with nine

Oak Leaf Clusters, the French Croix de Guerre and three Palmes, and then the French Légion d'Honneur. He eventually received the US Medal of Honor, but he had to wait until 1930 for that to be bestowed upon him. A full life in aviation, including tours of the various battle fronts in the Second World War, brought him the Certificate of Merit. He died in July 1973.

Whatever tactics could be or were used, there was always the easy 'kill', and because surprise was always the best way of downing an enemy aircraft, pilots felt no guilt that the opponent had might not have seen them approach. Rickenbacker claimed an Albatros scout in just these circumstances over Metz. He was running short of fuel so had cut his engine, taking a few minutes to glide down to save petrol. He later wrote in his autobiography:

> I saw, far beneath me, three graceful German Albatroses taxi out into the field and take off, one by one. They headed straight southward, climbing steadily, obviously unaware of my presence above them.

Rickenbacker, Douglas Campbell and Ken Marr of the 94th Aero. Campbell became the first US-trained ace of the USAS but was wounded on 5 June 1918 whilst gaining his sixth victory. Rickenbacker went on to become America's 'ace of aces', with 26 victories, although his last was not confirmed until 1960.

I continued circling, afraid even to breathe, until the last of the three was well on his way, with his back towards me. I put the Nieuport into a shallow dive to start the propeller going and turned on the ignition. The engine caught, and I gunned my plane after the three Germans. I hoped to time it so that I would make my attack over the lines, rather than over German territory.

Closer, closer. My eyes were glued to the leather-jacketed shoulders of the German flying the rearmost Albatros. That is where my bullets were going to go. I was so intent on the pursuit that I completely forgot about a German stratagem. In front of the planes ahead, but higher, a black puff appeared in the sky, then another, and another. The German [AA] batteries had seen me, and it was their way of warning the three pilots in front of me. They were setting the fuze so that the shell would burst [at] approximately my altitude.

The pilot in front of me turned his head to look behind him. I saw the sun glint on his glasses [goggles]. All three pilots immediately put their planes into a dive. I was now within 200 yards of the last plane, and I had no intention of letting him get away. I knew the Nieuport's fatal weakness of shedding its wing covering in a dive, but in the excitement I did not think of it at all. I gunned the plane up to a speed of at least 150 mph and closed in on the man in front of me.

At 50 yards I gave him a 10-second burst of machine gunfire. I saw the bullets hit the back of his seat. I felt no sympathy. He had made a stupid mistake in diving rather than trying to out-maneuver me.

By then the other two pilots had had an excellent opportunity to pull up and get on my tail. At that moment either of them could be sighting down my back. But I still wanted to make sure that I had killed my man. Not until I saw the plane go out of control did I try to pull my own out of the dive. I had to come out of it in a hurry, put the ship into a sharp climb and have it out with the other two. I pulled the stick back into my lap.

A ripping, tearing crash shook the plane. The entire spread of linen over the right upper wing was stripped off by the force of the wind. I manipulated the controls, but it did no good. The plane turned over on her right side. The tail was forced up. The left wing came around. The ship was in a tailspin. With the nose down, the tail began revolving to the right, faster and faster. It was death. I had not lost my willingness to fight to live, but in that situation there was not much that I could do.

The two remaining Albatroses began diving at me, one after the other, pumping bullets into my helpless Nieuport. I was not angry at the two men for trying to kill me; I simply thought that they were stupid. Why waste ammunition? Did they think I was playing possum, with the framework of one wing hanging in the breeze?

In the end, Rickenbacker succeeded in getting out of his fix, and followed this by landing back at base with his damaged machine,

Jimmy Meissner, also of the 94th Aero, had, like Rickenbacker, the fabric of his Nieuport 28's top wing rip away while diving—which was disconcerting to say the least. The Americans were happy when the Spad XIIIs arrived.

despite having to run a gauntlet of ground fire at low level. However, on 4 June 1918 his career was nearly brought to an end once again. His fifth victory had not yet been confirmed officially, and while on patrol this day with another pilot, he had seen white AA bursts virtually over his own airfield and quickly had visions of not only a confirmed victory over 'his own backyard' but also of nailing a piece of the German aircraft's fabric up on his bedroom wall. Closing in, and making sure that the sun was behind him, he carefully put his gun sights right on the pilot's cockpit. At 100 yards, unobserved, he pressed the trigger. Three rounds shot forth, then his guns jammed.

Cursing everything and everyone, especially his armourer, he pulled up and began trying to clear the jams, while the two-seater Rumpler headed east and down. Fixing his guns, Rickenbacker headed again for the fast disappearing two-seater, closing gradually, intent on its destruction, even though all thought of a trophy over his bed had, to his annoyance, now evaporated. Totally absorbed in closing with the Rumpler, he took five minutes to begin to reduce the space between them, and as the target gradually came within range, he began to line it up in his sights once more.

Suddenly bullets began to whizz by his face, crackling like popcorn kernels on a hot griddle. It took a moment or two for him to realise what they were, but as soon as things became clear, he kicked his rudder with his right foot and shoved the stick to the right in a single spasmodic jerk. The Nieuport fell over on to its top wing and slid sideways for a few hundred feet, then, seeing space, he straightened out, looked back and saw two German fighters that moments before had been right behind him, still diving.

Rickenbacker wrote that he had not looked behind as the bullets zipped by—which was just as well. As Arthur Gould Lee once told me, if you took that second or two to look behind, rather than react, you would probably be shot down. Experienced pilots of both sides knew, too, that if a fighter pilot in your sights did take a look round, he was probably inexperienced—which, if you had missed, gave you that extra edge in continuing the attack.

Eddie Rickenbacker quickly flew back across the lines, a wiser man— and a live one! He resolved never again to permit premature elation or circumstances to rile his temper that had so affected his judgement that morning. He knew fate had been kind to him, but also that he could not hope to be so fortunate again.

THIRTEEN

Year of Victory

TWO VERY successful British fighter pilots during 1917–18 were Edward Mannock and George McElroy. Both were of Irish descent, and they had served together in No 40 Squadron during 1917, flying Nieuport Scouts.

Mannock, the son of a serving army NCO, was aged 27 when the war began, but was working in Turkey for a British telephone company. Repatriated after a spell of internment, he joined the RAMC in 1915, was commissioned into the Royal Engineers and then transferred to the RFC. One of his instructors was none other than James McCudden.

Mick Mannock joined No 40 Squadron in the spring of 1917 as previously mentioned, and by 1918 he was the senior Flight Commander with No 74 Squadron. Owing to hero-worship on the part of his biographer, James I. T. Jones, DSO, MC, DFC and Bar, MM, who himself was credited with around 40 victories, stated that Mannock had 73 victories. This was because 'Taffy' Jones wanted to ensure that Mannock's score was higher than that of the Canadian pilot Billy Bishop, whose score of 72 was known even then to be suspect. As far as can be ascertained, Mannock achieved around 61 victories, broken down as 35 destroyed or shared destroyed, 20 out of control, one balloon and five brought down on the Allied side of the lines, of which two were also shared.

As far as Jones and No 74 Squadron were concerned, Mannock was one of the greatest patrol leaders of the war, and, although he had no love for the Germans, he nevertheless took care to attack after carefully positioning himself and his men. Once committed, he was a hard and relentless fighter. His persistent dictum to all in No 74 Squadron, and later 85 Squadron, was: 'Always above, seldom on the same level, never underneath.' It was something Second World War fighter pilots advocated once they had read about such men as Mannock. A good leader was one who had good eyes, could size up a situation quickly and could keep calm, and one who knew the capabilities of his own and his opponent's aircraft. Despite the stories that Mannock was virtually blind in one eye, his ability to see the enemy first and prepare for the action that was sure to come was not hindered. 'Height', 'speed' and 'sun' were the leader's watchwords.

Mannock had joined No 74 Squadron with sixteen victories, and with it had raised this to 52 by the time he was given command of No 85 Squadron on 18 June 1918, taking over from a tour-expired Bishop. He was also given the DSO and Bar. With his new command he added eight more victories before his death on 26 July. It is often said that he gave 'kills' away to new pilots, and pilots who had been around for a while but had failed to achieve a victory. This is very romantic, but not strictly true. If he shot down a German machine and then promptly 'gave' it to another pilot, surely that pilot would not be happy with the situation. No— in actual fact there was no need, owing to the RAF's policy of sharing victories. So long as the other pilot had also opened fire on the downed aircraft, Mannock could always say the youngster had assisted in the 'kill', so they could share the victory, and each pilot would have received credit.

G. E. H. 'Mac' McElroy hailed from Donnybrook, near Dublin, and, born in May 1893, was six years younger than Mannock. When war came he joined the Royal Irish Regiment, and within weeks he was in France. Commissioned in May 1915, he was later badly gassed, which put him into garrison service in Ireland. To get back to active duty he transferred to the RFC in February 1917, thence to No 40 Squadron. By the time he left No 40 in February 1918 he had scored elevenvictories and won the MC, with a Bar, a second Bar quickly following.

His new squadron was No 24, and within weeks he had downed a further sixteen Germans, bringing his score to 27. Moving back to No 40 Squadron, he continued his scoring rate, so that by the end of July the total number of victories had progressed to 46, and with it had come the DFC and Bar.

On 20 July Mannock attended a farewell dinner for No 40 Squadron's Gwilym Lewis, DFC (twelve victories). Both Mannock and McElroy had admonished each other for being too aggressive, and for often going too low in pursuit of hostile aircraft. One of the golden rules of air combat was never to follow a victim down, no matter how badly it was thought to be hit: the danger always was that another German could easily follow the victorious pilot down and have him at a distinct disadvantage. It was good advice, if obvious, and the two friends laughed about it, although no doubt both meant it as a friendly warning.

Six days later Mannock did just that. Out with one of his pilots, he attacked an armoured two-seater that was trench strafing. Their combined fire set the German aircraft ablaze, but Mannock had followed it down just that much too far and his S.E.5a was hit by ground fire. With his fighter in flames, a crash was inevitable, and he went in south of Calonne-sur-la-Lys. He had always had a horror of burning and had often threatened to shoot himself if ever he was set on fire with no chance of survival. Whether he did during his fall will never be known.

Just five days later, on the 31st, McElroy shot down a German two-seater near Laventie at low altitude, and his S.E.5a, too, was caught by ground fire. The Germans later dropped a note announcing that McElroy was dead. Both men had fallen in the same area, both attacking two-seaters and following them down too low.

Mannock's record was later accepted as exceptional, and in 1919 a belated award of the Victoria Cross was promulgated for him, after 'Taffy' Jones had mounted a campaign for his former friend and Flight Commander. McElroy, too, deserved a DSO, and would no doubt have received one had he survived, but of course only the VC and a Mention in Dispatches could be awarded posthumously.

Another of the great British aces to fall in the early summer of 1918 had been Major R. S. Dallas. Born in July 1891, Roderic Stanley Dallas came from Queensland, Australia, and had been in the Army since 1913. Once war came, he immediately put in a request to join the RFC. This was rejected, but in 1915 he succeeded in joining the Royal

Lt H. S. Wolff flew with No 40 Squadron. Note that his wing-gun mounting is affixed to the bracket which also holds the Aldis gun sight in place.

Naval Air Service. By the end of that year he was with No 1 Naval Wing at Dunkirk, flying both single- and two-seaters. His first victory came on 22 April 1916, and by February the following year he had seven 'kills', two whilst flying the prototype Sopwith Triplane (N500) on trials at the front.

With the RNAS fighter squadrons helping the RFC during the 1917 battles on the British front, Dallas moved to 1 Naval Squadron, equipped with Triplanes, and by August his score had increased to twenty, gaining him the DSC and Bar as well as the command of the Squadron. Following the amalgamation of the RFC and RNAS on 1 April 1918, Dallas, now flying Camels and with a score of 23, not only moved to command an ex-RFC Squadron—No 40—but also converted from rotary-engined fighters to water-cooled, in-line-engined S.E.5as. However, he took it in his stride and soon increased his score to 32.

At various periods during the war, RFC Headquarters refused permission for Commanding Officers to fly operationally, so that their experience and knowledge would not be lost if they were shot down.

However, there are many instances of forthright and aggressive COs ignoring these edicts, and Dallas was one. Not that he flaunted it so that HQ would make it a direct order, but he often flew out to find trouble.

Most single-seat squadrons by this time were, in any event, being led by Flight Commanders, who daily led their Flights on patrols or ground-attack missions. Only if a squadron show was ordered might the CO fly too, and often he would not lead, leaving that job to his senior Flight Commander, but flying within the group. It was only men like Mannock who might lead patrols, but then his experience was current. On 1 June 1918, Dallas' squadron were out on patrol and he took off alone, but, rather than risk a problem with authority, he remained behind the lines, happy to be flying and just watching out for any action in far-off enemy territory, probably hoping to see his pilots in action somewhere.

What he did not see was three Fokker Dr .I Triplanes from Jasta 14, led by its leader, Johannes Werner. 'Hans' Werner had flown two-

Wolff's CO was Major R. S. Dallas, DSO, DSC, a former RNAS pilot. He is seen here in his earlier RNAS days, in front of a Nieuport 11 of No 1 Naval Wing.

seaters, then been with Jasta 7 prior to commanding Jasta 14 with effect from September 1917. He scored a modest five victories by the end of May 1918, but on 1 June he had led two of his pilots out on this cloudy day to attack the British balloon lines. Sneaking across, he then spotted the lone S.E.5a and attacked, shooting down the luckless Australian, who for once had his guard down. Dallas fell near Lieven and was killed outright.

One of his pilots in No 40 Squadron was H. S. Wolff, whom we met earlier. He recalled for me:

> There is one incident concerning Dallas that is quite outstanding in my memory. One day we were alone in the Mess, chatting about things in general, and our SE5s in particular, when he suddenly suggested that we should go out on a 'joy-ride' together. Up we went with him leading, gained height and turned east over the lines, gaining more height all the while.
>
> I formated perfectly until [at] about 17,000 feet my engine became slack and I was unable to keep level with him and was about 100 feet below him, still in good formation, but I just couldn't get level. We flew on and on east, with nothing in sight except exploding 'Archie'.
>
> When we eventually returned and landed, with a scratch here and there through our wings, I explained to him about my engine and why I was unable to keep level. I really think that in his mind he wanted to test out his pilots individually. He was the type that would not ask any of his squadron to do anything that he would not do himself. During what to me seemed a very long flight, I really was hoping that we would not meet a bunch of Huns and become engaged in a scrap long enough to use up valuable petrol.
>
> He was completely fearless, happy in personality, cheerful, a born leader with a most likeable personality. Everyone in the squadron thought the world of him. His death was a great loss to the Service.

The Fokker D.VII

By the early summer of 1918 the Fokker D.VII biplane was becoming firmly established as Germany's main front-line fighter. Jastas still had a smattering of Albatros and Pfalz scouts, generally flown by the newer pilots until either the older machines became too worn out or further supplies of the D.VII arrived. A few Fokker Triplanes remained too, but the type had mainly been withdrawn. However, Josef Jacobs liked the Triplane so much, and, as leader of Jasta 7, he rarely flew anything else.

Jacobs was a Rhinelander, born in May 1894, and learned to fly in 1912, enlisting in the German Air Service once war began. With a two-

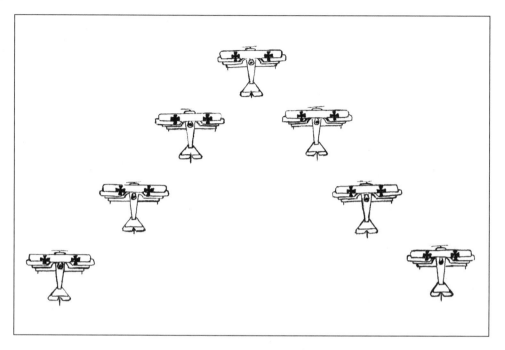

Jasta formations. As the air war developed it became clear that specific tactical formations represented the way forward. Whilst Allied airmen often referred to German formations as 'gaggles', many in fact had a good tactical grouping. Flying in a 'vee' formation, the leader would fly at the point of the 'vee', his less experienced pilots fanning out from him, whilst at the extremities of both would be the more experienced men. In this way, the whole Jasta could still support the leader during an initial attack, while the experienced 'outriders' were able to keep a watchful eye on the novices as well as the sky around and behind the whole formation.

seat unit he also flew Fokker Eindeckers before moving to Jasta 22, beginning to score regularly in 1917. In August he moved to command Jasta 7, by which time his score had reached a modest five but with another ten unconfirmed.

Leading Jasta 7 for the rest of the war, he fell in love with the Triplane, and although von Richthofen is always associated with the Driedecker, Jacobs scored many more 'kills' on this type than did the Red Baron. In point of fact, well into the summer of 1918 Jacobs had two, possibly three, personal black Triplanes, in which he led his Staffel pilots in their Fokker D.VIIs. Because by this time rotary engines for the Triplane were scarce, he let it be known that any front line German troops who could salvage a rotary engine from an Allied aeroplane which he could then use would be rewarded with a crate of champagne.

Although von Richthofen gave fame to the Fokker Dr.I Triplane, it was Josef Jacobs of Jasta 7 who scored the most victories on the type. He preferred it to all other fighter aircraft—even the Fokker D.VII—and had three machines at his disposal long after it had been withdrawn from service. In all, Jacobs had around 30 victories flying Triplanes, out of his total of nearly 50.

He apparently never went short of engines! He ended the war with 48 victories and the Pour le Mérite.

Jacobs liked the Triplane because he knew he could out-turn and out-climb anything he came up against, even if he was slower. Moreover, of course, with a slower aircraft there was no danger of his causing his pilots to struggle to keep up with him. He personally liked to use the slip turn, a turn made with just the rudder, although to perform the flat turn considerable opposite aileron was needed to keep the wings level. Thus with the wings level, anyone behind would not realise he was turning because his Triplane gave the wrong impression. A normal turn with aileron and rudder banked the wings and turned the rudder at the same time. With the slip turn the Triplane skidded round a turn, level, and was difficult to detect by an opponent unless he were a very experienced air fighter. More than once while using the slip turn Jacobs was able to see his attacker's tracers go by, while the attacking pilot thought he was on target.

Jacobs also told his pilots not to rely on loops and rolls, which did little to help if a '*Lord*' (the German's word for British airmen) or a Frenchman was on one's tail, and only reduce speed, which, in a combat situation, was not good; steep turns with engine full on was a far better manoeuvre. To many Allied pilots, the German formations seemed to be little more than a gaggle, but the more disciplined Jastas tried to fly in set 'vee' formations, with the leader at the point. The less experienced pilots would fan out to either side, with the Staffel's best pilots at the extremities. In this way, everyone could protect the leader, who would have first crack at the enemy, while the best pilots had the experience both to look after the less experienced men ahead of them and at the same time to be able to keep a watchful eye on the sky above and behind.

Keith Caldwell, MC, DFC, the New Zealand ace and CO of No 74 Squadron in 1918, once told Ray Collishaw that on one occasion he was the victim of the tactics used by Jasta 7. Caldwell and another pilot were on patrol, keeping a sharp look-out, but of course they could not observe the area immediately below them quite so easily. Suddenly Caldwell's companion waggled his wings, and almost immediately the New Zealander's machine was severely hit. Jacobs taught his pilots (if the situation arose) to climb and to attack from below, using the 'hanging on the prop' tactic of firing. Jacobs claimed that shooting was much more accurate that way.

★　★　★

The first Fokker D.VIIs to arrive at the front had 160hp Mercedes engines, virtually the same as previous motors used in Albatros and Pfalz Scouts. However, by mid-summer, and especially in time for the battles of August and September on both the British and French/American fronts, some D.VIIs were arriving fitted with the BMW 185hp engine. The immediate external view of the BMW-engined machines was no different as far as the Allied airmen were concerned: the difference, they found, was in combat. It was rather like the Germans finding in 1942 that the Spitfire Mk V looked just like the new Spitfire Mk IX—until that is, they got into a fight.

The BMW engine, with its high compression, gave the D.VII a marked improvement in performance over the Mercedes-powered machines. Ernst Udet, who would survive the war with 62 victories—second only to Manfred von Richthofen's score of 80—wrote:

The DVII with the 160 hp motor was a technically outstanding aeroplane. However, its efficiency decreased considerably at altitudes above 13,000 feet. [The BMW-ngined DVIIs] began to arrive and I was amazed at the remarkable increase in power over the 160 hp Mercedes. The engine was very smooth and throttled down easily. I used the BMW-powered machine for the first time [on 30 June] on a line patrol, and noticed more than ever its tremendous advantage over the other machines of my staffel. In order to stay with them I was forced to use half throttle only. My speed was much higher, particularly during powered descents, even at low altitudes, and at 16,000 feet the machine was nicely balanced. There was still ample power reserve, and in a fight it is good to know that more power is available when desired.

I then led my staffel onto a squadron of Spads and was soon able to obtain another victory. Because of the power available I could attack from below, a technique that I began to employ. With the extra speed I could easily overhaul my staffel and they could not keep up with me.

Udet, by this time, was leader of Jasta 4 within JG I, and the Spad he mentions was his 36th victory. From Frankfurt, Udet was born in April 1896, and it took several attempts for him to get into the military before becoming a mere motorcyclist. He eventually joined the Air Service, flew two-seaters and later Fokker monoplanes. He moved to the new Jasta 15, then Jasta 37, before catching the eye of the Red Baron, who invited him to join Jasta 11 in the spring of 1918. Shortly after the Baron's death, Udet took over as leader of Jasta 4. He was among those pilots lucky enough to have his life saved by a parachute when he was shot down on 29 June with his score at 40.

The British still flew the S.E.5a, Camel and Dolphin single-seat fighters, with the Bristol F.2b remaining, for the Germans, the troublesome two-seater. The only new fighter that would see limited service in the final weeks of the war was the Sopwith Snipe, which equipped just two squadrons, No 43 RAF and No 4 AFC. It had been produced with long-range escorts in mind, and, had the war continued, No 45 Squadron, which had returned to France from Italy, would have provided such missions for the Independent Force bombers attacking the Ruhr.

The French now had virtually all their escadrilles equipped with the Spad XIII, and the Americans, too, had shed their Nieuport 28s for the Spads, although the 17th and 148th Aeros retained their Camels. Up in the north, the small Belgian Air Force, which had flown a variety of machines during the earlier war years, had now standardised on the Camel and Hanriot HD.1.

Bristol Fighters were efficiently used in a number of ways, pure air fighting not being among the first. Fighter reconnaissance was their forte, since they were able to look after themselves more readily than previous pure Corps machines. They could also fly light bombing missions and ground-attack sorties and even, on occasions, go after balloons. The two-man team in a 'Brisfit' had ideally to become as one in the air. Each put his trust in the other's ability, and the more two men flew and fought together the better they became. It was fairly rare for either a new pilot to go up with an 'old' observer, or an 'old' pilot to have a new back-seater. With no common bond both were in danger, so it was usual for a new pilot to start out with a new observer.

In combat, the Bristol Fighter crew worked as a team, although in a fierce air battle it was not always possible to advise each other of present danger, so each relied on the other to do the right thing. If there was time, and the observer spotted a hostile aircraft starting to make an

attack, he would tap his pilot's flying helmet and point to the danger. Being in close proximity, with their cockpits virtually touching, was a great aid. However large or small the formation, there was always a leader and a deputy leader, each with two wingmen. The rear three would fly slightly lower so as to avoid the others' slipstream, and so that the rear pilots could clearly see the leading three. To have flown behind and

The advent of the parachute for German aircrew saved many lives, although, except for balloon observers, the Allied airmen were refused them on grounds that they may take the easy way out! Here Leutnant Gustav Frädrich of Jasta 72 (with six victories) puts on his parachute apparatus, July 1918.

above would put the leading three in a blind spot. In this way, too, the observers in the leading three had a clear view and shot behind and above, with no danger of hitting the other Bristols. Once an air battle developed, however, it was usually every man for himself, but, if attacking, each section would engage in turn, the rear sections delaying just enough to make certain other hostile aircraft would not suddenly appear overhead.

Parachutes and Balloons

Parachutes had been developed before the war, but the early ones were bulky, heavy and difficult to accommodate in the small confines of a cockpit. Balloon observers had them almost from the start, the pack being attached to the side of the observation basket, so that should the man have to jump out upon being attacked by an aircraft, an attached line simply pulled the canopy free of its knapsack. In this way scores of balloon observers were saved, but the same consideration was not given

to the airmen—certainly not Allied airmen, although the Germans got them in small numbers by the early summer of 1918. Even so, it was not obligatory for German airmen to use them, and sometimes there were not enough to go round anyway.

Nevertheless, there were any number of men who did use them to escape from a burning aeroplane, Udet and another top ace we have already talked about—Josef Jacobs—were both saved by using them. Franz Buchner, leader

Erich Löwenhardt of Jasta 10 became the third-ranking ace of the First World War, with 54 victories, including nine balloons. He met his fate by colliding with another German Fokker during a combat on 10 August 1918. Although he baled out, his parachute failed to deploy and he fell to his death.

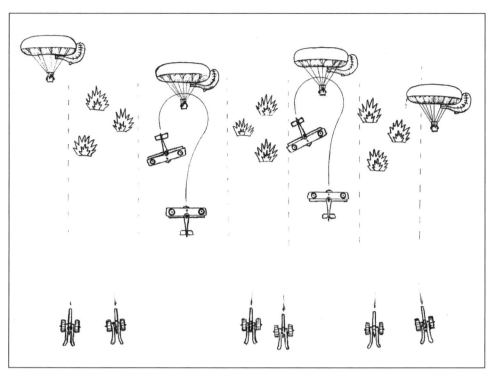

Balloon attack—low-level. Whether solo or part of a squadron effort, the aircraft flies headlong across the lines towards the balloon area, the pilot hoping that speed and surprise will bring him to within range of the target without being hit by ground fire, and without the balloon having been pulled down. Once in range, he simply zooms up to the balloon's height and opens fire. After the attack he can either make a tight turn and make another pass, or, more sensibly, climb away and go home at height. During organised unit assaults, support by artillery would hope to keep German heads down during the approach, the artillery men leaving avenues of approach along which the attacking aircraft would fly, its pilot safe in the knowledge that he would not be in a segment of sky filled with shells—provided the artillery were on target and he was on the right course.

of Jasta 13, who would end the war with 40 'kills', also baled out successfully following a collision with one of his men on 10 October 1918. Those who did make successful jumps had their parachutes re-packed and used again.

Not that using a parachute guaranteed salvation. Several pilot baled out and either had their parachutes fail completely or open too low. Two top German aces, Erich Löwenhardt, leader of Jasta 10 (54 victories) and Hans Pippart, leader of Jasta 19 (22 victories), both died baling out of crippled Fokker D.VIIs during August 1918, while the following month Fritz Rumey of Jasta 5 (45 victories) died when his

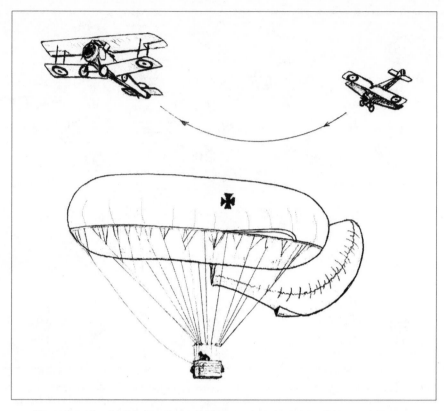

Balloon attack—high-level. As Captain W. M. Fry, MC, wrote: 'Balloon strafing was one of our occasional jobs, and anyone was always free to have a go at one or more if he felt like it. The normal and about the only way to attack a balloon was to dive suddenly at it full out, and pump bullets into it and then zoom away and home. As soon as an attack took place, the occupants of the balloon and the ground crew went into action, the balloon being pulled down rapidly on its winch much faster than one would have thought possible. Generally the observer took to his parachute, as he did not want a blazing balloon coming down on top of his basket.' Diving from height had the advantage of racing through or by any enemy aircraft lurking over the balloon line, and ground fire would be faced with a speeding target whose height was changing. However, nearer the ground an attacking pilot needed to pull out of his headlong dive and for several seconds was vulnerable to AA and small-arms fire from enemy troops.

'chute failed to deploy after his aircraft collided with an S.E.5a. In fact, the success rate was sixty per cent.

The British could have had parachutes, but by some twisted logic applied by the men in power, it was thought that if airmen had the use of parachutes they might use them too liberally, or even 'chicken out', thereby becoming less aggressive. Surely a pilot would be more aggressive, knowing that if all else failed, he did at least have an escape route? I have mentioned this before and make no apologies for stating it again: where does stupidity end and accessory to murder begin? I will wager that none of these decision-makers had sons in the Air Force! Major-General Sir David Henderson, who commanded the RFC in France, did, but it is not known how much input he may have had in the debate, which may have taken place in London. His son, Ian Henderson, MC, had ended his immediate war flying in mid-1917, but was killed in a collision at Turnberry in June 1918.

Attacking balloons had become something of an art to some air fighters, while others, as mentioned earlier, left them well alone. There seems to have developed a sort of balloon-mania with some men, who appeared to be drawn to them like magnets. Many of these became so successful at destroying balloons that they obviously felt either they had either a charmed life, or they had found a method of destroying them and getting away with it.

Balloons were expensive items, so the armies of both sides did not like to lose them too readily and had them well defended by anti-aircraft guns and machine guns, and, because of necessity they were usually tethered to their mobile and motorised winches a few miles behind their respective front lines, casually protected by fighter patrols. There did not seem to be one foolproof method of attacking them, and pilots experimented with various ideas.

No 40 Squadron in 1917 had attempted the direct approach from fairly low level, and attacked en masse. Others decided that a full-blown screaming dive from high level, out of the sun for preference, would do the trick, while still others attacked from the east, hoping that all enemy eyes would be looking the other way (or, for the Germans, from the west, having, like their British or French counter-parts, flown well behind the enemy lines at height prior to starting an attack).

Among the British, Captain A. W. Proctor (known also as Beau-champ Proctor), a diminutive South African serving in No 84 Squadron, destroyed sixteen balloons out of his score of 54 victories. His achievements brought him the VC, DSO, MC and Bar, and DFC. Henry Woollett, a Sopwith Camel pilot with No 43 Squadron, scored eleven balloon 'kills' in his 35 victory claims, to earn the DSO and MC and Bar. Tom Falcon Hazell of No 24 Squadron was third on the

RFC/RAF list of balloon-killers, with ten of his 43 victories being *Drachen*.

Of the German aces, Fritz Röth of Jasta 34b, 23b and 16b, claimed twenty balloons, with eight aircraft shot down. Heinrich Gontermann, of Jasta 5 and 15, got seventeen out of a score of 39, while Oskar Hennrich of Jasta 45 got fourteen balloons in his total of 22 'kills'. In all, 27 German aces downed more than five balloons each.

Richard Wenzl of Jasta 6 was not a balloon-hunter ,but he had attacked two. On both occasions he had flown out and only attacked them because he was suddenly confronted by them. Each time he recorded that he pretended to 'play Americans', by heading into French airspace and then come down on the balloons from the Allied side. On 5 September he had flamed one near Croiselles, but during another encounter he had again headed west, then turned and come back towards the lines, again trying to act like an American, and

Heinrich Gontermann scored seventeen balloon victories out of his total of 39 whilst flying with Jastas 5 and 15. He died testing a new Fokker Triplane on 30 October 1917.

On the British side, Henry Woollett, DSO, MC, of No 43 Squadron, achieved eleven balloon 'kills' out of his total of 35 victories. His Camel is daubed with white in an effort to disguise it amidst the clouds.

although his fire had holed the target, and both occupants had baled out, the balloon was hauled down rapidly and he was unable to finish it off, even though he was certain he could see a glow through the holes he had puntured in the side of it. In the end, the AA fire was too severe to linger around, and he dashed for the lines and home. At least the tactic of approaching from the west had given him a clear run without being fired on by the ground defences until he was actually attacking.

Erich Löwenhardt described his own views on balloon attacks. During his first combats he had downed nine. He knew one either attacked a balloon alone, or with a formation:

> If I fly alone to the front, twilight is the most favourable time to attack. Near Ypres I have shot down three balloons in the evening and have always followed the same tactic with success. I go deeply into the front line, take note of the position and heights of the balloons and watch out for enemy aircraft. When the sun has set, on days of major battles, there are usually one or two balloons standing, probably doing evening reconnaissance and which will eventually guide the heavy artillery. I carefully keep these balloons in view, fly away from the front, and climb to a height of about 3–4,000 metres. Then I return to the front and, when I think I can reach the balloon in a glide,

Frank Luke Jr, of the 27th Aero, shot down fourteen balloons and four aircraft between 12 and 29 September 1918, but was killed on the latter date. He received the DSC with Oak-Leaf Cluster, and a posthumous Medal of Honor.

cut the engine. Usually the English can then neither see nor hear me any more.

A short burst at very close range—not more than 50 metres—has always been sufficient to ignite a balloon. In my experience, a night flight home is best made at full power since the English anti-aircraft gunners assume that you will dodge about and will thus shoot too low.

With heavy cloud cover, one can too easily be surprised by enemy aircraft; the balloons are difficult to find, because as a rule one has to fly above or in the clouds. Normally, the English balloons sit 3–4,000 metres below the clouds. A burst of speed in the clouds, which stretch 2–3,000 metres from the height of the balloons, can sometimes be very favourable.

The Staffel attack. Early mornings and evenings are the best times because you can achieve surprise and there are usually less enemy aircraft about. For attacks at this time of day, I arrange my force so that I have as many machines as there are balloons. I see no advantage in allocating the attacking aircraft before reaching the target because the enemy's protective aircraft will not immediately recognise the purpose of our flight. Thus, whoever is first to a balloon, shoots it down, and he should continue the attack until it is on fire. In this way, everyone will be caught up in the ambition to be first to a balloon and thus have the force in close formation on arrival at them. In this way an unexpected attack by enemy aircraft will be avoided and anti-aircraft fire is divided amongst individual machines and its effect on each will be reduced.

The French, too, had their 'balloonatics'. Leon Bourjade of Spa 152 accounted for one aircraft and 27 balloons in 1918; Michel Coiffard, Spa 154, downed 24 out of his 34 claims; Maurice Boyau, Escadrille Spa 77, 'killed' 21 balloons plus fourteen aircraft; and Jacques Ehrlich of Spa 154 was credited with nineteen victories, of which no fewer than eighteen were balloons.

The most manic—or bravest, depending on your point of view—was the Belgian ace Willy Coppens, or, to give him his eventual full title, Willy Omar François Jean Coppens, Baron de Houthulst. Born in a small town near Brussels in July 1892, he moved from the Army to the Air Service and saw combat in 1917, but without having any victories confirmed. By the spring of 1918 he was flying the Hanriot HD.1 with Escadrille 9, and, after downing his first confirmed aeroplane on 25 April, began his war against German balloons. Over the next six months he shot down a total of 35 balloons and one other aircraft, before being seriously wounded in an attack on 14 October, hit by AA fire which caused him to lose his left leg. As well as all the awards his country could bestow upon him, the British gave him the DSO and MC, and Serbia their Order of the White Eagle.

So well known was his pale blue Hanriot to the Germans that they once set a trap for him, sending up a decoy balloon with its basket full of explosives, set to detonate as he got close to it. However, for some reason the balloon did not blow up, and he set the gasbag alight and it fell to the ground, only then exploding the ordnance—among the men who had set up the trap.

This was not an isolated occurence. In Macedonia, the Geman ace Rudolph von Eschwege gained a reputation for downing Allied aircraft and balloons, although mostly aircraft. The British put up a balloon with a basket packed with explosives which the German attacked on 21 November 1917, although this time the trap worked and the German's machine was destroyed, along with its pilot. The watching Germans assumed he had fallen whilst downing his twentieth combat success, but, although he had reached the magic figure, the Pour le Mérite was not an award given posthumously.

While Willy Coppens scored the most balloon 'kills', probably the most famous and best-remembered 'balloon buster' was the American Frank Luke Jr. Luke came from Arizona, from a poor family, one of nine children of German immigrants. His grandfather, had, nevertheless, fought for the Union in the American Civil War. Joining the US Air Service, Luke eventually found himself in France, a member of the 27th Aero, flying Spads.

He does not seem to have been wholly accepted by his fellow pilots: perhaps his brash Arizonian outlook, or perhaps his background, was against him. His reputation was certainly not enhanced following a fight in which he claimed a German aircraft shot down, and nobody believed him. This appears to have stung him into stubborn action, and he and another fighter pilot, Joe Wehner, also a bit of a loner, teamed up to destroy balloons.

Balloons, of course, were important targets, and often needed to be knocked out or destroyed during pre-offensive phases, and while offensives were taking place. With the Allies holding air superiority over their side of the lines, it was often difficult for the Germans to obtain good reconnaissance of what was going on behind the front-line trenches. So while the Allies could use their balloons too, and could also rely on verbal and photographic help from their Corps crews, the Germans relied heavily on their balloon observers.

Luke's first balloon 'kill' came on 12 September 1918, followed by two more on the 14th. Three more balloons burned on the 15th, two on the 16th, two (plus three aircraft) on the 18th, a balloon and an aircraft on the 28th and finally three on the 29th. This brought his score to four aircraft and fourteen balloons in eighteen days, or, to be precise, in seven days of action. However, in attacking his last batch of balloons, his Spad had been hit by ground fire, and he himself (probably) wounded in the chest. Forced to land behind the German lines, he either died in a shoot-out with German soldiers or was shot while firing his sidearm trying to attract attention to his plight. Whatever his end, he did not live long enough to receive his DSC and Oak-Leaf Cluster, nor to know that his bravery had won for him his country's highest award, the Medal of Honor. He was 21 years old.

Another American 'balloonatic', but one who flew with the RAF, was Louis Bennett Jr, from West Virginia, born on 22 September 1894. A former Yale student, he joined the RFC in Canada, and by the summer of 1918 was with No 40 Squadron in France. It was nearly a month before he made his first claim, a Fokker D.VII on 15 August, followed two days later by an LVG two-seater, and his first balloon 'kill'. He then went mad for balloons. On the 19th he downed four, with two more on the 22nd, another aircraft on the 23rd, and finally two balloons on the 24th, to bring his score to nine balloons and three aircraft. However, in his last action he was going for a third balloon but was hit by ground fire. His S.E.5a caught light, forcing him to jump out at 100 feet, and he broke both legs hitting the ground, dying in a German field hospital. In his brief career he had only flown 25 sorties, his victories occurring on just seven of them—another example of the burning meteor.

Lancing C Holden Jr flew with the American 95th Aero Squadron in 1918 and five of his seven victories were over balloons. On 23 October 1918 he gained his third victory and his second balloon. In his diary he recorded the event, and also noted that becoming an 'ace' was something he was striving hard for:

> October 23, 1918. Another balloon! It is certain to be confirmed and that will make three!—two official—three more and I am an official ace. That is my dream and I swear I shall accomplish it.
>
> This balloon was troublesome so they telephone in for someone to get it—Ted Curtis, Tom Butz, Al Weatherhead and Buck Church were to be my protection. Tom and Buck dropped out with motor trouble. We three were flying over one of our balloons when I saw two observers jump out. That meant something was attacking it. In another instant I saw the German set it on fire. I dived on him firing from long range. It was a stern chase and he got away, but later Rickenbacker got him. The nerve of that Hun—I certainly admire him—right under our noses.
>
> I flew around waiting till it got darker then made for five German balloons all in a row. If I could get all five . . . I picked the end one, which proved to be a fake with no basket. It didn't burn, and both my guns jammed. I fixed them on the way to the next one, and oh, the barrage they put up all the time, looked like the Fourth of July. Not many 'archies,' but millions of flaming onions and incendiary bullets. The second one the observers jumped from but that didn't burn either and the guns jammed again. The third I attacked twice. They had pulled them all down—this one was about 50 metres up—again the guns jammed, but as I turned away two little red holes like bloodshot eyes were burning on the side. Slowly the fire spread then up she went. Gee I felt good, but my dream of five didn't pan out.

On 4 November he scored his last victory—another balloon—making six 'kills' plus a shared Fokker D.VII in all. Five balloons and two aircraft made him an ace, an accomplishment which he duly recorded in his diary:

> At last, at last! I am an ace!—and one over. I burned another balloon last night and one tonight. That makes five official balloons and one official plane. Ted Curtis and myself are the only men with six official victories in the squadron.

Two Naval pilots pose with a Nieuport two-seater which has some local 'mods', such as an upward-firing Lewis gun, and two stripped-down guns for the observer. Note the variation in the observer's method of moving his guns. Both the men in the photograph later became fighter aces— S. M. Kinkead, standing, and E. V. Reid scored heavily, although Reid was killed in action. (Bruce/Leslie Collection)

Last night I dodged over the clouds and burned the balloon just as the observer jumped. Poor devil, the whole burning mass of balloon must have fallen on his parachute. I am getting this job down pretty fine now—the balloon burned after one burst of 30 shots.

Tonight Al Weatherhead, Sumner Sewell and I went over. They were to protect me. I went down and burned mine. They saw another and burned that also. Pretty good party?

They [the German ground crews] can pull those balloons down 30 miles an hour. I didn't catch it till it was on the ground. It is more fun to see them burn up in the air, but it burned and fell on all its machine gunners, which must have been annoying. If there is any one class of human beings I heartily detest it is the German 'flaming onion' shooters. Flaming onions are great fun to dodge. They are fireballs on strings about ten feet apart; they come sailing up. If the string hits your plane it wraps all the balls round you.

On the way home some especially unintelligent German ripped my aileron up with an explosive bullet and put a hole in the propeller, but otherwise all went well.

Holden came from New York and went home with the DSC and Oak-Leaf Cluster. He died in a plane crash in 1938.

The Last Fighters to See Action

On the British side, the last fighter to see action was the Sopwith Snipe, which to all intents and purposes looked like a bigger and more robust Camel. It only equipped two fighter units, Nos 43 and No 4 Australian

FC Squadrons in the last weeks of the war, with No 208 Squadron taking them on charge as the war ended.

Captain W. G. Barker, DSO, MC, won the Victoria Cross flying one while attached to No 201 Squadron for an action on 27 October 1918, in which he was badly wounded after hitting several Fokker D.VIIs in a wild single combat. He had flown this Snipe to France and was attached to No 201 for combat experience, his previous service having been in France and then on the Italian Front with Camels.

The Snipe had a 230hp Bentley engine and proved a winner, but it came too late to have any real influence on the air war. It did however, remain in RAF service for some time after the war.

On the German side, two other fighters saw limited action in 1918, the Pfalz D.XII and the Fokker E.V. The Pfalz looked very similar to the Fokker D.VII, and probably the Allied airmen fought them thinking they were indeed Fokkers. Only the odd one or two that were brought down inside Allied lines that positively identified them as an aircraft other than the D.VII. Several Jastas used examples of the Pfalz, but no doubt the more experienced pilots preferred the D.VII if available.

The other machine, the very distinctive Fokker E.V, was a high-wing monoplane. It arrived at the front in August 1918, and in fact equipped Jasta 6 for several days, but its Oberusel seven-cylinder rotary engine needed castor oil lubrication, and as this was in short supply the machine was mostly withdrawn. Some were used by the Marine Jagd-

Another good view of the top-wing gun arrangement on a Nieuport Scout. This is a No 6 Naval Squadron aircraft, with Squadron Commander J. J. Petrie, DSC, looking nonchalant.

233

geschwader, Theo Osterkamp, for one, gaining his 25th and 26th victories in an E.VIII, but they were never seen in large numbers. The type also had some wing problems.

Theo Osterkamp was a Rhinelander, born in April 1892, and saw service with the Naval Flying Corps, first as an observer and then as a pilot. His first fighter unit was Marinefeldjasta 1 (MFJ 1) in the spring of 1917, and his first six victories were scored in that year. He then took command of MFJ 2, which he led till the war's end. In all, he achieved 32 victories and won the Pour le Mérite. In the mid-1930s he joined the Luftwaffe , and during the Second World War he was a fighter commander. In fact, in 1940 he led from the front and gained a further six victories over the Low Countries, over Dunkirk and in the early stages of the Battle of Britain. He died in January 1975.

The second highest Marine fighter pilot, Gotthard Sachsenberg, gained 31 victories in the First World War. From sea cadet in 1913 to leader of MFJ 1 in February 1917, he ended the war as leader of Marinejagdgruppe I, and was also awarded the Blue Max. He lived until August 1961, aged 69.

The Final Battles

In the final weeks of the war the pilots of the German Air Service, while having the best fighter yet in the Fokker D.VII, did not have the depth of training evident in earlier years. Petrol was also becoming a problem, and on a number of occasions patrols were curtailed because of supply shortages. Nevertheless, the German Jasta pilots were still a force to be reckoned with, and right up to the Armistice they were shooting down Allied aircraft in large numbers. However, replacement pilots were at a premium, while the Allied side had an almost bottomless barrel of aviators just itching to get into action.

In early August the Battle of Amiens began, and this signalled the beginning of the end for Germany. The British 4th and French 1st Armies pushed into the German lines on the 8th, supported by massive air cover, with not only patrols to counter German aircraft but also low-level bombing sorties to harry troops and bomber raids to hit dumps, supply trains and bridges behind the lines. This battle raged for several days and pushed the German soldiers back some distance. Allied bombers and fighters were constantly in the air.

Ronald Sykes DFC (although the ribbon in this photo is upside-down) flew with 9 and 3 Naval and No 201 Squadrons in the First World War, achieving six victories. His flight commander in No 201 was Sammy Kinkead.

Ronald Sykes, DFC, a former RNAS pilot with whom I corresponded (as mentioned in the previous chapter), had earlier flown with Roy Brown. By August 1918 he was flying with No 201 Squadron. He remembered two scraps in which he flew with Sammy Kinkead. S. M. Kinkead was also a former naval pilot, who by this time had scored over 30 victories, flying Bristol Scouts, Nieuports, Triplanes and now Camels. 'Kink' was a South African from Johannesburg, born in February 1897 of an Irish father and a Scottish mother. Ron Sykes related:

> I was flying in my place at the right rear of Kink's close formation on an H.O.P at 16,000 feet on 11 August. A lone Fokker D.VII came down in a long, gentle dive from behind and picked on me. As he closed he began to fire and I looked to Kink for orders. He waved for me to fly straight and keep formation, which I did very reluctantly as the *kak-kak-kak* behind was loud and clear. Fortunately, I had great confidence in Kinkead's judgement.
>
> When the Fokker was quite close to my tail, Kink yanked his Camel into a sharp climbing turn and half-rolled back over my head and confronted the Fokker head-on, firing as he did so. I made my Camel split-arse as only a Camel could, and pulled up and fired the burst which I felt entitled to, as the Fokker 'peeled off', and so did the other three Camels. The Fokker went 'fluttering' down to the ground.
>
> Kink told me back at the airfield that the Fokker's aim was very low and from Kink's viewpoint he could see tracer bullets passing down well under my tail, and he thought we could coax the German pilot down within striking

distance. He would have signalled me to turn if the German's aim had been more accurate!

Sykes' matter-of-fact description of this engagement probably shows less emotion than was present at the moment it happened. It also shows how much trust some pilots put in their proven leaders. Most pilots in this situation would have started to turn as soon as the German began firing, and not look for the leader's instructions. In this way, of course, the Geman pilot might easily have turned with the Camel, adjusted his aim, and scored hits. It still took some courage to continue in a straight line and hope, in the first instance, that his leader had actually seen the danger, and that the German would not be on target.

It was paramount to see the enemy first—or, at least, quickly. Good eyes and quick reactions were essential for the fighter pilot. A certain amount of calm was alsop needed, in order to size up the situation and decide rapidly how to handle a developing scenario. By 1918 flying was virtually all patrol work: long gone were the individuals of 1916 or even

French 'ace of aces' was René Fonck, of Spa 103. He claimed 75 official victories, with another 69 which he termed 'disabled'.

Charles Nungesser was the third-ranking French ace, with 43 victories, although his exploits took their toll: he was wounded and injured several times, and it is understood that at one time or another he broke every major bone in his body at least once.

early 1917. The sky was just too dangerous now for the 'lone wolf' tactics that Ball, Guynemer and Immelmann had employed. Ron Sykes continued:

On 12 August 1918 the day bombers expected a lot of opposition due to the ground battle, so they asked for an escort and were allotted one Flight of five Camels from 201 Squadron led by Captain S. M. Kinkead. After the raid was over, the D.H.9s were heading for home with noses down and throttles wide open, going as fast as scouts. The Camels were behind and above them in a 'vee' formation, staying up at 12,000 feet, for behind the Camels was a formation of ten Fokker D.VIIs and closing in from the north was another formation of twelve Fokkers. To the south we could also see another twelve German fighters, at our height, on a course to converge with us. Slowly the German fighters came nearer on both sides, with their third ragged formation keeping up at the back.

For the Camels, the direct course home was still open, and the bombers were now all far ahead, nearing the security of the lines. So the five Camel pilots headed for home too, and we got little comfort by closing up into a very compact near-'vee' formation. We were literally escorted to the lines by over thirty German fighters which did not attack: it was contrary to their usual aggressiveness.

The lines came into sight below, as a solitary Fokker DVII dived from the group on our right and came directly under us, obviously asking for a fight. I was in the right, rear Camel, and at my Flight Commander's signal I peeled off and dived for the German's tail. I immediately found I had taken on a most skilful enemy who could anticipate my every manoeuvre. and I could not get him in my sights. Finally I pulled up into a near climbing turn towards my Flight above but, as I did so, down came Captain Kinkead, and he flashed past me on to the tail of the Fokker. I half-rolled over and went down to protect my leader's tail, and as I gave a quick glance astern I saw a general dog-fight was on with the three remaining Camels staying up in circling matches among a lot of Fokkers.

Kinkead and his German, with me just above them, kept together, circling, half-rolling, diving; I had a real bird's-eye view of the deadly aerial combat between two of the most skilful of pilots, beginning at about 11,000 feet and ending at ground level. I do not think that either of them ever got their gun sights lined up on each other on their way down, owing to their extraordinarily clever flying. I know that the German easily evaded the few attacks I made, so I kept my duty of protecting my leader's tail, for during rearward glances I could see, at first, many circling Fokkers above us.

Later, as we circled for a time and dived lower, I could not see other aeroplanes above. There were only a few Germans and Kinkead with the Fokker in front. Kinkead pulled hard back on his stick and for a second got his guns to bear on the Fokker's rudder, which was hit and put out of action. The German levelled up and crash-landed unhurt not far from Bayonvillers, among Australian troops. Kinkead and I landed at our field at Bertangles and Kinkead returned by road to the scene.

The German pilot had asked the Australians to give his gold cigarette case to Kinkead (before he had been driven away), whose machine number was taken as being that of the winner and duly reported by the Aussies who had been excited spectators of the fight. The cigarette case was handed over and used by Kinkead. The Aussies said the German had told them he had no idea that he had reached the lines or he would not have given such a futile demonstration to his squadron of trainee pilots by asking for a fight in his decidedly chivalrous manner.

The French had continued with their tried and proven tactics of keeping pressure on the German Air Force along their sectors of the front. They had for some time grouped their escadrilles into Fighting Groups—Groupes de Combat—and GC 12 appears to have become the French élite outfit. GC12 comprised the Cigognes squadrons— 'The Storks'—which had progressed from the Nieuports of 1916– 17 to the Spad VIIs and XIIIs of 1917–18. Escadrilles Spa 3, Spa 26, Spa 67, Spa 73 and Spa 103 had been the main components, and the Groupe had amassed a total of 286 aircraft and five balloon victories, with Spa 3 and Spa 103 claiming 107 and 108, respectively. These, of course, were all confirmed 'kills', with no 'probables' like the British 'out of control' claims. Exactly why this élite group only achieved five balloon victories between 1916 and 1918 probably says something about the dangers these targets posed. The majority of the successful aces, like Baron von Richthofen and James McCudden, never attacked balloons.

After Guynemer fell in September 1917, the two names that were to feature most in French aviation folklore were those of Charles Nungesser and René Fonck. Nungesser came from Paris, born in March 1892, and when war came he joined the Hussars. After some early action as an NCO, being decorated too, he transferred to aviation and by the spring of 1916 was flying two-seaters, but he soon moved to scouts with Escadrille N 65. By the end of 1916 he had achieved 21 confirmed victories, including three balloons. He moved to Escadrille V 116, which, despite its Voisin designation, continued to fly single-seaters, and by August 1917 his score had reached 30. Back with Escadrille 65 in 1918, by which time the unit was flying Spads, he shot down his 43rd victim on 15 August, having claimed no fewer than four balloons the previous day.

These successes had not come without a penalty—in his case several severe injuries. In fact, the story goes that, at one time or another, Nungesser had broken every major bone in his body at least once! These injuries occurred on 6 February and 22 June 1916, and again in September 1917. He lost his life attempting to fly the Atlantic on 8 May 1927.

Fonck was destined to become the French and Allied 'ace-of-aces', with 75 confirmed victories and an astonishing 52 'probables' and another seventeen damaged. He was born in March 1894, at Soulcy-sur-Meurthe, and also joined up in August 1914, though directly into aviation. His first unit flew Caudron two-seaters, but with his gunner he claimed two 'kills', the first on 6 August 1916 and the second on 17 March 1917. Moving to scouts, he joined Spa 103 in the spring of 1917, and by the end of that year his score had risen to nineteen. In 1918 he was active in every month until the Armistice. He often scored or claimed multiple victories, for example six two-seaters on 9 May and six more—three Fokkers and three two-seaters—on 26 September. His last six claims were made on the three days 30 and 31 October and 1 November.

Gunships

In trying to protect their bombers, the French experimented with what might be described as 'escorting gunships' in the last months of the war. These were large Caudron R.11s. The original design was the R.4 bomber, but this was found to be too heavy and so it was employed as a photo-recce machine. By 1918 the R.11 had been developed, which had two 220hp Hispano-Suiza engines, a 58ft 10in (17.9m) wingspan, a duration of three hours and an armament of five machine guns. Two guns each were for an observer and a gunner, with the fifth fitted to fire forwards. The cream of the Air Gunnery School at Cazaux manned the two main gun positions, one in the nose and the other just behind the pilot. The aircraft eventually equipped eight escadrilles to escort Bregeut XIV bombers.

RAF Wings

Had the war lasted into 1919, which was expected, the RAF may well have increased its organisation into more active Wing operations, such as Louis Strange's No 80 Wing. Strange we met in an earlier chapter, but by 1918 he was a colonel and commanding this Wing, which comprised seven squadrons, Nos 92 and 2 AFC with S.E.5as, 46, 54 and 4 AFC with Camels, 88 with Bristol Fighters and 103 with D.H.9 bombers.

Colonel Louis Strange had definite ideas on tactics, and his orders were to attack German air bases and lines of communications, especially railways. By the time No 103 Squadron had become part of No 80 Wing, its commander had suggested that, as his D.H.9s took the longest to get to their operating height, these aircraft should lead the raids at the lowest level, whereas the Australian Camels had usually led. Strange therefore had his Wing squadrons staggered upwards and back, with No 103 Squadron at 2,000 feet, No 2 AFC at 3,000 feet, No 46 Squadron at 4,000 feet, No 88 Squadron at 6,000 feet (these aircraft would also take photographs of the attack) and No 4 AFC's Camels, and later their Snipes, at 7–8,000 feet. This way, if they met fighter opposition, the Camels or Snipes would protect the Bristols, while the lower Camels and S.E.5as would protect the bombers.

German airfields and railway stations were heavily attacked during the final weeks of the war, and several German aircraft were claimed during fierce combats. Strange himself was credited with a Fokker biplane on 30 October, almost four years after he and his observer had forced an Aviatik to land inside British lines back in November 1914, using a Lewis gun (although mounting such a weapon was against orders at that time).

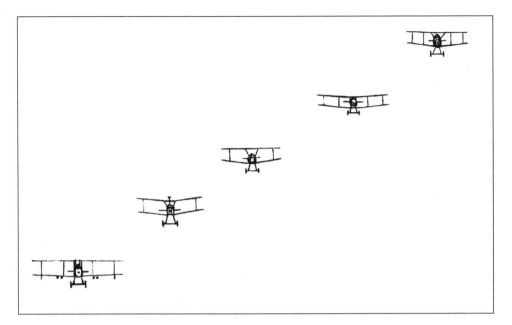

Wing formation. Colonel Louis Strange's No 80 Wing formation consisted of four squadrons, initially formed up with Camels at 5,000ft, S.E.5as behind at 5,500ft, D.H.9 bombers behind at 6,000ft and Bristol Fighters behind them at 6,500ft, with overall cover by another S.E.5a unit at 7–8,000ft. Later this was amended with the arrival of another bomber squadron, its CO arguing that as his D.H.9s, while carrying 230lb bombs, took longer to gain height, they should lead at the lowest level. The Wing formation therefore changed, once the machines had crossed the lines and the AA guns, to D.H.9s at 2,000ft, S.E.5as at 3,000ft, Camels at 4,000ft, F.2bs at 6,000ft and finally S.E.5as (later Snipes) at 7–8,000ft. To a degree, the German AA gunners over the lines and over the target were confused by the staggered groups of aircraft, and their gunfire took no effect in the first raid.

Armistice

The guns along the Western Front fell silent at 11 a.m. on 11 November 1918. The aeroplane and air power had grown out of all recognition since the days of 1914, and aviation in general had leapt ahead an at amazing pace.

Airmen of each of the belligerent nations had gradually developed their aeroplanes, their engines, and their training. Strategy and planning were developed by the commanders; the men in the field were the ones who had to try to carry them out. In doing this, the front-line airmen gradually learned to get the best from their machines and, if inferior, did their best to develop tactics to stay alive until a better machine came along.

As mentioned throughout this book, in the early years tactics were not always appreciated or developed quickly enough. Once common sense prevailed and tactics were formulated, however, these could only be implemented if the correct circumstances presented themselves. One might say that in Nelson's day, tactics at sea could be put into practice almost every time a sea battle became imminent, simply because both sides had ample time to manoeuvre into position. In the air things happened far more quickly, and whereas a Nelson or a Villeneuve could, during a sea battle, take hours in preparing for action, the fighter pilots in the First World War had only minutes—and sometimes just seconds.

One sad aspect was that most of which had been learned during the First World War—often at a very high price in human life—was, seemingly, almost forgotten by the time the Second World War began twenty-one years later. Very few of the high-scoring fighter aces who had survived the Great War were in command positions in September 1939, and those who were in such positions were not always listened to, or even asked. A new breed of air leader had emerged, and often the newly developed technologies helped to blind, or certainly obscure, logical thinking, not to mention memory. There were a few exceptions. One was Keith Park in command of No 11 Group, Fighter Command, during the Battle of Britain in 1940, although his ideas were sometimes in conflict with those of less knowledgeable men. Another was Quentin-Brand, who commanded No 10 Group in 1940. One problem in the 1930s was that the speed of modern fighters seemed to confuse people into thinking that First World War tactics were totally obsolete, whereas the young fighter pilots of the day discovered that much of what they could read from pilots' biographies still held good, despite the faster speeds.

I shall not go into the errors that were made and which could have been avoided by recalling recent history, but I might mention as an example the offensive stance taken by Trenchard, which was later taken by the air leaders and War Cabinet after the Battle of Britain. Trenchard's doctrine of taking the war to the enemy may well have helped shape the path to victory, but the cost in lives was immense. As Oliver Stewart, a Sopwith Pup ace, once noted, in 1914–18 everyone was learning and things might be excused, but by 1939 lessons should have been learned and understood. One might therefore question the policy of the 'non-stop offensive' which began in 1941 and continued into 1942–43. Over these years, RAF Fighter Command and No 2 Group of Bomber Command constantly took the war to the enemy over northern France and the Low Countries, in order, we are told, to keep the Luftwaffe pinned down—especially after Hitler invaded Russia in June 1941. The fact that Hitler got to the outskirts of Moscow with his army and air force does not tend to support any pinning-down motive. All it achieved was to boost the morale of the British public, although the cost in fighter pilots shot down over France or over the grey waters of the English Channel was high. Even with parachutes, baling out over France mostly meant a loss to a prison camp. Where the fighter pilots were really needed was in the Middle East, although one accepts that 'the powers' in Air Ministry, felt that they must defend the homeland first.

My contention is that, although on paper the German Air Service was taking a beating in 1918, actual losses were much less significant. Moreover, the air leaders must have known, through their intelligence services, that the RAF, French Air Force and US Air Service could not be destroying more aircraft each week than the Germans had in total. In 1941-42, too, with far more sophisticated intelligence-gathering, they had to know that Fighter Command's claims of enemy aircraft destroyed were over-optimistic.

In September 1941 one set of figures produced by the C-in-C Fighter Command, Trafford Leigh Mallory (who commanded a Corps squadron in the First World War), showed that while 273 fighters and 39 light bombers had been lost, German losses amounted to 460 destroyed, plus at least 192 'probables' and 240 damaged. Actual German losses on the Western Front, *from all causes*, for the *whole* of 1941 totalled under 200! Thus while someone was trying to persuade someone else that the RAF were winning the air battles by a possible margin of two to one, they were actually losing it by around three to one.

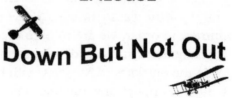

Down But Not Out

THE GERMAN Air Service was not defeated in the First World War: right up to the end they were still a force to be reckoned with, especially the fighter pilots. Short of men and aeroplanes (not to mention aviation fuel) they might have been, but the fighter pilots were still scoring against British, French and American aviators until the end. As an example, seven pilots of No 65 Squadron, in company with pilots of No 204 Squadron, became embroiled in a terrific air battle on 4 November 1918, just one week prior to the ceasefire. The combat report tells the story:

Time: 08.30
Locality: S.E. of Ghent
Height: 15,000 ft – 7,000 ft
Claims: 8 destroyed, 6 out of control, 1 driven down.
Remarks on Hostile Aircraft: Fokker Biplanes, Yellow & Green Tails, Chequered and Light Fuselages.

Narrative:
Whilst leading an Offensive Patrol of 65 and 204 Squadrons, Captain J. L. M. White with his Patrol encountered about 40 E.A., in two formations, at 12,000 ft over Zohleghem. The E.A. were above the Patrol and attacked. Captain White turned under them and a dog fight ensued. An E.A. got on the tail of Captain White's machine. He did a quick right hand turn and got on the tail of the E.A. He fired a long burst into him at about 20 ft. E.A. turned over on to its back, when both planes folded up, and the tail fell off. Confirmed by Captain M. A. Newnham, 2/Lieut A. J. Cleare and by several other pilots. As Captain White finished with this E.A. another got on his tail; he did two turns of a spin and came out into a right-hand turn.

The E.A. was still attempting to shoot him down and Captain White completed the right-hand turn and got on the tail of the E.A. The E.A. attempted to climb away, but Captain White fired a burst into him, and he went down vertically with volumes of white smoke coming from him, bursting into flames at about 2,000 ft. Confirmed by 2/Lieut W. H. Bland. Captain White had several more combats but could not observe results. He then singled out a Fokker who was taking head-on shots at nearly every Camel, and, placing himself in his way opened fire. The E.A. came straight at him firing also, Captain White saw his tracers striking the front of the enemy machine, which ceased firing and passed over his top plane. Captain White doing a quick turn, fired a short burst at the E.A. who was flying straight. E.A. then went down vertically and burst into flames. Confirmed by Lieut W R Allison.

He then got onto the tail of another, firing a short burst into it when E.A. went into a spin. Following him down to 6,000 ft, Captain White saw E.A. come out of the spin and begin to glide East. He then fired another burst at E.A. when, turning over on to its back, and falling about 1,000 ft, E.A. went into a very rapid spin. Captain White watched him down to 500 ft but did not observe him crash as he was attacked by several more E.A. His machine was badly shot about, but he succeeded in getting away and returned over the lines to his aerodrome through a very heavy A.A. barrage.

Two E.A. got behind Captain M. A. Newnham's tail, but pilot was able to shake one off and, in turn, got on the tail of the other E.A., who had lost sight of him for the moment. He approached to within 10 yards and fired a long burst right into the cockpit. E.A. made a half loop and then spun onto its back. The machine nearly came out once, but Captain Newnham immediately attacked it again, which was unnecessary, as E.A. made a stall turn and again spun on to its back. Captain Newnham watched it from 12,000 ft down to about 3,000 ft when it was still completely out of control. The pilot of this machine appeared to be the leader of the formation. Confirmed by 2/Lieut A. J. Cleare.

Captain Newnham then 'zoomed' up underneath another Fokker, firing short bursts into him. This machine did a half roll, and Captain Newnham was able to get dead onto his tail at point blank range. He fired about 100 rounds when the machine went up into a vertical 'zoom'. Captain Newnham was still directly on its tail and continued firing. The pilot fell forward and the machine went down in a vertical dive. Captain Newnham followed it down to 7,000 ft and then watched it right down, practically to the ground. He was unable to see it crash as he was again attacked from above. He also had four indecisive combats. The enemy pilots were undoubtedly from a crack Squadron as they were all exceptionally good [reported Newnham].

Lieut W. R. Allison saw a Fokker Biplane on the tail of a Camel, and, getting onto its tail, fired about 75 rounds into the cockpit at 10 yards' range. The E.A. then emitted a lot of white smoke and went down vertically, later breaking into flames. Pilot then saw another Fokker on a Camel's tail and shot at him from 50 yards. E.A. then went down vertically. Lieut Allison continued on the tail of the E.A. and fired altogether about 200 rounds into him, and later saw him still going down vertically and crash. He then observed a Fokker on the tail of Captain White's machine and fired into him. The Fokker pulled out of dive coming head-on for Lieut Allison, having ceased firing. Lieut Allison continued to fire head-on until at about 10 yards range, when Fokker pulled up and [Allison] went under him. E.A. went over on to its back and spun down. Pilot could not follow him down owing to pressure of other E.A. He fired about 150 rounds into this E.A.

An E.A. dived underneath 2/Lieut W. H. Bland, who half rolled on to E.A.'s tail ,firing two or three bursts at about 50 yards' range. E.A. stalled, fell over on to its back, and went down out of control in a flat spin. 2/Lieut W. H. Bland was unable to see him crash owing to the presence of the remaining Fokkers. A dog-fight followed, during which 2/Lieut W. H. Bland attacked another E.A. broad side on and put 5 bursts into him at point blank range. E.A. immediately went down in a vertical dive and clouds of smoke came out of the machine. 2/Lt Bland followed him down to 4,000 ft when E.A. burst into flames.

Several E.A. attacked 2/Lieut R. C. Stiven from different points during the fight but he got them off his tail. An E.A. dived on him from the right rear, and 'zoomed' up to the right in front of him. He put a burst of about 50 rounds into E.A. at point blank range. E.A. was seen to go down in a vertical dive to about 2,000 ft.

2/Lieut A. J. Cleare observed an E.A. diving and firing at Lieut Walno [No 204 Squadron]. He got on his tail, firing about 100 rounds from 25 yards' range into his cockpit, when he observed the pilot to fall over on to his 'stick', apparently killed. The enemy machine turned over on to its back, spun on its back for a while when 2/Lt Cleare got a burst of 50 rounds or so into it, and observed the machine crash on the ground from about 5,000 ft. Confirmed by Lieut F. J. Wolno. He was dived on by another E.A. and, doing a climbing turn, he got on E.A.'s tail, getting several bursts into the pilot's cockpit from point blank range. The E.A. stalled, turned over on to its back, and when 2/Lt Cleare last saw it from 7,000 ft, it was doing a flat spin on its back. 2/Lieut A. J. Cleare is positive that this machine was destroyed, though he could not follow it until it crashed owing to pressure of other E.A.

2/Lieut Pemberton attacked a Fokker at 12,000 ft and fired at him from 50 yards' range. He kept firing until he was within 20 yards' range of the E.A., when enemy machine fell over on to its back and went down into a spin. It continued spinning down to 2,000 ft when a piece of the machine broke off in the air. 2/Lieut F. R. Pemberton fired 100 rounds at this E.A. and had several other indecisive combats in which he fired 200 rounds.

This air battle appears to have been fought with Jasta 29, the latter's markings of yellow noses (cowlings) and green fuselages agreeing with

The glory days are over: a Fokker D.VII in the hands of the men of No 85 Squadron, on a Brussels airfield. Second from the right is Captain M. C. McGregor, DFC.

No 65's report of seeing colours of yellow and green. Records of some Jastas were incomplete in the last days of the war, but it is understood that Jasta 29 claimed five Camels in this action. Although there was a comment that the German pilots were good, the five victorious pilots only recorded their third (two pilots), second (two pilots) and first (one pilot) victories. Another German unit involved in this combat was Marinefeldjagdstaffeln 4, from which Flugmeister Gerhard Hubrich claimed his eleventh and twelfth victories.

In total, seven Sopwith Camels had been claimed (the only Camels claimed this date), all on the German 4th Army front, which is where the fight took place, this Army holding the further sector north which bordered the Channel coast, and where, of course, the German Marine fighter Staffeln operated. Jasta 29 was part of Jagdgruppe 3, led by Harold Auffahrt, who had by this time achieved 29 confirmed 'kills'. He was another whose victory tally was enough to have his name recommended for the Pour le Mérite, but its approval had not been made before Kaiser Wilhelm abdicated. After two-seaters and a spell with Jasta 18, he had led Jasta 29 since November 1917. The other units in JG 3 were Jastas 14, 16 and 56. It is possible that some of these were in the 4 November fight too, as their records too are sparse after mid-October, although none records any pilots killed on the 4th except Jasta 29, which lost Unteroffizier Paul Schönfelder killed in action over Oosterzeele, Belgium. Hubrich and MFJ 4, of course, could have been the 'good' pilots the Camel boys referred to.

The losses sustained by Nos 65 and 204 Squadrons in this action were one No 65 Squadron pilot killed, one taken prisoner, and one wounded, while No 204 had one pilot killed with another forced to land on the Allied side. It is unfortunate that no aircraft loss records by the Germans have survived, although from the combat report it does seem that more than one pilot would have been killed. However, the eight destroyed and six 'probables' does seem a trifle excessive. Furthermore, No 204's pilots claimed two more destroyed and a further five out of control. In total therefore, there are ten destroyed and eleven probables—21 claims.

Captain Joseph L. M. White, aged 21, came from Halifax in Canada, and his four claims brought his final score to 22. His reward was the DFC and Bar, and the Croix de Guerre. He had begun scoring in May 1918, and although he survived the war to join the RCAF, he was killed in a flying accident in 1925.

Maurice Newnham received the DFC for his eighteen victories. His two credits on the 4th brought his score to seventeen, his eighteenth being a balloon that he burned on 9 November. He, too, was 21. He had started his RFC career as a dispatch rider in 1915, finally becoming a pilot and opening his scoring with No 65 Squadron in May 1918. He later rose to be a Group Captain in the RAF in the Second World War, at which time he commanded the RAF Parachute Training School. Although he was in his late forties, by that time he still made parachute experimental training drops, at night, in fog and into water, while fully laden with equipment. He died in 1974.

That 4 November 1918 saw the Germans claim 38 aircraft and two balloons, all but three of the aircraft being confirmed. Only three Jasta pilots were reported killed. The actions included a fight between Jasta 2 (Boelcke) and the new Sopwith Snipes of No 4 Squadron, Australian Flying Corps. No 4 AFC lost four Snipes, two of which had been flown by aces—Captain T. C. R. Baker and Lieutenant A. J. Palliser.

Thomas Charles Richmond Baker DFC, MM and Bar, came from Smithfield, South Australia, and was aged 21. He had claimed his twelfth victory on 30 October, and eight of these had been Fokker D.VIIs. His MM and Bar had been won with the Field Artillery in 1915–16, the first award being made for repairing broken telephone lines while under fire. Arthur John Palliser came from Tasmania and was 28. His seven victories had been Fokker D.VIIs apart from one balloon.

All four Snipes had been victims of Karl Bolle, who was born in June 1893 and came from Berlin. He had attended Oxford University in 1912, and as the war began he was in the German cavalry, seeing duty in Poland and Courland. Once in the Air Service, and after two-seater action, he went to Jasta 28 in the summer of 1917. With five victories, he was given command of Jasta 2 in February 1918, and his four 'kills' on 4 November brought his score to 36. In August 1918 he had received the Pour le Mérite. He died in his native Berlin in 1955 after a lifetime in aviation, including service in the Luftwaffe as a special adviser in training and air transport.

Postscript

As the war ended in 1918, only fifteen years had passed since the Wright brothers had made their tentative first flight. It was only nine years since Blériot had flown the English Channel, and only six years since the formation of the Royal Flying Corps. Yet in those few years aviation had grown rapidly, and so had the knowledge of how to survive in an air war. Boys who had been at school when the above events occurred were, by 1918, exceptionally knowledgeable in air strategy and air tactics—what to do and what not to do in most given situations. These were things that were unknown to them just a few short years earlier, and that they could never have dreamed they would be experts at in their immediate future lives. They had also emerged from a late Victorian world into a very different place. Wars would never be the same again. War in the third dimension had arrived.

Appendix

Main Fighter Types: 1914–15

Type	Seats	Powerplant	Speed (mph/kph)	Armament
Morane Type N	1	80hp Le Rhône	144/230	1 × Lewis*
Morane Type L	1	80hp Le Rhône	125/200	1 × Lewis
Vickers F.B.5	2	100hp Gnome	70/112	1 × Lewis
Bristol Scout	1	80hp Gnome	92/147	1 × Lewis
Fokker E.I	1	80hp Oberursel	130/208	1 × Spandau
Pfalz E.I	1	80hp Oberursel	90/145	1 × Spandau

Main Fighter Types: 1916

Type	Seats	Powerplant	Speed (mph/kph)	Armament
Nieuport XVI	1	110hp Le Rhône	165/264	1 × Lewis
Nieuport XVII	1	110hp Le Rhône	165/264	1 × Lewis
Airco D.H.2	1	100hp Gnome	93/149	1 × Lewis
F.E.8	1	110hp Gnome	80/128	1 × Lewis
F.E.2b	2	160hp Beardmore	92/147	2 × Lewis
B.E.12	1	140hp RAF 4a	102/163	1 × Vickers, 1 × Lewis
Spad VII	1	150hp Hispano-Suiza	150/240	1 × Vickers
Fokker E.II/III	1	100hp Oberursel	88/140	2 × Spandau
Fokker D.II/III	1	100hp Oberursal	88/140	2 × Spandau

Main Fighter Types: 1916–17

Type	Seats	Powerplant	Speed (mph/kph)	Armament
Nieuport XXIII	1	120hp Le Rhône	103/165	1 × Lewis
Spad XIII	1	200hp Hispano-Suiza	136/218	2 × Vickers
Sopwith Pup	1	100hp Gnome	111/177	1 × Vickers
Sopwith 1½-Strutter	2	130hp Clerget	105/168	1 × Vickers, 1 × Lewis
Fokker D.II	1	100hp Oberursel	94/150	1 × Spandau
Halberstadt D.III	1	120hp Mercedes	90/145	1 × Spandau
Albatros D.II	1	160hp Mercedes	110/175	2 × Spandau

Main Fighter Types, 1917

Type	Seats	Powerplant	Speed (mph/kph)	Armament
Nieuport XXVII	1	130hp Le Rhône	107/172	1 × Lewis, 1 × Vickers
Spad XIII	1	200hp Hispano-Suiza	136/210	2 × Vickers
Sopwith Camel	1	130hp Clerget	108/173	2 × Vickers
S.E.5	1	150hp Hispano-Suiza	114/182	1 × Lewis, 1 × Vickers
Bristol F.2a	2	190hp Rolls-Royce	110/176	1 × Lewis, 1 × Vickers
Sopwith Triplane	1	130hp Clerget	112/179	1 × Vickers
F.E.2d	2	250hp Rolls Royce	94/150	2–3 × Lewis
Albatros D.III	1	160hp Mercedes	103/165	2 × Spandau
Albatros D.V/Va	1	180hp Mercedes	103/165	2 × Spandau
Fokker Dr. I	1	110hp Oberursel	104/165	2 × Spandau

Main Fighter Types, 1918

Type	Seats	Powerplant	Speed (mph/kph)	Armament
Spad XIII	1	220hp Hispano-Suiza	136/218	2 × Vickers
Nieuport 28	1	160hp Gnome	128/206	2 × Vickers
Sopwith Camel	1	150hp Bentley	124/198	2 × Vickers
S.E.5a	1	200hp Wolseley	117/187	1 × Lewis, 1 × Vickers
Sopwith Dolphin	1	200hp Hispano-Suiza	123/197	2 × Vickers, 1–2 ×Lewis
Bristol F.2b	2	190hp Rolls-Royce	113/180	1 × Vickers, 1–2 × Lewis
Hanriot HD.1	1	130hp Le Rhône	116/185	1 × Vickers
Sopwith Snipe	1	230hp Bentley	125 /200	2 × Vickers
Pfalz D.III/IIIa	1	160hp Mercedes	102/163	2 × Spandau
Fokker D.VII	1	160hp Mercedes	116/186	2 × Spandau
Fokker D.VIIF	1	185hp BMW	124/198	2 × Spandau
Fokker D.VIII	1	110hp Oberursel	127/203	2 × Spandau
Siemens-Schuckert D.IV	1	160hp Siemens-Halske	112/180	2 × Spandau
Pfalz D.XII	1	160hp Mercedes	106/170	2 × Spandau

* Allied aircraft are shown with RFC/RAF machine guns; the French Air Force used Hotchkiss guns as well.

Select Bibliography

Arms & Armour Press, (pub.), *Fighting in the Air*, London, 1978.

Balfour, Capt. Harold, *An Airman Marches*, Greenhill Books, London, 1985.

Bodenschatz, Karl, (trans. Hayzlett, J.), *Jagd in Flanderns Himmel*, Berlin, 1935. (Published under the title *Hunting with Richthofen*, Grub Street, London, 1996.)

Bruce, Jack, *Aeroplanes of the Royal Flying Corps*, Putnam, London , 1982.

Fry, W. M., *Air of Battle*, Williamm Kimber & Co, London, 1974.

Gibbs, G. E., *Survivor's Story*, Hutchinson, Lodnon, 1956.

Lee, A. S. G., *No Parachute*, Jarrolds, London, 1968.

———, *Open Cockpit*, Jarrolds, London, 1969.

McCudden, J. T. B., *Flying Fury*, John Hamilton, London, 1930.

MacLanachan, W., *Fighter Pilot*, Greenhill Books, London, 1985.

Macmillan, Capt. Norman, *Into the Blue*, Duckworth, London, 1929.

Mittler, E. S., & Sohn, (pub.), *Rittmeister Manfred Frhr von Richthofen: Sein militärisches Vermachtnis*, Berlin, 1936.

Rickenbacker, E. V., *Rickenbacker*, Prentice-Hall, New Jersey, 1967.

Rochford, Leonard, *I Chose the Sky*, William Kimber & Co, London, 1977.

Taylor, Sir Gordon, *Sopwith Scout 7309*, Cassell, London, 1968.

Udet, Ernst, *Mein Fliegerleben*, Newnes 1937.

Cross & Cockade (various edns).

Over the Front (various edns).

Index